The Dark Side of Lyndon Baines Johnson

JOACHIM JOESTEN

Copyright © 1968, 2013 Joachim Joesten

All rights reserved.

Published 2013 by Iconoclassic Books

www.iconoclassicbooks.com

ISBN: 1771520094

ISBN-13: 978-1771520096

CONTENTS

CHAPTER 1: His Own Worst Enemy	1
CHAPTER 2 - The Roots of Illegitimate Power	12
CHAPTER 3 - The Texas Power Grab	31
CHAPTER 4 - 'To Get Our Man Elected'	44
CHAPTER 5 - The Wealthiest President Ever	51
CHAPTER 6 - The Rich Fruits of a Monopoly	69
CHAPTER 7 - 'Just a Little Ranch'	90
CHAPTER 8 - Wheeler-Dealer's Merry-Go-Round	101
CHAPTER 9 - Texas Billie	107
CHAPTER 10 - The Senator from Lobbyland	120
CHAPTER 11 - Bobby and LBJ: Like Rocket, Like Booster	128
CHAPTER 12 - A Case of MAGIC (How the 'F-80 Club' Took Care of Its Own)	136
CHAPTER 13 – Serv-U—Bobby	145
CHAPTER 14 - Sweet Tunes of Payola—And a Jarring Note	153
CHAPTER 15 - A String of Murders - or a Rash of Suicides?	164
CHAPTER 16 - Bobby's White Elephant: The Carousel	178
CHAPTER 17 - The Dignity of Senator Dirksen	189

CHAPTER 18 - Thank God, The Marines Are Coming!	199
CHAPTER 19 - Of Murchisons and 'Finders' Fees'	218
CHAPTER 20 - Sex and the Solons	231
CHAPTER 21 - Adventures of Elly Rometsch	237
CHAPTER 22 - Guess Who?	247
CHAPTER 23 - The Short, Sweet Life of Carole Tyler	255
CHAPTER 24 - Sing No More, Don Reynolds!	270
CHAPTER 25 - Master of the Cover-up	286
CHAPTER 26 - The Trial of Bobby Baker	301
CHAPTER 27 - The Ways of a Usurper	315
CHAPTER 28 - Johnson's Phony 'Red Conspiracy'	333
CHAPTER 29 - What's the Hurry, Mr. Johnson?	344
CHAPTER 30 - Why All This Secrecy?	349
CHAPTER 31 - Why Do the Kennedys Hate Lyndon Johnson So Much?	360
CHAPTER 32 - Sabotaging the Garrison Enquiry	368
CHAPTER 33 - The First *coup d'etat* in American History	375
Epilogue	386
THE MURDER OF ROBERT KENNEDY	388
About the Author	390

CHAPTER 1: His Own Worst Enemy

'The President... is ours, and we exercise the right to destroy him'.

-John Steinbeck

No one ever set out to destroy Lyndon B. Johnson with the fierce determination the bearer of that name himself has evinced all his life.

A man who desperately wants to be believed and respected while his whole political career is built on the use of The Big Lie and organized fraud;

A man who covets popularity with every fiber of his soul yet who would never for one moment hesitate to crush underfoot anyone who got in his way;

A man to whom the attainment of power by any and all means is the supreme ambition of his life;

A man unmoved by any principle except that of expediency;

A man who in a lifetime of public service manages to amass a private fortune of 14 million dollars;

A man who callously sacrifices millions of lives in order to win the most senseless war in history.

Such a person cannot succeed, in the long run, in anything but self-destruction. In our generation, Hitler and Mussolini have set the pattern and Lyndon B. Johnson, ideologies apart (he has never had any), has followed in their footsteps.

And so the 36th president of the United States will go down in history as one of the most unloved and unlamented, if not indeed the most unloved and unlamented of American presidents, in striking contrast to the near-exalted status of his predecessor, John F. Kennedy.

For many years the world has been beguiled about the true nature of the Johnson regime by the horde of professional sycophants, parasites and myth-makers, which operates out of Washington, D. C. Regrettably, this Toadies, Inc., which will glorify any president, sight unseen, as long as he holds the reins of power and the purse-strings, also includes a large segment of the foreign press corps in Washington.

Even some of the shrewdest and most knowledgeable observers in that capital have at times eulogized Johnson with an effusion which one finds hard to credit solely to genuine conviction.

Take, for example, the panegyric which Henry Fairlie published in the *Sunday Telegraph* of October 10, 1965, under the headline 'Lyndon, the Leader Extraordinary'. It contained such passages as these:

"He was harried... by such irrelevant comment, but he rode it (and this has never been adequately acknowledged) with calm and common sense. The result... has been the growth of an easy and normal relationship between him and the country: a relationship without exaggeration, without charisma, without too much sensitivity on either side...

'The continuity which President Johnson made it his first and main task to establish after Dallas was not only a striking and personal achievement for that moment: it has shaped American politics in the past two years...

'At least as important as the style of the Presidential leadership in public... is the exercise of that leadership within the administration itself and within Congress. It is impossible to have any contact with any department or bureau of the Administration without realizing that each of them is now working directly and sensitively to a leadership from the White House which it understands. It is a leadership which is personal, in terms both of Mr. Johnson himself and of a staff which (to say the least) would be disjointed if he had to be replaced... If the Presidential leadership in the past year has been exceptional, the fact remains that what matters, and what one looks forward to with fascination, is the growth of that leadership in the next three years... It is a common observation that a President meets his real test, his greatest challenges and greatest opportunities, in the second and third years of his term... it is a matter of speculation—but of speculation which, I believe, excites only optimism—how Mr. Johnson will employ the rest of his Presidency. What can at least be acknowledged is that, as he turns his talents, not to the comparatively obvious tasks of the past year, but to situations requiring more political invention, as he makes more and more imaginative use of the responsive administration which he has created, as he becomes more familiar with the handling of foreign affairs, as he moves towards the full exploitation of the politics he has created—as, in short, his Presidency takes on its full shape, he could prove to be one of the great Presidents of all American history, and in ways that have not yet been considered...'

Compare to these fervent outpourings of Mr. Fairlie what *Newsweek* magazine (generally a loyal supporter of the Administration) reported less than two years later in a cover story entitled 'LBJ in Trouble' (Sept. 4, 1967):

'He (Johnson) is the first President in U.S. history to be beset simultaneously with a major war abroad and a major rebellion at home—neither of them going well or holding forth any promise of the kind of sudden and dramatic improvement that alone could reverse the rising tide of anger, frustration and bitterness that is cresting around the White House. He is also a President whose own personality has become an issue in itself—an issue, indeed, that seems increasingly to be producing almost as much criticism and contention as the war in Vietnam and the tumult in the ghettos.

'In Pocatello, Idaho, a sixtyish but sprightly grandmother and good Democrat said: "I'm beginning to hate that man." In Portland, Ore., Charles Snowden said: "I've switched. I'll vote for almost anybody except Johnson." In a modern office off New York's Fifth Avenue a young executive said: "Johnson's too clever. He's always got something up his sleeve." In Los Angeles, Mrs. Aljean Harmetz said: "I don't think I like Johnson now. I don't think he's an honest man."

So much for what Mr. Fairlie has described as 'the growth of an easy and normal relationship between him (the President) and the country'. Now let us see how his claim that Johnson is a 'leader extraordinary' stands up in the light of facts. On this score, *Newsweek*: said:

'On the President's Asian battlefront last week, U.S. ground forces were stalled and American airmen took their heaviest casualties—(thirteen planes in seven days) since May. At home, after the worst summer of riots in the nation's history, a dozen (or could it be a hundred?) Negro ghettos seethed with hostility. On Capitol Hill, where Lyndon Johnson once reigned almost supreme, some of his most faithful followers had deserted him. There were reports that important segments of his own Democratic Party were turning against him, and there was no question that he had lost much of his support among the American people.

'What has happened to Mr. Johnson's popularity is almost unprecedented. In the brief two months after his summit talks with Soviet Premier Aleksei Kosygin, the polls showed that one in five Americans had turned against Mr. Johnson. The latest Harris poll and Gallup poll showed that only 39 per cent of the country's voters approved of the way the President is handling his job—and this was the man who won the Presidency less than three years ago by the biggest landslide in U.S. history.

'Down, Down, Down. For the country's No. 1 trader of polls, this was a bitter blow, for it meant that his rating was lower than it had been since he became President 45 months ago, a level lower than Dwight Eisenhower or John Kennedy had ever reached.

'Woe and dismay hung over the President's own official family like Washington's terrible humidity. To a colleague the usually stoic Dean Rusk confided recently: "I'm very tired." In the aftermath of the Newark and Detroit riots, another Cabinet officer (he would be instantly asked to resign if his name were used) talked at great length one day about the lack of leadership in the White House. "Things seem dreadful," he said wearily...

'...An ex-Johnson assistant telephoned a presidential aide not long ago to ask: "What's the situation?" The weary reply: "Bewildered."

'When one Cabinet deputy was asked recently if it was correct to say that "the Administration seems to be coming apart at the seams," he replied wryly: "No, it already has."....'

It is a far cry, indeed, from this sober analysis to Mr. Fairlie's vagaries about 'Lyndon, the Leader Extraordinary'. It is not that the picture had radically changed in the intervening two years, though undoubtedly it had grown worse. Basically, the total lack of genuine leadership qualities in Lyndon B. Johnson (as distinct from his unquestioned abilities as a political manipulator) has been apparent from his first days in office to any observer not purblind.

Lyndon B. Johnson never had wisdom, style or grace. He was possessed of ambitious zeal, dynamic energy and relentless drive, a typical go-getter who combined the craftiness of the political pro with the insatiable appetites of a Southern 'wheeler-dealer'.

His leadership—if the term applies at all—never amounted to anything but the outstanding ability to manipulate Congress, to bend reluctant Senators and Representatives to his will, and to pull parliamentary strings to keep the puppets dancing.

True statesmanship, as distinct from political trickery, has always been a foreign art to him. That is the deep underlying reason why the presidency of Lyndon Johnson could never succeed, even though his long career as a Congressman was moderately successful. As head of one of the two mightiest nations on earth, he was a poor substitute for a Kennedy or even an Eisenhower and an even poorer match for a Khrushchev or even a Kosygin.

His most effective weapons have been throughout his career an intimate knowledge of the inside workings of the Washington powerhouse, the ability to exert irresistible pressure through secret blackmail and that peculiar form of persuasion that has come to be known as the 'Johnson treatment', a mixture of cajoling, veiled threats and incubus-like oppression which once was described in these terms by a Senator who had been subjected to it:

'...by this time, Johnson had risen from his high-backed chair and was on his feet towering over the interviewer, one hand on the latter's knee, his face a few inches away, his right forefinger wagging emphatically, and his voice rising and falling from persuasive tones to emphatic declaration.

'One could well believe the remark of a Senate colleague who said: "If I spend a half-hour with Lyndon, he can convince me of anything. I've never known of anyone who out-argued him in a face-to-face discussion or who ever claimed he had."'

It was Johnson's regrettable mistake—and the even more fateful error of those influential political leaders who put their trust in him—to believe that this kind of 'treatment' could influence the course of world affairs or that it could induce the American Negro to accept crass inequality as a matter of course.

When real, life-size problems started to crowd in on him, as in Vietnam and in the racial revolt, the man in the White House showed that he was no Machiavelli but only an out-traded horse-dealer from the Pedernales.

The true nature of Lyndon B. Johnson has long been hidden from the public through the frenzied efforts of highly paid P.R. wizards and artificial image-builders. Even among those almost in daily contact with him, only a few were able to discern the extraordinarily mean streaks in that man's character.

William Manchester came closer than most other people to seeing through the benign public relations mask of Lyndon Johnson, but one wouldn't know it from scanning the pages of *The Death of a President*.

Manchester's knowledge of what really makes Johnson tick was not firsthand, for he had little, if any, personal contact with him, but he was able to draw on the vast store of information and impressions available to the Kennedy clan. If there are two persons in the world who have really come to know Johnson at close quarters, outside of his own family, they are Robert and Jacqueline Kennedy. Manchester interviewed both of them at length and they told him, without mincing their words, what they thought of That

Man in the White House. But when Manchester, having faithfully recorded everything the Kennedys had told him, rushed into print with his story, years ahead of schedule, they both got panicky and practically forced him to 'revise' his story out of recognition.

Edward J. Epstein, the author of *Inquest*, somehow managed to get hold of a copy of the original, unedited manuscript of the Manchester book, then entitled *Death of a Lancer*, and revealed in the July issue 1967 of *Commentary*, some of its contents.

In his original draft, Manchester, it seems, made some very pungent remarks about Lyndon Johnson whom he described, among other things, as a 'chameleon who constantly changes loyalties'; 'a capon' and 'a crafty schemer who has a gaunt, hunted look about him'.

He also pictured Johnson as 'a full-fledged hypomaniac' and 'the crafty seducer with six nimble hands who can persuade a woman to surrender her favors in the course of a long conversation confined to obscure words. No woman, even a lady, can discern his intentions until the critical moment'.

By far the most interesting aspect of this matter, however, is Epstein's contention that Manchester's original theme, which gave unity to his book, was 'the notion that Johnson, the successor, was somehow responsible for the death of his predecessor'.

'This concept', Epstein commented, 'gave the original melodrama much of its thrust and such structural coherence as it had'.

Several quotations from the original draft bear out this

contention. At one point, the *Lancer* version states, 'The shattering fact of the assassination is that a Texas murder has made a Texan President'.

At another, Kenneth O'Donnell, Kennedy's appointments secretary, is quoted as exclaiming 'They did it. I always knew they'd do it. You couldn't expect anything else from them. They finally made it'.

Then Manchester comments: 'He didn't specify who "they" were. It was unnecessary. They were Texans, Johnsonians'.

All of which is a far cry, indeed, from the version presented by Manchester in the published book which not only hews to the Warren Report, in making Lee Harvey Oswald appear as the sole culprit, but even embellishes upon it. For Manchester, in *The Death of a President*, goes so far as to tell his readers the exact hour when Oswald went mad and decided to shoot Kennedy and he even implies, strongly, that the impulse to kill the President overwhelmed Oswald that night because his wife had refused her love to him.

The authenticity of Epstein's disclosures is not in doubt for both Manchester himself and his editor, Evan Thomas, of Harper and Row—the man chiefly responsible for the total emasculation of the work—have confirmed the accuracy of the material, the first implicitly, the latter explicitly.

Both men, of course, were annoyed. Thomas called Epstein's technique 'dirty pool', while Manchester complained that it was 'equivalent to digging in a reporter's wastebasket'.

But what is one to think of an author who allows his most important work not only to be castrated, but to be turned completely upside down by a publisher more committed to the dictates of expediency than to the search for historical truth?

In any event, this is one of the strongest indications yet that the Kennedy family, for all the restraint and even pusillanimity they have exhibited in the matter, have been well aware all along of the true background of the assassination. I'll revert to this aspect of the Lyndon Johnson story in subsequent chapters. But first let us take a searching look at the beginnings of that unsavory story.

CHAPTER 2 - The Roots of Illegitimate Power

FOR a number of years America has been a victim of fear. She is now ruled by an illegitimate government.

By defalcation of Congress on the one hand and Judicial usurpation on the other—with the connivance and ready support of the Executive branch—the Federal Government has been corrupted into a vehicle of vast unrestrained power over the lives, the effects and the affairs of the American people.

'Just at this fateful period in our national life, as if by diabolical design, there has been thrust into the presidential office a man who knows the meaning and the uses of power; not power based on mutual confidence and consent, but the power of political pressure and of blackmail. Thus we are faced with illegitimate power in the hands of a ruthless ruler'.

These hard-hitting lines are from the Preface to the most remarkable book that has ever been written about the life and times of Lyndon B. Johnson. Entitled *A Texan Looks at Lyndon*, and subtitled *A Study in Illegitimate Power*, it was published in the summer of 1964 'under semi-clandestine circumstances,' as *The New York Herald Tribune* of Sept 13, 1964, remarked. It achieved an enormous sale throughout America in that election year.

The author is J. Evetts Haley, a crusty Texan who describes himself as a 'cowman and historian' who, with his son, is 'the active cowboy owner-operator of three Southwestern cattle ranches'. As for the historian's part in this unusual combination, it is represented by twelve books of history and biography concerned with Texas and the Southwest and also documented by the fact that the author was a member of the Department of History at the University of Texas in the mid-thirties.

As I intend to quote repeatedly and at some length from this exceptionally informative book, which is a real fountainhead of inside knowledge on the antecedents of Lyndon B. Johnson, a few more details about the author, his work and the way I chanced to come across it are in order.

In the wake of the publication, in June 1964, of my first book about The Kennedy Murder Fraud, *Oswald: Assassin or Fall Guy?* which contained a chapter pointedly entitled 'CUI BONO?', I received voluminous fan mail which one day included a curious pamphlet with the title 'LBJ - A Political Biography'. Published by 'Liberty Lobby', a notorious ultra-right outfit, this pamphlet would not normally have retained my attention except for the eye-catching unsigned note attached to it which read:

'If you wish to broaden your speculations on CUI BONO? - read this!'

So I read the pamphlet which turned out to be an extract from the book *A Texan Looks at Lyndon* by J. Evetts Haley. My appetite whetted, I got hold of a copy of the book itself which I read in one sitting from cover to cover and have reread many times since, with growing fascination.

Haley's book may not be a masterpiece in the strictly scholarly sense, and it is certainly not a bible of my political creed, but as source material it is invaluable. For the author is not only a fellow-countryman of Lyndon B. Johnson, but an insider of Texas politics and an old political pro in his own right. A self-styled 'Jeffersonian Democrat' and conservative, Haley has been for years active in regional politics and in 1956 he unsuccessfully sought the Democratic nomination for Governor.

That this biography of Lyndon B. Johnson is colored to a considerable extent by bitterness at his own failure in the political game, as well as by an ingrained dislike of the Rooseveltian tradition (which, alas, also produced LBJ) and a generally ultraconservative stance, I do not doubt. Still, even after making generous allowance for possible exaggeration due to these factors, there remains in his book so much well-documented fact that it cannot possibly be bypassed by anyone seeking enlightenment about the dark recesses of the Johnson story.

The principal merit of Haley's *A Texan Looks at Lyndon* lies in exploring those parts of Johnson's past that have been most zealously kept from view by the official biographers. In particular, the author relates in great and obviously authentic detail how Lyndon B. Johnson got started on his long and crooked road to the White House through a fraudulent vote. No one who has closely followed Lyndon Johnson's shifty Congressional career, his ascent to the presidency through a well-planned murder camouflaged as the demented action of a lone Communist and the endless chain of deceptions that have marked the Vietnam war, will doubt that the 'turbulent run-off primary' of 1948—to use an expression favored by the official biographers—was indeed the blatant vote 'steal' Haley makes it out to be.

Johnson, a Congressman since 1937, had failed in his first bid for a Senate seat in 1941. He was determined not to lose out again when he got into another race seven years later with the popular Governor Coke R. Stevenson as his opponent in the primary battle which to all practical purposes decided the election as everywhere in the then still 'solid' South.

The final count in the primary poll, held on July 24, 1948, showed Stevenson, with 477,077 votes to 405,617 for Johnson, far out in the lead by a seemingly safe margin. However, since Stevenson's lead of 71,460 votes did not constitute a majority over the entire field, a run-off became necessary and it was set for August 28.

The wily Johnson quickly spotted his chance to reverse the comfortable majority his opponent had piled up on the first ballot. In the south-western portion of Texas, where many people of Mexican parentage live, for the most part in primitive conditions, the master of an entrenched political machine can easily swing a large 'controlled vote' one way or the other. Some of these Latin-populated counties are ruled in almost medieval fashion by 'dukes' who lord it over vast areas by means of a well-established hierarchy of ward-heelers and 'jefes politicos'.

One of these key figures was, in the words of Haley, 'an affable, blue-eyed, multimillionaire criminal' by the name of George Parr, 'Duke of Duval Country'. To the political power and riches inherited from his father, Archie Parr, who had been for many years a Texas Senator, George had added a great deal of his own through a variety of shady deals which repeatedly landed him in jail—without damage to his political influence and social standing.

At Parr's first trial, in 1932, for criminal evasion of income taxes, the Federal Attorney of the San Antonio District, Wm. Robert Smith, proved that George Parr, in 1928, had an income of more than $45,000 only $2,700 of which had come 'from a legitimate source'.

About $17,000 represented pay-offs for protection of illegal liquor and gambling operations and houses of prostitution. The protection provided by Parr in return for these payments was well worth the money, it seems, for the defendant was, in the words of the prosecutor, 'the political dictator of Duval County' who 'controlled the action of practically every other office-holder in the county'.

The remaining $25,000 of Parr's 1928 income, the U.S. Attorney showed, represented a kickback on a county road contract which the defendant, as County Judge, had thrown to the Pierson Construction Company in return for $25,000 in cash delivered to his home 'in a little black bag'. Uncle Sam got none of that loot.

In the face of the incontrovertible evidence which Smith had mustered against him, Parr gave up and pleaded guilty. He drew a $5,000 fine and an 18-month probated sentence. When two years later he got involved in a fraudulent oil deal, Parr's probation was revoked and he was sent to a federal reformatory.

Although Parr had originally been in the Stevenson camp, he found it to his advantage to make a deal with the Johnson forces after the run-off primary of 1948 had been set. His political influence at the time extended far beyond Duval County, but especially into adjoining Jim Wells and Starr Counties.

'The switch that Parr engineered in his area of influence and control was absolutely fantastic', Haley writes. 'His immediate tri-county returns gave Johnson a *thirty to one* lead—10,547 to 368, with heavy majorities in many other counties adjacent to them and along the Rio Grande'.

Needless to say, such an incongruous majority, coming after a fairly even split of votes in a primary held only a few weeks earlier, is evidence *per se* of a rigged election. But there was even worse to come.

'When the count from the run-off election was in'. Haley relates, 'Parr had delivered for Lyndon. But though he had dallied in sending his returns while Lyndon kept in close touch by telephone, it finally turned out that they had closed their own count prematurely. Stevenson was ahead by 113 votes.

'Johnson made another frantic telephone call to Parr, who indicated that he might pick up what they needed in Precinct 13 at Alice (county seat of Jim Wells). Thereupon his henchmen "re-canvassed the returns," reporting on September 3 the "corrected" total of 202 additional votes for Johnson and one for Stevenson.

Thus Lyndon went into the lead by 87 votes out of nearly a million actually cast'.

The smell of fraud was so strong, Stevenson and his supporters swung into action. Accompanied by two of his aides, Kellis Dibrell and Jim Gardner, both lawyers and former FBI agents, the Governor went to San Diego, the seat of Duval County.

But when they called on Parr at his office, they found that Johnson's campaign manager, John Connally (later the Governor of Texas) had beat them to it. As Clyde Wantland, Texas newspaper man and historian (who published a detached account of the matter in *The Texas Argus*, April 1962, San Antonio, entitled 'The Story of George Parr's Ballot Box No. 13'.) wrote, "He had arrived the preceding day and was busily cementing the theft," though Parr publicly stated that the run-off in his district "was as clean an election as had ever been held." Possibly so, in his district.

Stevenson demanded that Parr show them the Duval poll lists and the returns of the election judges, which reported a vote of 4622 to 38 (!) in favor of Johnson. Parr feigned astonishment. Why should they ask him? He was not an election judge; he knew nothing about the returns.

The Stevenson party had somewhat better luck in Jim Wells County where in the meantime two new men had been elected chairman and secretary of the Democratic Executive Committee. The two new party officials took a dim view of the last-minute 'correction' of the returns from Precinct 13 and were already trying to upset this maneuver. Having seen the 'corrected' list with their own eyes, and sat in on the 'recount', they told Stevenson that the 202 new names had been added alphabetically in blue ink, whereas the original list was in black—clear-cut proof of fraudulent ballot-stuffing.

The list, however, was not available for Stevenson to inspect. The Committee's old secretary, Tom Donald, an employee in Parr's Texas State Bank, kept the list safely stored away in his vault. Although it was a public record, Donald refused to turn it over for scrutiny.

What followed then comes close to a scene from a Western movie.

When the bank opened the next day, Governor Stevenson, flanked by his former FBI man and some Texas Rangers headed by Captain Frank Hamer, were there, determined to storm the fortress. In front of the entrance to the bank, Parr's forces, equipped with Winchesters, were waiting for them. No blood was spilled, though, for, as Wantland tells the story:

'Governor Stevenson wisely ordered his forces to appear in public in only their shirt sleeves (to prove they were unarmed).

'As the hour approached for the bank doors to open, armed men sauntered onto the scene and took positions with an ominous stance.

'Governor Stevenson and his coatless investigators arrived, escorted by Ranger Captain Frank Hamer. Not a word was spoken as the Ranger Captain took position directly before the bank door. The veteran captain was well known to every man there. He was known as a stern, inflexible officer who exacted, one way or another, prompt and stern obedience to his orders.

'He waved the armed men to fall back from the bank door, and they did. Very promptly! The doors opened and Governor Stevenson and his men entered. Captain Hamer forbade any other to follow. None tried. Witnesses said later the Captain never lifted his pistol, nor even touched it, but Johnson charged him with force, threats and intimidation'.

Then, Haley continues, citing an affidavit by James Gardner to the Sub-Committee on Privileges and Elections of the United States Senate, November 12, 1948:

'Inside the bank Tom Donald produced the list for the Stevenson party to see. Dibrell and Gardner concentrated upon the added names, having determined in advance to memorize as many as possible. Donald conferred with the County Attorney who, after a few moments, gave the opinion that Stevenson should be allowed only to look at the record, not to copy or take notes therefrom. Donald repossessed the record and again locked it in the bank vault...

'Gardner and Dibrell, hurriedly scribbling down their remembered names, left on investigations of their own—the identity and whereabouts of the added "voters". They found grave difficulty in locating the addresses they had jotted down except three, "whose last known address was the cemetery," one of whom, according to the church records, had been there for four years. At least two of those they did locate swore they had not voted, while others shrugged off their questions with the frank admission that people in Parr's province who did not talk prospered better and lived longer than those who did'.

At this juncture, the scene of action shifted to the County Democratic Committee whose new chairman, Harry Adams, and secretary H. L. Poole decided to take over the poll lists and re-certify the returns. In view of the irregularities that had come to light, the two party officials planned to eliminate returns from Box 13 altogether, which would have thrown the election to Stevenson.

Johnson and Connally, having got wind of this plan, which was to have been put into force at a full committee meeting on the 10th of September, countered with an extraordinary move. From a friendly judge in faraway Austin, Roy Archer, they obtained an injunction which forbade the County Committee to meet and thus stalled Stevenson's drive.

'Johnson's petition and Judge Archer's restraining order are exceptional documents even in Texas jurisprudence,' Haley comments. Obviously Johnson was desperate. He contended that he had received a majority of the votes "in the recent election." He charged that Stevenson, Hamer and the Committee had "entered into a conspiracy" to have Box 13 "thrown out on the grounds of fraud and irregularity..." which would take from him enough votes to change the election.

Pleading that the 'resident Judge of Jim Wells County... cannot be reached in sufficient time,' Johnson's lawyer applied for a 'restraining order without notice' to the defendants, which Judge Archer granted forthwith.

Haley points out that in fact the resident Judge, Judge L. Broeter, of Alice, was in his district on the day the Committee scheduled to meet and was readily available, had Johnson desired him. He writes:

'This obvious perversion of the law, distortion of the truth, brazen action and political perfidy, were characteristic of Johnson. But even for Texas it was a high point in low and dirty dealing. It set something of a record'. And then the author quotes Clyde Wantland as follows:

'Just why Johnson and Connally presented the petition to Judge Roy Archer in Austin, two hundred miles distant from Jim Wells County, raised a serious question, not alone of honesty and fair play, but also the more serious fact of swearing to a falsehood when Johnson knew it was a lie.

'Just why Judge Archer was beguiled into signing this order in chambers, without notice, thus perverting the vast powers of a District Court to handcuff a victim while ruthless political hijackers mauled and stripped him clean, is a question still unanswered. Maybe it was the legendary Johnson charm and personality. Maybe the decision stemmed from the law of heteronomy than the law of Texas. Judge Archer alone has the answer'.

How the whole course of history would have changed if Judge Archer had at least taken a little time to ponder his decision! For, as Haley points out, 'Had the action in Judge Archer's chambers been delayed more than an hour, it is highly likely that the Jim Wells Democratic Committee would have met, thrown out Box 13, and restored electoral decision in Stevenson's favor. But with the State Democratic Executive Committee meeting in Fort Worth within three clays to canvass the returns and certify the candidates to the Secretary of State for printing of the ballots for the November election, the blow to the hopes of the Stevenson forces seemed fatal'.

The battle now shifted to higher political ground. On Monday, September 13, the State Committee met at the Blackstone Hotel in Fort Worth to decide the issue. Johnson, who had always had a flair for picking the best legal talent available, had his case eloquently presented by a topflight Texas lawyer, Charles I. Frances. After a daylong debate, the matter was put to a vote. Unexpectedly, the Committee split down the middle, with 28 members on either side. The tie, however, was broken when a Committeeman from Amarillo; who had flown in late, cast his vote in favor of Johnson. This meant certain certification of Johnson as the Democratic Party nominee by the Secretary of State at Austin and hence virtually certain election in November.

But Stevenson would not give up. He issued a statement saying, 'This race is not a matter of life or death for me. If I lost by one vote in an honest count the heavens wouldn't fall in. But some half million good solid Texans voted for me as their Senator and they have been defrauded and robbed. We can do no less than appeal to the Federal Courts'.

The Governor's lawyers then drafted a petition for a temporary restraining order that would prevent the Secretary of State from printing Johnson's name on the ballot until the evidence could be heard and presented it to Federal Judge T. Witfield Davidson of Dallas. The judge signed the order and set Federal Court for a full hearing in Fort Worth on September 21.

On this occasion, Stevenson, too, came up with a whole battery of able lawyers, led by a former Governor, Dan Moody. Gardner and Dibrell were standing by with the evidence they had dug up, ready to testify that 202 names of alleged voters had been mysteriously added in blue ink, and all in the same hand, to a poll list previously drawn up in black and in a number of hands. Also present were a number of Mexicans on the list who were supposed to have voted for Johnson and now stood ready to swear that they had not voted at all.

The clearest evidence of fraud, however, could be seen in the fact that only 600 ballots had been officially issued for Precinct 13, while the 'corrected returns' claimed 1025 votes had been cast.

In the face of such overwhelming evidence, Johnson's lawyer, Charles Frances and John D. Cofer, took the line that the Court lacked jurisdiction in the case which, they contended, was strictly a party matter which party officials had sole authority to decide.

They were overruled by Judge Davidson who angrily stated that:

'There has not been one word of evidence submitted to disprove this plaintiff's claim that he has been robbed of a seat in the United States Senate'. The Court then decided to appoint a Commissioner—former U.S. Attorney Robert Smith, the man who had previously investigated George Parr—to go into Jim Wells County, to summon and swear witnesses, to adduce evidence and to find out the truth about the voting in Precinct 13. Another Commissioner was appointed to look into the election procedure in Duval County.

'With the resolute Bob Smith, armed with the authority of the Federal Court, moving to dig out the voting records and take the sworn testimony of those involved,' Haley goes on to say, 'Johnson was in serious trouble. He frantically called George Parr... pleading: "George, don't burn those ballots. It'll be a reflection on me."

'But Parr, who like Harry Truman, knew the psychology of his henchmen and the code of loyalty in their protection, shouted back: "'To hell with you. I'm going to protect my friends."'

George was as good as his word. Both of the Commissioners sent by Judge Davidson ran into the same trouble. All their questioning of the mostly Spanish-speaking witnesses ended in frustration, with the eternal 'quien sabe?' (who knows?) or another form of evasion taking the place of an answer. And all the lists they asked for providentially 'showed up missing'.

This is a common hallmark of the Lyndon Johnson story. Documents of vital importance for the elucidation of some particularly sensitive aspect of that story invariably 'show up missing'. They are accidentally destroyed, burned by chance or by mistake, they get lost in the shuffle, they vanish into thin air or—most conspicuously in the case of the Kennedy assassination—they are consigned to the classified files of the National Archives, which is the worst of all fates.

In the particular case we are here concerned with, Haley thus describes what is supposed to have happened:

When Commissioner Burnett in Duval asked for the poll lists, he was told they couldn't be found. 'It developed later that County Chairman, T. C. King, a Parr enterprise employee, had grown nervous over the vast disparity between the election returns and the poll taxes issued—about two to one—and had taken the lists home for safe-keeping. There his wife, in her commendable zeal of housecleaning, had apparently consigned them to the fire...

'Over in Precinct 13 at Alice, in Jim Wells County, the investigations went little better. Commissioner Bob Smith issued a subpoena for Tom Donald, the Parr bank employee who was Democratic County Secretary at the time of the election, but he was in Mexico "on business". He issued another for Luis Salas, presiding judge in the election. He had also been called to Mexico "on business".

'The poll list, too, failed of subpoena. Commissioner Smith impounded the County's ballot boxes and found them empty. "Why?" Obviously, it was suggested, the industrious Mexican janitor, ignorant of what they were for, must have emptied the boxes and burned the ballots. Thus the same pattern of evasion and frustration prevailed as in Duval. "Nobody knew nothing."'

While all this was going on at the low levels of deceit, equally frantic maneuvering took place in the higher councils of the Truman Administration to make sure that the President's favorite, Lyndon Johnson, got the Senate seat 'at any price'. Now, to quote Haley again:

'...Johnson flew his case directly to that ex-Ku Klux Klansman and noted police judge on the Supreme Bench, Mr. Justice Hugo Black.

'Justice Black belonged to the club. At once, on September 29, 1948, he issued a sweeping order on behalf of Johnson, staying Judge Davidson's temporary injunction and ending the Fort Worth hearing...

'The Black order, hurriedly issued in chambers... has been likened to that of a judicial bulldozer. It over-rode one of America's foremost Constitutionalists and Judges, who had, in the light of fraud, simply stayed the election contest long enough to give each side time to present its case in evidence... It brazenly abridged the Constitution and the Bill of Rights, especially in their guarantees of States Rights and the limitations on jurisdiction. But perhaps most terrible of all, it sanctioned corruption as public policy. There is nothing in American history like it'.

Interestingly, the two high-placed Washington lawyers to whom Johnson took his case in his appeal to Justice Black have since both been appointed themselves to the Supreme court—by

President Johnson. They are Abe Fortas, a life-time crony of LBJ, and Thurman Arnold, the first Negro to sit on the Supreme Bench.

This, then, is the little-known behind-the-scenes story of how Lyndon B. Johnson in 1948 got his Senate seat, by a margin of 87 fraudulent votes. The 'winner' skillfully capitalized on the smallness of that majority by dubbing himself, in an apparently humorous vain, 'Landslide Lyndon'. His publicity experts made the nickname stick and thus, by causing people to chuckle at the nonsensical description of 87 votes as a 'landslide', helped to divert public attention from the underlying fraud. The whole operation is a perfect example of Johnson's political tactics, one that was to be matched, in various forms, over and over again on his road to the White House and beyond.

Two more brief quotations from Haley's *A Texan Looks at Lyndon* are in order. He writes that the vote steal, which he has amply documented, 'established his (Johnson's) illegitimate seat in the Senate, where his aptitude for compromise and chicanery put him into the crucial position from which a diabolical fate catapulted him into the presidency...'

Haley, for all his otherwise keen insight into the illegitimate nature of the Johnson regime, here completely misses a key element in its making. Diabolical as the force surely was that 'catapulted him into the presidency,' it wasn't fate and it wasn't Lee Harvey Oswald either.

Haley apparently was prevented by his ingrained political prejudices—and possibly by some of his political associates—from scrutinizing the Assassination of President Kennedy with the same cold eye which he has turned on other facets of Lyndon Johnson's career. To him, as to practically all other 'Conservatives' in America—and lots of so-called 'Liberals' as well, I am sorry to add—the Communist label cunningly and falsely pinned on Oswald by the Dallas conspirators was sufficient proof of the young man's guilt.

So blind is Haley on this subject that he even fails to catch the obvious implications of one of his own remarks, a most revealing one at that:

'What a strange coincidence that Lee Harvey Oswald, on his return from Mexico shortly before the Kennedy assassination, detoured from Laredo to stop and spent the night in "search of a job" at Alice, in Jim Wells County, Texas, before proceeding to Dallas and his world-shocking deed'.

I am satisfied that there was no coincidence at all. Even though Oswald was not Kennedy's assassin, he was implicated in the conspiracy that led to it. If he made a detour to and stopped off at Alice, early in October 1963, 'in search of a job', it is clear that he hoped to land one from kingmaker George Parr or one of his henchmen. This is an angle I hope District Attorney Jim Garrison in New Orleans some day will get around to looking into.

And here is a final quote from Haley's account of the 'Landslide Lyndon' episode: 'More than once in public addresses thereafter Governor Moody boldly charged, in the proper jurisdiction, that "if the District Attorney here had done his duty,

Lyndon Johnson would now be in the penitentiary instead of the United States Senate." And there was no action for libel'.

CHAPTER 3 - The Texas Power Grab

'NOWHERE is oil a bigger political force than Texas, producer of 35 percent of the nation's oil and possessor of half of its obtainable oil resources. As a Texan in Congress, Lyndon B. Johnson was a strong advocate of oil industry causes—low import quotas and the 27-and-a-half percent tax allowance for depletion of oil reserves...'

In these terms *The New York Times* of December 15, 1963 (The News of the Week in Review) cautiously defined Lyndon B. Johnson's unquestionable allegiance to the oil interests, the strongest economic power in America and the most important element in his background. It printed those words three weeks after Johnson had been 'catapulted into the presidency,' by a force which Haley correctly described as 'diabolical,' even though the Texas historian misunderstood, or pretended to misunderstand, its true nature.

Throughout his long political career, Johnson has been a tool of the Texas oil magnates in their drive for political influence with which to buttress and preserve their vast economic might. All his campaigns, from his first bid for a Congressional seat in 1937, and including his fraudulent 1948 election to the Senate and his 1960 attempt to win the Democratic nomination were financed by the Texas oil interests—and he paid them back lavishly in political gain. Johnson had many wealthy friends and 'angels' in the oil business—Richard Kleberg, A. J. West, Clint Murchison, John Mecom, among others—but none of them ever matched the closeness of his affinity with Haroldson Lafayette Hunt of Dallas, the wealthiest, most politically-minded, and most rightist of all Texas tycoons. Much of the H. L. Hunt story and its connection with Lyndon B. Johnson's sudden ascent to power has already been told in my book *How Kennedy Was Killed* (Chapter 5—'Case History of a "Psychotic" Oil Millionaire'). A good deal remains to be said.

Why is H. L. Hunt so important in the story of Lyndon B. Johnson's Rise and Fall? Because of the close association that has existed, over a period of many years, between the hate-mongering oil tycoon from Dallas and the Senator from Texas.

The New York Times, in its issue of August 19, 1964 (International Edition) carried a long feature story by its Dallas correspondent, David R. Jones, about 'H. L. Hunt: Magnate with a Mission' which contained some extremely significant and revealing passages such as these:

'Mr. Hunt has been friendly with President Johnson for several years. Booth Mooney, a Hunt public-relations man in Washington, was an executive assistant to Mr. Johnson from 1953 to 1958. He wrote Johnson's authorized biography, *The Lyndon Johnson Story* in 1956 and brought it up to date this year'.

Ponder this paragraph well. That was the period when the most vicious demagogue America has produced in our time, Senator Joseph McCarthy of Wisconsin, was riding high and roughshod through the land. McCarthy and Hunt, having first met in April 1952, had become close friends and political allies. Hunt's 'Facts Forum,' whose chief moderator at the time was the former FBI agent and ultra right-wing agitator Dan Smoot, went all out for McCarthy and became one of the principal driving forces behind the menacing spread of McCarthyism at that time.

According to *The New Republic* of February 16, 1954, 'In the fall of 1952, McCarthy and Hunt had another meeting, this time for dinner. They discussed the Senator's political situation and the Facts Forum. Shortly afterward, Miss Jean Kerr, then McCarthy's research assistant and now his wife, and Robert E. Lee, a close personal and political friend of McCarthy, went to work for Facts Forum. Their job was to organize the television project.

'Hunt himself has admitted that McCarthy's recent bride (Miss Kerr) "has done a great many things for Facts Forum," but has denied she was on the Facts Forum payroll at the time. "She and Robert E. Lee," Hunt said, "were instrumental in getting together the first Facts Forum programs, the television programs."'

A nice set-up, indeed. Here we have the wealthiest of the Texas oil tycoons, the man who has practically run nefarious Dallas for decades, forging close personal, political and business links with the very symbol of right-wing radicalism in America, Senator McCarthy.

And Lyndon B. Johnson, the Democratic Senator from Texas, a self-styled follower of the great Franklin D. Roosevelt tradition, picks that precise moment to select from this Hunt-McCarthy crowd an 'executive assistant' and 'authorized biographer' for himself. Indeed, nothing could illustrate more strikingly the intimate working relationship between Johnson and Hunt than the fact that Booth Mooney was for years operating simultaneously as an executive assistant to Senator Johnson and Washington lobbyist for oilman Hunt.

'Friends say Mr. Hunt finds it hard to break away publicly from Mr. Johnson,' the above-quoted article in *The New York Times* went on to report, 'because the President for years was such a staunch friend of the oil industry. But, Mr. Hunt says, Mr. Johnson has made "terrible mistakes" as President, including the selection of Chief Justice Warren to head the inquiry into President Kennedy's assassination'.

This almost naive statement shows that, Hunt, for all his evil cunning, has indeed basically remained a country hick, with an IQ way below that of his partner Lyndon B. Johnson. Actually it was a real masterstroke when the latter picked Earl Warren, until then the bearer of one of the most respected names in America, to lend his high prestige to the most ignominious cover-up operation in modern history. Hunt couldn't appreciate the extraordinary finesse of that move. He was shocked because Johnson had appointed Chief Justice Warren to head the Commission three days after the communist *Daily Worker*, in a front-page statement, has suggested it. That Johnson did not follow this advice in order to accommodate the Communists, but for a truly Machiavellian purpose, was something bound to escape the limited intelligence of an H. L. Hunt.

Hunt was scared to death, and for an apparently good reason, for Earl Warren had, immediately after the assassination, publicly expressed the opinion that this foul deed was the work of right-wing extremists. His anxiety grew when investigators for the Warren Commission found out that one of his boys, Nelson, had paid for that despicable ad in the *Dallas Morning News*, while another, Lamar, maintained a cozy business and social relationship with notorious pimp and murderer Jack Ruby.

What the old man didn't realize is that the Commission, in this as in a score of other cases, simply sought to establish the damaging facts in order to be better able to suppress them and to shield effectively those responsible for the assassination. How Lyndon B. Johnson ever managed to get a man like Earl Warren so abjectly to prostitute his great name and prestige, remains the only real mystery of Dallas. But he did it and thus managed to fool, at least for a few years, public opinion throughout America and the world.

After the Warren Report had been released, Hunt heaved a deep sigh of relief. When reporters asked him how he felt about it Hunt replied, 'It's a very honest document'. And that, coming from H. L. Hunt, is about the most damning thing anybody has ever said about the Warren Report.

One more quote from that article about the 'Magnate with a Mission' in *The New York Times* is in order:

'Mr. Hunt lists among those Americans whom he admires as patriots Gen. Robert E. Wood, former chairman of Sears Roebuck & Co., a member of the Life Line advisory board, and a strong Goldwater supporter; Gen. A. C. Wedemeyer, former chief of staff to Chiang Kai-shek, once a member of the John Birch Society advisory committee, and a Life Line advisory board member; Robert H. W. Welch, Jr., founder of the John Birch Society ; Maj. Gen. Edwin A. Walker, the ultraconservative former officer; Gov. Wallace, Senator Goldwater and President Johnson'.

This is about as complete a collection of the top Fascist generals, Birchers, Ku-Klux-Klansmen and reactionary politicians one could muster at a glance in America today. Charming company for Lyndon B. Johnson.

These and other retired generals and active militants of the extreme right form the backbone of that pernicious military-industrial establishment against which even a conservative military man like former President Eisenhower has found it necessary to warn the nation. Many of them have close links with the so-called 'intelligence community' and, in particular, the CIA.

No wonder Hunt and his likes detest Eisenhower. According to Robert G. Sherrill, Hunt has said: 'Eisenhower was no good. Eisenhower was the worst President, the most harmful President we have ever had...'

Hunt takes great pride in having helped to push through (or so he claims) the Twenty-second Amendment, which forbids a third presidential term.

He makes one exception, though: 'Johnson,' he says, lighting up, 'is the kind of President who can lead Congress around by its nose. I wouldn't mind seeing him in there for three terms'.

Indeed, Lyndon B. Johnson is the ideal President for the Hunts of America. And they made him President.

'Since the late 1940s,' Sherrill writes, 'Hunt has fancied himself in the role of kingmaker and as a shaper of national policy. He tried his hand at the making of various "kings," in particular General Douglas MacArthur and then, in 1960, went all out for his fellow Texan, Lyndon B. Johnson'.

In this endeavor, Hunt enlisted the help of one of those bigoted rabblerousers of the cloth who abound in the Dallas area, the Reverend W. A. Criswell, pastor for of the First Baptist Church of Dallas. Since about 1957, Hunt and Criswell had been working hand-in-hand, with the former sponsoring the pastor's printed outpourings and the latter peddling Life Line pamphlets to his parishioners. Now, to quote again from Sherrill's illuminating article in *The Nation*:

'Not long before the 1960 Democratic Presidential Convention Criswell mounted his pulpit and sounded an alarm against the threat of Romanisn in politics that was heard around the country: "The election of a Catholic as President would mean the end of religious liberty in America." Kennedy had gone on record as favoring a review of the oil industry's tax benefits, including the depletion allowance. A "review" could only mean a lessening of benefits. The Reverend Criswell's message sounded useful indeed to Hunt...

'That's why Hunt promptly had 200,000 reprints of Criswell's sermon printed and mailed out, after which he sat back to watch a wave of aroused Protestantism wash Kennedy out of the running. Instead, the wave was one of indignation from editorial writers and the general public at this artificial injection of hysteria into American politics.

'The Senate took an even sterner approach. The Criswell flier did not name its source and there is a federal law against distributing this kind of anonymous circular after a campaign is officially underway. In Dallas, the perpetrators panicked. Hunt ducked out entirely and could not be found. Criswell denied that Hunt had paid for the leaflets, but Ralph B. Raughley, a partner in a Great Neck, L. I. printing firm, told a Senate subcommittee that an employee of Hunt's had paid $10,000 for the printing and mailing of the sermon to Protestant ministers.

'Fortunately for Hunt, Raughley also swore that the order had been placed before the Democratic convention closed in Los Angeles. Thus Hunt was legally, if not morally, in the clear...'

After their attempt to torpedo the Kennedy candidacy on religious grounds had failed, the Johnson-Hunt clique, before and during the Los Angeles convention, tried a dozen more low tricks from their well-filled bag. In particular, they berated the front-running Kennedy for the alleged Nazi affiliations of his father (this coming from Hunt & Co.!); they hinted darkly that he was incurably sick (Addison's disease); they spread false rumors about Kennedy's supposed earlier marriage; and they even peddled fancy tales of alleged sexual escapades by him at Convention time. It was a real witch's brew, but all to no avail.

Even the staid *New York Times*, in an article by Russell Baker published on November 23, 1963, wrote: 'Although Mr. Johnson arrived at Los Angeles with the Kennedy nomination a virtual certainty, he nevertheless attacked with a ferocity that startled his admirers and seemed to create a permanent chasm between himself and Mr. Kennedy'.

That ferocity turned into a boomerang, just as the previous Hunt-Criswell production had done. Kennedy won the nomination hands down.

'The history of the Vice-Presidential nomination that followed is still garbled,' Mr. Baker went on to say. 'It came as a shock to Mr. Johnson's family, his advisers, his staff, his Senate colleagues, everyone who had assumed that he had alienated himself permanently from the Kennedys. It was also a shock to Mr. Kennedy's liberal convention supporters.

'When Mr. Kennedy first proposed it, the Johnson camp seemed to receive the offer as an insult. The late Sam Rayburn, then Speaker of the House, and Mr. Johnson's closest friend and confidant, advised against accepting. His family was opposed. Most of his staff and most political veterans on the scene assumed that the man who ran the Senate would scarcely surrender his position of power for the anonymity of the Vice-Presidency...'

Since then, a good deal of light has been thrown on the backstage manuvering that went on in Los Angeles. Arthur Schlesinger, Jr., Theodore White and other well-informed political writers have brought out that the Kennedy offer to Johnson was no more than a gesture in the interest of party unity, made in the belief that there was practically no chance Johnson would accept.

But, in the words of J. Evetts Haley, 'Johnson wanted power and with all his knowledge of political strategy and his proven control of Congress, he could see wider horizons of power as Vice-President than as Senate Majority Leader. In effect, by presiding over the Senate, he could now conceive himself as virtually filling both high and important positions—and he was not far from wrong. Finally, as Victor Lasky pointed out, Johnson had nursed a "lifetime dream to be President. As Majority leader he never could have made it. But as Vice-President, fate could always intervene."'

Fate could always intervene... 'Diabolical fate' as Haley elsewhere put it. Fate, coincidence, chance—Hale, Lasky, the Warren Commission, *et al*, seem to have the same blind spot, for they always talk about supernatural forces, when the crass reality of ruthless human scheming is so self-evident.

'Corriger la fortune, 18th century French gamblers used to call the process by which deft brainwork or nimble fingerwork are substituted for the all-too-slow interventions of Fortune.

Nothing was left to chance in Dallas on November 22, 1963. And the groundwork of what happened then had been laid well over three years earlier.

The question why Lyndon B. Johnson, at the Los Angeles convention, so dramatically reversed himself—for he had previously proclaimed that he would never take the second spot on the ticket—against the advice of all his friends and counsellors, will have to be examined conscientiously some day by historians.

Or by a court of law.

'There are many theories about his reasons for stepping into what most observers at Los Angeles considered oblivion,' Russell Baker wrote, conspicuously overlooking the most obvious one.

H. L. Hunt has not been so reticent.

What prompted Hunt, ostensibly against his own interests—for Johnson's acceptance of the Vice-Presidency was bound to deprive the oil interests of their most influential voice in Congress—to urge Johnson to take the second spot?

And how could his lone opinion prevail over the opposite counsel of so many tested Johnson advisers, including Sam Rayburn?

History has given a clear-cut answer to that question. It is an answer as yet fully understood only by a few, but more eyes are opening every day.

Besides H. L. Hunt, there was only one other Johnson intimate who advised the reluctant candidate to accept the second spot on the Democratic ticket. That was young Bobby Baker, Johnson's favorite protégé, about whom a great deal more will have to be said in subsequent chapters.

Bobby Baker, whose chief, natural asset is a nimble mind and who is as totally devoid of scruples as any other member of the Johnson clique, immediately understood the possibilities H. L. Hunt had in mind even at that early moment. A great believer in cash philosophy, he also instantly realized why Hunt, after having done everything in his power to block the Kennedy nomination, now stood ready to fork out over $100,000 to help the Kennedy-Johnson team to win over the Republican competition.

It was one of Bobby Baker's closest friends and business associates of that time, Don B. Reynolds, who three years later was to spill the beans on that score. That's why Edward J. Epstein, in a long article in the December 1966 issue of *Esquire* magazine, included Reynolds, along with Joachim Joesten, Barbara Garson, Jack Ruby and a few others as proponents of the 'Johnson theory':

'Although not one shred of hard evidence has been uncovered to prove them right, many people have taken the "Who benefited?" line of pursuit and point an accusing finger at Lyndon Johnson'.

Says Epstein about Don Reynolds' finger-wagging:

'In January of 1964 the Warren Commission learned that Don B. Reynolds, insurance agent and close associate of Bobby Baker, had been heard to say the FBI knew that Johnson was behind the assassination. When interviewed by the FBI, he denied this. *(Says the FBI -J. J.)* But he did recount an incident during the swearing in of Kennedy in which Bobby Baker said words to the effect that the s.o.b. would never live out his term and that he would die a violent death'.

Bobby Baker said that, mind you, in 1961. Now was that supernatural vision—or could it be that Mr. Baker chanced to have exact knowledge of something that was going to happen at the opportune moment?

CHAPTER 4 - 'To Get Our Man Elected'

ELECTIONS cost money, an awful lot of money. The way the American plutocracy works in our time, one has to be either a millionaire or to be able to draw on the financial assistance of millionaire 'angels' in order to have a minimum chance of being elected President. That is axiomatic.

Those who contribute funds for a presidential campaign (or a Congressional one or even one on the level of state and local elections) invariably expect something in return. That is axiomatic, too.

Even the best of American presidents, men like Franklin D. Roosevelt and John F. Kennedy, indulged in the practice of political payoffs. The worst of the lot, like Lyndon B. Johnson, have been busy throughout their stay in the White House reimbursing their sponsors out of the public till, in one way or another.

One of the most blatant examples of financial *quid pro quo* in contemporary electioneering came to light in the course of the Baker investigation (which will be discussed in detail in a later portion of this book). It was revealed to the three Republican members of the Senate Rules Committee—the six Democrats on the Committee didn't even want to listen, for good reason—by the afore-named Don B. Reynolds, a former business associate and pal of Bobby Baker who eventually turned star witness against the latter after Senator Williams had put the heat on him (See Chapter 14).

When Baker appeared before the Committee, in the last week of February, 1964, one of the most significant of the more than 100 specific questions fired at him was:

'Did you receive $10,000 from Fred Black for a 1960 *presidential* candidate's campaign contribution?'

Bobby didn't care to answer that question any more than the rest of the hundred. He maintained a stony silence in the protective shadow of the Fifth Amendment.

But, to quote *Time* magazine (March 6, 1964):

'Reynolds told the committee's Republican members that he was present when Black gave Baker $10,000 in cash "to get our man elected," and promised $90,000 more. Reynolds said that Baker later told him the money was for Johnson's campaign'.

Time, which during the Johnson Administration became practically a house organ of the LBJ-Ranch (on a par with its competitor, *Newsweek*), is here being as discreet as a news-magazine can possibly be without forfeiting the first part of its title. The magazine failed to enlighten its readers on the question of for which of Lyndon Johnson's 1960 campaigns his $100,000 contribution was intended. That's why I have italicized the word 'presidential' in the text of the question put to Baker by the Senate probers.

Johnson, campaigned first in 1960 for the presidency—against Kennedy who also sought, and won the Democratic nomination;

and then he campaigned for the vice-presidency, alongside of Kennedy who had won the top spot on the ticket.

The wording of the question put to Baker, at the committee hearing, in connection with Reynolds' identification of Lyndon B. Johnson as recipient of this campaign distribution, establishes beyond a shadow of doubt, therefore, that this $100,000 fund ($10,000 down, $90,000 promised) was intended to finance Johnson's battle against Kennedy for the presidential nomination at the party convention, not the joint ticket selected there. It was not a campaign contribution made to the Democratic Party, but one to Lyndon B. Johnson personally.

And those who handed out, or pledged, this huge campaign fund were interested not in seeing the Kennedy-Johnson ticket win out over the Nixon-Lodge team, but wanted to make sure, at the earlier stage of the contest, that 'their man' would get the presidential nomination over the front-runner, John F. Kennedy.

Who were these well-heeled wire-pullers behind the scene?

Fred Black, a professional lobbyist, had many irons in the fire, but he was first and foremost the Washington representative of North American Aviation, Inc., a huge aerospace concern which, in the Johnson era, was able to wangle the largest slice of the U.S. Government's fantastically costly and, to industry, immensely profitable lunar exploration program.

There can be little doubt, therefore, that most, if not all, of that $100,000 which was to pass through Bobby Baker's hands, on its way to Lyndon B. Johnson's pockets, came from North American

Aviation and was designed to pave the golden way for a presidential candidate who, once elected, could be relied upon to favor this giant corporation, along with its countless affiliates and subcontractors, over competitive firms.

In this regard, some quotes are in order from an article entitled 'Miller Taunts Johnson on Baker', which appeared in the February 13, 1964 issue of *Newsday*:

'Washington—Republican National Chairman William E. Miller raked President Johnson over the still-flaming coals of the Bobby Baker case yesterday and called for a Teapot Dome type of investigation.

'"How many times did North American Aviation (a big defense contractor) advertise over the LBJ TV station (in Austin, Tex.)?" Miller asked a National Press Club luncheon audience without further explaining or answering his own question. He said, further, that was only one of the many questions about the Baker case that needed checking. Johnson, he added, just a bit cryptically, "has done very well since he came to Washington with one suit." And, amid laughter from the audience, he added, also without spelling it out, that the war on poverty began long before Johnson's State of the Union message...'

Indeed, Lyndon B. Johnson's war on poverty—his own—began the day he hit Washington in the wake of his rancher-friend Richard Kleberg, late in 1932. It is the only war on poverty he has ever pursued with vigor and success. And one of his means towards this end was building fruitful business and political relationships with such big corporations as North American Aviation.

It is too bad, really, that the Republican high command did not follow up on the suggestion of its National Chairman Miller and check how many times North American Aviation did advertise over the eminently successful TV station of the LBJ Broadcasting Company in Austin—which will be the subject of the next chapter. His 'rhetorical' question, however, indicates an awareness, among the Republican leadership, that there was plenty of such advertising and that it would have been their duty to the nation to lay the facts on the line.

However, the spread of corruption among American politicians is so great and so thoroughly bipartisan—as the Baker case among many others has demonstrated—that Johnson apparently was able to stop this particular line of attack through the simple expedient of threatening counter-exposure of some equally corrupt bigwig in the Republican camp.

According to *Newsday*, 'Miller said that the Baker situation struck him as "pretty sickening" and added: "I wish we could campaign on issues which do not strike at the personal integrity of officials in high places." Despite that wish, Miller said, the Baker case should be used by the GOP as campaign ammunition in the presidential election'.

It was, but very lamely. Vague oratory aside, the Republicans did very little to exploit the immense possibilities inherent in that scandal, just as they deliberately ignored the even larger issue of

Johnson's illegitimate accession to power. The reason for such restraint was in both cases the same: too many big wheels of the Republican Party would have been tarred with the Baker brush, if the attack had been pressed; and too many of them had been involved, one way or another, in the right-wing agitation that had led to the assassination in Dallas.

So, by a sort of gentleman's agreement (if one can speak of gentlemen under the circumstances) both these sordid issues were swept under the rug, with the inevitable result that Johnson, in November 1964, won by a landslide. Had the American people really learned the truth about the Baker scandal and, even more importantly, about the Oswald Hoax, they would certainly not have returned Johnson to the White House, even at the risk—God forbid—of putting a Goldwater in his stead.

Thus are American politics conducted in our day. The people have the choice only between the greater and the lesser evil and it is often hard enough to see the difference.

In the light of the above disclosures concerning the ties between Lyndon B. Johnson and North American Aviation, the fact that Bobby Baker's own business venture, 'Serv-U', had an equally happy business relationship with that industrial giant (as will be detailed in a subsequent chapter) assumes special significance.

Here, indeed, you have a real wheeler-dealer's merry-go-round whirling before your eyes:

One of the nation's biggest industrial concerns, North American Aviation, employs as its Washington representative a topflight lobbyist, Fred Black, who also happens to be a close friend and business partner of the powerful Senate leader and later Vice-President, Lyndon B. Johnson.

Through the Black-Baker conduit, North American channels $100,000 into this private campaign chest of LBJ; it also showers lucrative advertising on the Austin TV monopoly of the Johnson family.

And who do you suppose happens to be, at that precise moment, Chairman of the Senate's Aeronautical and Space Committee, which is supposed to act as Congressional watchdog over Government profits and expenses in that lucrative field? Well, Lyndon B. Johnson, of all people!

To round out the picture, Bobby Baker, right after 'our man' has been elected, starts from scratch a vending machine business (See Chapter 13) and promptly finds a first-class customer: North American Aviation, which, according to *The New York Times* of April 22, 1964, did an annual gross business worth an estimated $3 million with Bobby Baker's Serv-U Corporation.

And, coincidentally, North American Aviation snatches the biggest slice of America's multi-billion-dollar aerospace program.

CHAPTER 5 - The Wealthiest President Ever

On the early afternoon of November 22, 1963, a mechanic in the West Texas oil town of Odessa, upon hearing the news, thoughtfully paused and remarked:

'That means Lyndon Johnson is President. He's stolen out half of Texas; I guess now he'll steal out half of the United States'.

From J. Evetts Haley: *A Texan Looks at Lyndon*

IN *The New York Times* of August 13, 1964 (International Edition), the noted columnist James Reston took a critical look at 'Johnson's Money: An Underground Issue' and wrote:

'President and Mrs. Johnson, according to published reports, seem to be getting richer and richer. In May, *U.S. News and World Report* estimated their net holdings at over $7 million. In June, the *Washington Star* made it $9 million, and this week's *Life* magazine puts it at "approximately $14 million."

'This fortune, whatever its size, is gradually becoming an underground issue in the election campaign. Each article implies that it was amassed partly as a result of Mr. Johnson's political influence and the White House answer to all queries is merely that the President has put everything in an irrevocable trust and has no control over it whatever'.

Referring to Johnson's opponent, Senator Barry Goldwater, who had just released an accounting of his family's holdings, showing a net worth of about $1.7 million, Mr. Reston went on to say:

'Pending a similar disclosure by the Johnsons, the newspapers and magazines are within their rights to try to find out what they can about how a man who has been on the public payroll for 33 years could build a fortune of any king...'

Later on in his piece, Mr. Reston discussed the question why the public was curious about Johnson's personal fortune and was entitled to some explanations:

'The budget of the Federal Government now totals almost $100 billion, about half of which is for defense. The allocation of defense contracts now often determines whether major cities and even regions of the nation prosper economically or decline, and the fight for these contracts has produced wholly new temptations and possible conflicts of interest for both executive and legislative employees.

'Throughout this last year, the Senate has been engaged in a savage controversy over charges of influence-peddling on the part of Robert

'Baker, the former secretary to the Democratic majority in the Senate. Also, in this same period, the Senate has been in a turmoil over the allocation of a vast military airplane contract—the TFX— to a firm in Texas rather than to another in the state of Washington.

'Before that, the Congress divided over the Federal Government's decision to locate the new space headquarters in

Houston rather than in Boston, and these are only the most prominent of the recent cases involving Federal contracts.

'At no time has there been any charge that President Johnson has used the White House to further his own financial interests, or that, as majority leader of the Senate he ever did anything illegal. But because the space agency and the TFX contract did go to Texas, and because Robert Baker was his personal protégé in the Senate, his name has repeatedly been brought into these controversies and added to his reputation as a highly successful political manipulator...'

In this last paragraph, Mr. Reston engages in the familiar double talk and whitewash technique of all Johnson supporters (which he is, in spite of his occasional veiled criticism). If there had been no public charge that Johnson had feathered his own nest by using his political influence, that certainly does not mean that there is no basis for such a charge.

And Reston's statement that there was no charge that Johnson 'used the White House to further his own financial interests or that, as majority leader of the Senate, he ever did anything illegal' evidently leaves open the question of whether Johnson used his Senate position to further his own financial interests and even the corollary one of whether, when in the White House, he didn't do something illegal. *Time* magazine, on August 21, 1964, put it this way:

'Lyndon Johnson was born hard-scrabbling poor in a ramshackle Texas farmhouse, but he soon learned the value of hard work, good luck, quick wits and bold maneuver. After 27 years of service in modestly paid public offices, he has managed to become one of the richest Presidents in U.S. History'.

That is, indeed, the Lyndon Johnson story in a nutshell and if it does not constitute *prima facie* evidence of corruption on a massive scale, all words have lost their meaning.

The United States Internal Revenue Service, in combating the attempts of wealthy gangsters to enjoy their ill-gotten riches tax-free, has successfully employed over the years the so-called 'net worth theory'. Basically, the theory consists in using as yardstick of assessment not the annual income claimed by the mobsters (they couldn't really be honest about it, even if they wanted to be, because so much of it is from illegitimate sources) but the visible, palpable increase in their wealth and living standards.

Discarding the mobster's income tax declaration *a priori* as worthless, the sleuths of the Internal Revenue Service apply themselves instead to finding out, among other things, how much real estate this person owns; how many automobiles, of what model and year of make he has; how many servants and mistresses he keeps (and how affluent the latter are); how much money he has recently gambled away and how much he spends on high living etc. etc. Then, working back from these expenditures and assets, which can be verified with comparative ease, the investigators conclude—in most cases irrefutably—how much that particular gangster must have really earned in a given period. The discrepancy between that figure and the one given by the man himself in his income tax declaration is usually so big that it leads to prosecution for income tax evasion and a heavy jail sentence.

Unfortunately, the IRS's 'net worth theory' is seldom, if ever, applied to successful politicians. But it serves as a perfect yardstick for measuring the integrity of such people.

To be sure, Johnson and his faithful keep pointing out that all that money doesn't really belong to the President, who is as pure as Caesar's wife, but that it is perfectly legitimate income earned by Lady Bird and her two daughters, mostly through their television station (see the following chapter). But one would have to be inordinately naive to accept these 'explanations' at face value.

Any affluent mobster who told a judge that he never made a penny but that the missus and the kids were the real business geniuses would get the book thrown at him. But clever politicos like Lyndon B. Johnson can get away with absolutely everything.

The way the American press has reported the engrossing story of Johnson's road from rags to riches suggests that some of the old spirit of muckraking is still alive, but dampened, if not crushed by a healthy respect for the powers in Washington.

Take for example *The Washington Evening Star* which on June 9, 1964 shocked the country by revealing not only that the size of the Johnson family fortune was well above what had previously been conceded, but also that the secrecy surrounding it was heavily guarded.

After stating that the Johnson holdings in radio stations, land, banks and stocks were reliably calculated at $9 million, the paper noted that this huge fortune 'was amassed almost entirely while Mr. Johnson was in public office; mainly since he entered the Senate and began his rise to national power in 1948'.

Recalling that, according to the common version, this fortune was mainly the result of Mrs. Johnson's business acumen and energy, *The Star* wrote:

'Mrs. Johnson doubtless has made impressive contributions. But there is strong evidence that Mr. Johnson himself has participated vigorously in the family business ventures.

'Several Texans who dealt with the Johnsons prior to last November say they always dealt with Mr. Johnson, never with his wife'.

This is, of course, the crux of the matter. The legalistic fiction, strictly adhered to by 'authorized' biographers, White House spokesmen and assorted press agents, was presented by *The Star* in these terms:

'Mr. Johnson, it should be noted, owns no stock in the company which has title to most of the Johnson property and has provided the family with such amenities as limousines, an airplane, a cabin cruiser and the LBJ Ranch itself. A majority of the family company stock, 84.45 per cent, is owned by Mrs. Johnson and her daughters.

'Last Nov. 29, a week after Mr. Johnson entered the White House, the family relinquished control of the company by putting the stock in trust.

'The trust agreement stipulates that neither the President nor his wife shall receive any information on how the family property is administered.

'Since then, according to Washington attorney Abe Fortas, an old friend and personal legal adviser to the President, Mr. Johnson has not engaged in or discussed any family business. But in gathering material for this article, *The Star* has received allegations to the contrary'.

Fully conscious, apparently, that the origins and development of his unconscionable wealth could give rise to adverse comment, Johnson has taken great care to dissuade any and all of his business contacts from talking to the press. *The Washington Star* noted in this respect:

'Reliable businessmen, knowledgeable about the Johnson wealth and how it was acquired, generally are most reluctant to talk about it. Those who will usually extract an oath that their names never will be mentioned'.

That's the way authentic gangsters keep the world from knowing how rich they are and how they got that way: Anybody they deal with must give a solemn pledge to keep his mouth shut— or else. America's cemeteries are full of prematurely deceased people who talked too much about where Lucky Luciano, Frank Costello, Alberto Anastasia, Vito Genovese, Thomas Luchese and others of their ilk got their money from.

But for a President of the United States to put such pressure on his former business associates that they feel compelled to extract oaths of anonymity from inquiring newsmen surely was something unheard-of until Lyndon B. Johnson came along.

The Washington Star went on to illustrate that pressure with this almost comical episode:

'After some 30 minutes of conversation with a reporter, an Austin oilman abruptly halted the interview. He refused to continue it until he had verified the reporter's identity by calling Washington and receiving a physical description of him from an editor'.

Obviously the story of how Lyndon B. Johnson became the richest President in the history of the United States is *TOP SECRET* and anyone who wants to have a peep at it must first get clearance from Washington.

The Star, parenthetically, thought there had been wealthier occupants of The White House than Johnson:

'About former Presidents, one estimate is that it would take $20 million at today's prices, to buy the land George Washington owned. But he was frequently short of cash.

'President Kennedy is reported to have left $10 million when he died. Herbert Hoover is said to be worth much more than that. It is known that Mr. Hoover had about $6 million as far back as 1914'.

In the first place, however, none of the afore-named presidents started out from 'hard scrabbling poor', as Johnson did; as a matter of fact they all were multimillionaires before they got into politics. And, secondly, Johnson, according to the *Life* estimate, which is by far the most detailed and well-documented (see below), is worth at least 14 million, not 9 as *The Star* has it. Thus he is, without question, the wealthiest President that ever sat in The White House.

One of the most illuminating exposés of Johnson's road to fortune was published in May 1964, in a series of articles written by Thomas Collins of the *Newsday* Washington Bureau. *Newsday*, at that time, was still something of a fighting liberal and hard-hitting newspaper, whereas it is now, under the editorial supervision of Johnson's ex-aide Bill Moyers, just one more bubble in an ocean of consensus papers.

The Collins series began with these words:

'Time after time in recent weeks President Johnson, with scarcely veiled exasperation, has publicly declared his total divorcement from the flourishing radio and television station that is in his wife's name and—unfortunately for him—also in the files of the Federal Communications Commission (FCC), which must regulate it.

'It is a problem that will not disappear, not merely because this is a political season, but also because the facts that were of little interest in the political career of a representative, a senator and a vice president are properly of public concern in the career of a President.

'After an exhaustive investigation in Austin and Washington, one fact becomes clear: the President's disclaimer may be letter-of-the-law correct, but in ordinary English, the President and the television station company are almost as connected as the corner grocer and his grocery store'.

That this is, indeed, the case is amply demonstrated by each and all of the various sources cited here in evidence. Johnson's 'divorcement' from his business interests has always been no more than a lawyer's gimmick which is designed primarily to hide the fact that a government-regulated enterprise has been, thanks to a long string of favors from the regulating agency (see the following chapter), a source of immense profits to a top Government official. Such a state of affairs is, no matter how lawyers dress it up, blatant corruption.

When President Johnson, at a press conference on April 16, 1964, was pointedly asked by a bold reporter about the ethics of a federal official (himself) being connected with a government-regulated business, he replied in the typical Johnsonian style which is, as a rule, a mixture of double-talk and outright lying:

'...I don't have any interest in government-regulated industries of any kind and never have had. I own no stocks. I own a little ranch land, something in excess of 2,000 acres... Mrs. Johnson inherited some property, invested that property in the profession of her choice, and worked at it with pleasure and satisfaction until I forced her to leave it when I assumed the presidency... I see no conflict in any way...'

The time-honored dodge Lyndon Johnson employed when he had made up his mind that he was going to be both a senator or better and a millionaire was to set up in 1947 a family concern named The Texas Broadcasting Corporation. He invested control of his company, with 52 per cent of the shares, in his wife, and 16.5 percent in each of his daughters, for a total of 85 per cent held directly by the family. The remaining stock—it has dwindled since then to 11 percent and the family's share has increased correspondingly—is owned by company officials of long standing—all of whom are pledged to sell it back to the company if they wish to dispose of their holdings.

While the cornerstone of the Texas Broadcasting Corp. has been the immensely successful radio station KTBC in Austin, whose operations will be described in the following chapters, its broadly phrased charter also allowed it to engage in land ventures, ranching operations, oil exploitation, banking and all kinds of other business enterprises.

Subsequently, the name of the Texas Broadcasting Corporation was changed to that of 'LBJ Co'., but after Johnson had become President the company reverted to its old name.

The first of these two changes of name occurred at a time when Johnson, as senator, gave free rein to his vanity and put his LBJ stamp on everything he owned or acquired, from his ranch near Johnson City which, incidentally, was not named after his family though Lyndon Johnson has made that claim to his shirts and neckties. The second of course was prompted by the overriding desire for concealment which overcame Johnson after he had at last fulfilled his life's greatest ambition and had become President of the United States.

A few days after moving into the White House, Mrs. Johnson ostensibly divested herself of company control, which she had exercised for years from a second-floor office in the Johnson's $200,000 home in the Spring Valley section of Washington. To this effect, she filed an application with the FCC to turn over her 313 shares (52.8 per cent of the stock) to two trustees, A. W. Moursund and J. W. Bullion, both of Johnson City, Texas. At the time the two men also held 184 shares in trust for the Johnson daughters, Lynda Bird and Lucy Baines.

A. W. Moursund, general counsel of the Citizens State Bank of Johnson City and real estate dealer, is an old crony of LBJ, who has played a leading part in screening the First Family's wealth and continuing business operations from public view. According to *Life* magazine (21-9-64), Moursund has a direct telephone link to the White House. This telltale fact alone disposes of the fiction that he Johnsons exercise no control over their business interests while the head of the family resides in The White House.

The whole operation, of course, was never anything but a blind, designed to hoodwink the public, as is almost anything Johnson does or says. Plenty of witnesses, and even more telltale facts, clearly indicate (a) that Lyndon B. Johnson, not his wife has been all along the business genius behind the Texas Broadcasting Corporation; and (b) that he continued to run his far-flung business empire from the White House, managing it far better than the nation's affairs.

Life took care to point out that there was nothing intrinsically wrong with a Chief Executive who got on to the public payroll practically as a pauper and stayed there for 33 years to become the richest President in U.S. history.

In the first paragraph of the article, which was written by Keith Wheeler and William Lambert and entitled 'How LBJ's Family Amassed Its Fortune', the magazine set the tone by stating:

'The family of President Lyndon Baines Johnson has grown notably wealthy during his 27 (*sic*) years in high public office. This process of accumulation violated no tradition in a republic which is founded on the principles of free enterprise and which has never demanded of its servants—whether at federal, state or courthouse level—that they practice economic celibacy'.

In other words, it's perfectly all right in America to be a grafter and a wheeler-dealer in office, because corruption is a national tradition. Even if one were to accept this outrageous premise, a line must be drawn between the practice of 'economic celibacy' and the practice of economic debauchery. Even *Life* had some second thoughts on the matter:

'But every man who has amassed personal substance while simultaneously holding the public trust has had to tread a delicate, almost invisible line between his private interest and the public interest. The Johnson family story furnishes a fascinating study in how and where one man has handled that problem...'

It may be fascinating to the editors of a multimillion-dollar publishing concern which has certainly never practiced 'economic celibacy' either, but to me it seems that there are a lot of adjectives in the dictionary that would apply better to the 'Johnson family story'.

Messrs. Wheeler and Lambert then went on to explain how they arrived at placing the $14 million figure on 'the Johnson family's total accumulation of wealth'—an estimate far higher than all the preceding ones. The article was accompanied by an itemized 'Trustee's statement of the Johnson's holdings', drawn up by Albert W. Caster & Company, a firm of certified public accountants, and specially prepared for *Life* by Mr. A. W. Moursund.

According to this statement, the financial net worth of Lyndon B. Johnson was, in mid-year 1964, 'under $400,000.00', that of his wife 'slightly over $2,500,000.00', and that of the two daughters together $1,260,000.00 ($630,000.00 each), for a total family net worth of $4,160,000.00.

Goaded by the mounting public interest in his wealth, and apparently having gotten wind of the forthcoming *Life* story, President Johnson, on August 19, 1964, released through the accounting firm of Haskins & Sells, one of the biggest in the United States, still another assessment of his family's wealth, which arrived at an even lower figure.

According to Haskins & Sells, the President, Mrs. Johnson and their two daughters, as of July 31, 1964, had combined assets of $3,682,770. At the same time, the family had total liabilities of $198,672 which reduced their net worth to $3,484,098—about

$680,000 less than the figure Johnson's own trustee, A. W. Moursund, made public at almost exactly the same time.

The Haskins & Sells estimate was greeted with derisive laughter from coast to coast. *The Wall Street Journal*, surely an authoritative judge in such matters, considered the figure of $3.8 million as 'grossly understated'. *The New York Times* called it 'undoubtedly conservative if market, rather than book, value is made the yardstick'.

The most pungent comment came from the then National Chairman of the Republican Party, Dean Burch. Explaining that the modest figure in the Haskins & Sells valuation had been arrived at by a generally accepted accounting technique by which the original cost is used instead of current market value, Mr. Burch said that, in this instance, it was 'like listing the value of Manhattan Island at $24'—the price paid to the Indians for it by Peter Stuyvesant.

Nobody bothered to explain how two firms of certified public accountants, both employed by the Johnson family, could arrive at the same time at net worth estimates differing from each other by the huge sum of $680,000.

Life magazine, contrasting both these disparate accountings with its own valuation of $14 million, commented:

'There may be a number of reasons for the disparity in the figures. Basic to any financial appraisal is how the worth of the holdings is measured—by "book" value (the way it appears on the books for accounting purposes) or by "market" value (current resale value).

'For the purposes of this article, *Life* has applied the broader measure, to establish a businessman's evaluation of what the total Johnson accumulations are worth by a conservative calculation of present market values'.

After presenting a detailed picture of these 'accumulations', *Life* came up with this balance sheet:

Market value of the Johnson family's total broadcasting interests - $8.6 million

Real estate worth (conservatively) - $3.6 million

Assets held by specified funds and foundations, including bank stocks - $0.6 million

Cash and municipal bonds - $0.5 million

Plus miscellaneous personal property (upward of) - $0.4 million

In the words of *Time* magazine, (28-8-64) 'the (Haskins & Sells) audit offers some interesting glimpses into the President's capital progress since 1954, when his family's worth was listed as $737,730, scarcely a fourth of what it is today, even by the conservative Haskins & Sells evaluation.

'During the decade, Lady Bird handily out-earned her husband by drawing $570,856 as "compensation for services" from Texas Broadcasting, while Lyndon made $109,730 in salary and expenses as Senator, Vice President and President. In the same period, the Johnsons shelled out $587,515 for "living, office, travel, entertainment and sundry expenses," $365,955 for federal income taxes, and $178,578 for charitable donations'.

Parenthetically it must be stated that any ordinary taxpayer who, over a ten-year period, deducts from his federal income tax $178,578 for 'charitable donations'—almost half as much as he pays in income tax during the same period—would soon feel the hot breath of an IRS sleuth on his neck.

Could it be that Lyndon B. Johnson who, as this book shows, has practiced deceit in all domains all through his life, also cheated Uncle Sam out of his due? Some day when he has ceased to be President and has reverted to ordinary taxpayer status, we may get an authoritative answer to that pertinent question.

Before we go into the details of how Johnson, the public servant, amassed a $14 million fortune in various fields of endeavor—mainly broadcasting, ranching, land speculation and banking, as far as the overt side of it is concerned—one inure quotation from the above-cited *Life* article is in order:

'It has never been entirely clear to the general public who deserves what share of the credit for accumulating the Johnson holdings. The family has favored a legend that Lady Bird Johnson possesses the Midas touch and has run up most of the family wealth virtually single-handed. People who have had financial dealings with the family credit Mrs. Johnson with an astute business head. But they say that invariably, when it came to the hard bargaining, they sat down with the head of the household'.

J. Evetts Haley also plugs that family legend full of holes in a chapter of his book ironically entitled 'Lady Bird's Business', from which I again shall quote to some extent in the following pages.

And *Newsday* headlined the second article of its series, published on May 28, 1964: 'They All Barter With "The Man'.

CHAPTER 6 - The Rich Fruits of a Monopoly

REPUBLICAN National Chairman Dean Burch had a point when he sardonically remarked, in mid-August 1964, that Lyndon B. Johnson must be 'the greatest free-enterpriser in the world' to have amassed so much money while on the public payroll.

Mr. Burch had another point when he found it 'peculiar that the bulk of his (Johnson's) fortune was made in areas subject to federal control'. The reference was, of course, to Johnson's broadcasting interests, the cornerstone of his towering fortune.

If Mr. Burch's comments may sound partisan, especially since they were made in the course of an election campaign, take the word of *The New York Times* instead. This august newspaper wrote on August 22, 1964, in an editorial on 'The President's Accounting':

'The only legitimate issue posed by the riches of political candidates is the way in which they have been acquired. On this score, the Johnson family audit raises more questions than it answers. It is clear that a major part of the Johnson wealth, real and potential, stems from the family's ownership of a broadcasting corporation that operates under the regulatory authority of the Federal Communications Commission. This property, bought by Mrs. Johnson when the President was in Congress, has appreciated enormously in value as a result both of the growth in television and of regulatory decisions by the FCC'.

For anyone who takes the trouble to study the origins and the mode of operations of the Texas Broadcasting Corp., alias the LBJ Co., two facts of cardinal importance stand out crystal-clear: (1) Notwithstanding all that has been said to the contrary by Johnson himself and his toadies, the FCC did a lot of favors for LBJ, especially during the period when he was the most influential Senator in Congress; and (2) Johnson swapped political influence in Washington on a massive scale for lucrative advertising over his radio and television stations by business concerns and individuals; he did not even hesitate to exert massive pressure to compel people to favor 'Lady Bird's business' with advertising, as one specific case related in detail and under oath by Don B. Reynolds (See Chapter 24) conclusively shows.

The New York Herald Tribune noted on August 2, 1964, in an editorial on 'The Johnson Money', that the Texas Broadcasting Corp., is the major source of Johnson wealth, which from an initial investment of $24,850 has grown into a multi-million-dollar holding. Much of this growth, which has been aided repeatedly by favorable Federal Communications Commission rulings, took place while Mr. Johnson was a member of the Senate Commerce Committee, which has jurisdiction over affairs of the FCC'.

That is the key to the whole situation, or one of them, anyway. The FCC, like any other government agency, is sensitive to pressure exerted by leading members of Congress, for to resist such pressure would be tantamount to inviting retaliation from the Congressional committee that has jurisdiction over the

Commission. And Johnson was not just 'a member' of the Senate Commerce Committee, but its most influential member. Just as he was the most influential member, or rather the chairman, of the Senate's Aeronautical and Space Committee, which has a large say in the allocation of highly profitable Government contracts in the aerospace field, at a time one of the biggest contractors in that field, North American Aviation, showered advertising on the Texas Broadcasting Corp., and contributed $100,000 to Johnson's presidential campaign (See Chapter 5).

To go back to the above-cited editorial in *The New York Herald Tribune*, the paper noted further that 'Much of it (i.e. the growth of the Texas Broadcasting Corp.), furthermore, resulted directly from the Johnson station's unusual FCC-protected television monopoly in Austin. These broadcast holdings were retained while he was majority leader and then vice-president. Even when he became president, with power to appoint FCC commissioners, they were not disposed of, but only put temporarily into a trust under the supervision of long-time Johnson business associates'.

Why did the FCC protect the 'unusual' television monopoly of the Johnson family in Austin, contrary to its very purpose as a government agency?

Life magazine, in its above-cited article on 'How LBJ's Family Amassed Its Fortune,' gave this cautiously worded answer:

'The FCC leans to a defensive attitude concerning its treatment of the Johnson's radio-TV interests and insists that the President—

either as representative or senator—has never tried to affect agency rulings. There is no evidence that he did intervene by word or deed [always that same hackneyed phrase 'there is no evidence', as though it were not easy for a powerful politician to efface all traces of his malfeasance - J.J.].

'Musing on the subtle problems involved here, an FCC official recently observed, "I've never once had anybody pressure me on behalf of Lyndon Johnson. The pressure there is an obvious one, though. It simply stems from the position occupied, particularly when you have a company named the LBJ Co."'

Very subtle, indeed.

Two circumstantial, but sharply conflicting versions exist concerning the genesis of the Texas Broadcasting Corp. *Life* magazine tells this story:

'The cornerstone of the Johnson holdings is KTBC, a spectacularly successful Austin radio-TV operation. KTBC was a small, 250-watt radio station—one of two in Austin—when Mrs. Johnson bought it as a bargain in January 1943. It added TV to its operation in 1952...

'Lyndon Johnson's talent for business dealing was impressively revealed when he first expressed interest in KTBC in late 1942. The station was then losing money and had been in trouble with the Federal Communications Commission for various violations of its regulations. A syndicate originally headed by J. M. West, a prominent Austin businessman and publisher, had held two successive options to buy the radio outlet—first at a price of

$50,000; later, after the FCC trouble, for $20,000 and an agreement to assume $12,000 of the station's debts. For some reason the FCC steadfastly refused to approve the sale. Although West died, the syndicate continued its efforts to buy.

'Just before Christmas in 1942, 34-year-old Congressman Lyndon Johnson invited a local businessman, E. G. Kingsbery, who was a member of the syndicate, to his Austin office. Kingsbery recalled that during the meeting Johnson reminded him that an appointment to Annapolis [the U.S. Naval Academy - J.J.] for Kingsbery's son, John, had been obtained through LBJ's good offices. Then, according to Kingsbery, Johnson brought up KTBC and said: "Now, E. G., I'm not a lawyer or a newspaperman. I have no means of making a living. At one time I had a second-class teaching license but it has long since expired. I understand you've bought the radio station. I'd like to go in with you or to have the station myself."

'Kingsbery first put Johnson in telephone contact with the attorney for the syndicate and then advised the congressman to "make his peace" with J. M. West's heirs. "Lyndon told me," said Kingsbery, "he was going up to the West ranch to talk business, and he did and he came away with KTBC."

'The purchase was consummated when Mrs. Johnson handed over a certified check for $17,500. The transfer was quickly approved by the FCC'.

So far the *Life* story. J. Evetts Haley gives an entirely different account of the operation, one I am inclined to credit because Haley was close to the scene and was even personally involved in some of the dealings.

In his chapter on 'Lady Bird's Business', Haley writes:

'...The first of his (Johnson's) early wealthy ventures, which likewise illustrates his business ethics, methods and policies, is the LBJ Company, the name of which had just been changed for obvious political purposes, back to its original title of The Texas Broadcasting Company.

'Its lucrative base is the Johnson politically and perhaps financially dominated capital city of Texas, where his monopoly of television has long rankled the citizens of Austin. Here the truth is in interesting contrast to the picture so carefully contrived in the public mind. For years this enterprise has been represented as the product of the inherited wealth and the rare business ability of Mrs. Johnson. Granted her sharp and practical business mind and "the iron beneath the velvet glove," this too hardly squares with the major recorded facts. Johnson acquired his original holdings in Austin through one of the foulest political deals, upon one of the greatest Texans, on record'.

The author then goes on to demolish 'the well-worn fabrication that the President's wealth is founded on his wife's inheritance'. Drawing on the Probate Records, Deed Records and District Court as well as County Court Records, of Harrison County, Marshall, Texas, Haley shows that the 'inherited wealth' of Claudia Alta Taylor, whom Lyndon Johnson married on November 17, 1931, is a myth.

'On the 6th of November, 1936,' Haley writes, 'Claudia Alta was joined by her husband, Lyndon B. Johnson, ...in acknowledging receipt of $21,000 in notes from her father, T. J. Taylor, to be paid off at $7,000 annually, beginning November 6, 1937, as settlement in full of her interest in her mother's estate. Thus her "inherited wealth" from her mother's estate, as repeatedly mentioned in the press, consisted of a total of $21,000 in notes'.

At this point, Haley presents an interesting sidelight on the way Johnson's first election campaign was financed:

'In 1937 Lyndon B. Johnson made his successful race for Congress, according to one of his intimate biographers, on $10,000 loaned by his wife out of her inheritance, though by the official records she had not yet been paid a penny from her mother's estate'.

Not his wife, but Brown and Root of Austin, a wealthy firm of building contractors, financed Johnson's 1937 election campaign and they in turn were richly rewarded with government contracts, Haley claims.

A little further on, Haley says:

'The author of this book happens to know, at first hand, its (KTBC's) history and the sequence of events by which it fell as a luscious financial plum into Lady Bird Johnson's lap. That history is as follows:

'On January 9, 1939, after three years of effort, an East Texas graduate of Yale, Dr. James G. Ulmer, associated with others as the Texas Broadcasting Company, was granted a permit by the

Federal Communications Commission to build and operate station KTBC at Austin, Texas. After long experience in communications, Dr. Ulmer had gone into the radio business in 1930 with a station at Tyler, Texas. Through the years he obtained additional permits and with local associates spread his operations to include stations in at least half a dozen other Texas towns and cities before acquiring the Austin permit.

'Then J. M. West, Sr., the rugged son of an East Texas tenant farmer, who had fought his way to the top from a hand in a lumber mill to become one of the richest men in Texas, heard of the Austin permit. He called in his general ranch manager, the author of this study, whom he used in various capacities, and sent him to Austin to see Dr. Ulmer, to investigate the station's potentialities, to learn whether Dr. Ulmer would sell and if so to ascertain his price...'

In August 1939, Haley went to Austin on behalf of Mr. West for talks with Dr. Ulmer. The latter agreed in principle to sell the station, subject of course to the approval of the FCC, as required by law. His asking price then was $150,000.

After Haley had reported back to his employer, the latter met with Dr. Ulmer late in August, at Houston, and, after some hard bargaining, a price of $125,000 was agreed upon. An option contract was drawn up to be signed on September 1, 1939.

As Dr. Uhner's bad luck would have it, however, on that same day war broke out in Europe and West, afraid of war time controls, informed Ulmer that the deal was off.

'Ulmer countered with a drastic cut in his price,' Haley writes. 'He offered to take $87,500; with $2500 in cash to bind the bargain and the balance upon approval of the transfer by the FCC. West agreed and the contract was signed on that fateful day...'

There was, however, an obstacle hard to overcome. 'Somehow the approval of the Commission was not forthcoming'. On this point, and practically on this point alone, the divergent accounts in *Life* magazine and in the Haley book seem to agree. Neither side seeks to explain, though, who offered opposition to the deal in Washington, or why and how.

Meanwhile, J. M. West, we learn, had been laying ambitious plans for the building of a far-flung communications empire. He again used Haley's services to negotiate the purchase of a struggling little newspaper, its circulation and its archaic plant in Austin. He then built a six-story structure next to the Texas Capitol grounds, equipped it with a modern press and launched *The Austin Tribune*.

Then Mr. West got again in touch with Dr. Ulmer and made him a broad offer to buy from him all of his radio interests for $750,000, while at the same time retaining him as general manager—but only after the sale of the Austin station had been approved by the FCC. And that approval still was not forthcoming.

'Thus the matter dragged until February 7, 1940,' Haley continues, 'when Dr. Ulmer, while driving from Austin to Houston, was astounded and appalled to hear the news on his car radio that the Commission had just revoked the license of every station in which he was interested. Hurriedly, from Huntsville, Ulmer called West at his offices on the 20th floor of the Sterling Building, in Houston, to discuss this sudden and startling turn in his affairs. West had already heard the news. The FCC was alleging violations of various administrative rulings, the chief complaint being that of "hidden ownership."

Haley does not contest that there was outside ownership with Dr. Ulmer in the Austin station, but, he says, that was 'well-known'. He lists an impressive number of personalities who had acquired an interest in the station, the foremost among them being Robert B. Anderson, then State Tax Commissioner, later director of the vast Waggoner Estate, one of the biggest in Texas, and still later a prominent Cabinet member under President Eisenhower. Mr. Anderson, it appears, was president of the company that owned KTBC.

While the matter was being investigated by the FCC, Ulmer was permitted to continue operating his stations. What with new wartime controls being imposed, and the strain of the FCC hearings, with attendant unfavorable publicity, Haley suggests, Dr. Ulmer's affairs went from bad to worse and he found himself eventually in desperate financial straits.

'In desperation he (Ulmer) turned to a source of influence, to Lyndon Johnson's old campaign manager and close friend, Austin attorney, Senator Alvin J. Wirtz,' Haley goes on. 'They went to the Driskill Hotel for dinner where they ate leisurely, talking long and late. Dr. Ulmer laid his legal and business problems before Wirtz in professional detail, especially in regard to KTBC and the contract for its sale to J. NH. West, and told Senator Wirtz he wanted to retain him in his efforts to get FCC approval of the sale'.

At this point, Haley lets his deep-rooted 'conservatism' get the upper hand over his detachment as a historian. He claims that all of Dr. Ulmer's difficulties basically stemmed from the Roosevelt Administration's dislike of such rugged characters as J. M. West and that the powers in Washington were determined not to let the affluent and conservative Texan build the communications empire of his dreams. In this political battle, Haley contends, Dr. Ulmer just happened to be the 'unlucky pawn' in the middle.

This seems rather far-fetched to me. The circumstances indicate pretty clearly that the FCC had a case against Dr. Ulmer, at least on the issue of hidden ownership, and that would have been enough to warrant the delaying action of the Commission.

'Wirtz showed interest,' Haley continues 'inquiring as to what KTBC was really worth. "A million dollars," Ulmer replied, which must have seemed ridiculous. But Ulmer was an imaginative operator who knew the business, and time has abundantly proved him right. He offered to pay Wirtz $10,000 if he could get the FCC to approve the sale; $2,500 down, $1,000 a month through five months and the balance upon approval. Wirtz agreed to the retainer and asked Ulmer to meet him at his office at nine in the morning.

'Ulmer went to his office at the appointed time, took a seat in the waiting room, and waited and waited. Prominent on the wall of Wirtz's office was a large and handsome picture of

Congressman Lyndon B. Johnson, warmly autographed with a sentiment which Ulmer probably never forgot: "To my friend, Alvin J. Wirtz," it read, "who can do anything better than anybody else."

'Finally a secretary came to report that Senator Wirtz was out and suggested Ulmer return in the afternoon. He did. The secretary said she was sorry; the Senator had suddenly left for Washington on urgent business "His address there? The Mayflower Hotel." For several days Ulmer tried to get him by phone. But he never returned the call and Ulmer never heard from him again'.

An amazing story—but also one fairly typical of the way people are destroyed in the financial jungle that is American society, if they happen to get in the way of more powerful ones. Clearly, Dr. Ulmer was the victim of a double-cross in which a very close friend of Lyndon Johnson played a prominent part.

Not the least astounding part of this story is the fact that none of it has transpired into the official biographies, nor even into *Life*'s account of the matter. How could two *Life* staff writers who, in other respects, did a thoroughly researched piece on 'How LBJ's Family Amassed Its Fortune', possibly miss such a key figure in this drama as Dr. Ulmer, even if perchance they chose to ignore the role of Senator Wirtz? Yet there can be little doubt that Haley's version is essentially correct, because of his own personal contacts with J. M. West and Dr. Ulmer.

The denouement of the drama is told by Haley in these words:

'J. M. West, Sr. died in 1942 and Dr. Ulmer was at the end of his rope, his station in dire debt, the man himself broke. His Austin associates, unable to put up cash for their agreed purchase of stock, had given him $15,500 in notes, which he had endorsed to his Tyler financial backer as collateral, who in turn assigned them to the Austin bank which was carrying KTBC's operating expenses.

'Meanwhile Lyndon Johnson had "discovered" the station's plight; Lady Bird had made application for its purchase with an accompanying statement of her net worth on December 21, 1942; an agent was sent to Wesley W. West to see that the West estate was out of the picture; the FCC approved the sale in January, 1943, and Lyndon and Lady Bird Johnson picked up the station for the $15,500 in notes against it and were at once on their way to immense wealth'.

In a footnote to this account, Haley adds:

'In further emphasis of the totally political nature of this business, it should be noted that the FCC subsequently granted and renewed a total of 14 permits for Dr. Ulmer, among them that for the 50,000 watt station KCUL at Fort Worth, which he sold to Gov. Ed Rivers, reportedly for $450,000'.

So, in the end, Dr. Ulmer wasn't quite the victim of ruthless spoliation Haley makes him out to be; he made out all right with the rest of his property. But it is evident, nevertheless, that he was stripped of a potentially highly valuable asset, station KTBC in Austin, through a combination of political power play and shady business dealings. And the beneficiary of that operation was Lyndon B. Johnson.

Now, to revert to the *Life* presentation of the matter, 'KTBC may have been in FCC trouble before the Johnsons bought it, but is has been completely free of trouble ever since... All of its requests have been acted upon favorably and with dispatch by the agency—beginning with an early application to increase its power and the length of its broadcasting day'.

That is, of course, the crux of the matter. The FCC, after dragging its feet for years, as long as Dr. Ulmer and J. M. West were in the picture, was not only favorably disposed to the new station owners, the Johnsons, but even discovered the usefulness of acting with dispatch in granting their requests, beginning with the transfer itself, which was approved with record speed, in a matter of a few days. Such wonders of bureaucracy rarely, if ever, result from an impartial change of heart. In this case, there cannot be the slightest doubt that the FCC's dramatic change of heart, and especially of speed, was prompted by the fact that Congressman Lyndon B. Johnson had what it takes to get ahead in Washington—plenty of pull in the right places.

'The choicest plum of all fell in 1952,' *Life* continues, 'when KTBC was granted the right to broadcast over Channel 7, the only VHF (very high frequency) channel allocated to the Austin area by the FCC. This single outlet contracted to carry programs of all three major TV networks—CBS, ABC and NBC—with whom affiliation is the open sesame to success.

'True, the FCC also assigned to Austin three prospective UHF (ultra high frequency) channels; but at that time almost no TV receivers existed to pick up a UHF signal. Many sets can receive UHF now, but no one has moved to build a UHF station in Austin. Since KTBC holds the network contracts, it retains, on one VHF channel, an effective telecasting monopoly in a city of 186,000 and its environs. There are 107 other single-channel communities in the U.S., but since most are located in "overlap" areas where advertisers can reach the set owners via other nearby stations, few of them enjoy monopoly status'.

The almost unique monopoly status enjoyed by the Johnsons' Austin station is also underlined by *Newsday* in the last article of its series, published on May 29, 1964:

'Over the years, a number of FCC decisions have insulated KTBC from competition. KTBC remains the only commercial station in Austin.

'FCC officials are somewhat sheepish in discussing these decisions, particularly one in 1959 that resulted in the allocation to Corpus Christi, Texas (population 176,000), 160 miles from Austin, of a third TV channel while Austin (population 212,000) remained with one. "I suppose you could argue favoritism on that," said one official. "Because if we exercised a little ingenuity, we might have put in a second channel in Austin... I don't know..." Another official said, "It looks fishy, even to me."...'

The rich fruits of a well-guarded television monopoly such as the Johnson family have exercised in Austin for a period of many years, are readily apparent from a comparison of advertising rates. According to *Life*, KTBC, which is within viewing distance of 205,700 TV-owning homes, has a network base hourly rate of $575. By contrast, KROC in Rochester, Minn.—which has 204,600 TV homes in its viewing area even though it is a smaller city—has a rate of only $325.

High monopoly prices for advertising; the ready willingness of big industrial concerns like North American Aviation to advertise over a station owned by a man with plenty of influence on the allocation of government contracts; and direct pressure applied to individuals, as the Don B. Reynolds case shows—all these factors have contributed mightily to making KTBC one of the most prosperous radio and television stations in America.

And how prosperous it is! By the end of 1956, the station the Johnsons had picked up for $15,500 was able to report to the FCC total assets of $1,516,516 and a surplus and profit for the year of $1,029,531. Thereafter, each year yielded higher profits. The balance sheet for 1962 which the LBJ Company filed with the FCC, for instance, showed assets of $3,992,902.39, of which $965,289.78 was cash.

In 1959, KTBC, having grown into a multimillion-dollar operation moved out of the Driskill Hotel in Austin, where it had been located, into shining new headquarters at the intersection of 10th and Brazos Streets. Ever since, the handsomely modernistic KTBC Building in Austin has been one of the city's landmarks and chief attractions, along with the University of Texas Tower and the Capitol.

After making their first pile with KTBC in Austin, the Johnsons before long began to cast covetous eyes on other promising properties in the broadcasting field. Over the years, they acquired a 78.9 per cent interest in a Victoria radio station; one of 75 per cent in a TV station at Ardmore, Okla., one of 50 per cent in a TV station at Bryan; and one of 29 per cent of KWTX in Waco, Texas.

This last-named acquisition is of particular interest because it highlights another aspect of the Johnsons' way of doing business. In 1954, the LBJ Company applied for, and promptly obtained from the FCC, permission to purchase the television station KANG in Waco, 98 miles north of Austin. Due to a lack of UHF sets in that early period of television and in that particular region, KANG, a UHF station, had been losing money and was deeply in debt. Then a syndicate moved in to set up a rival station KWTX which operated on a VHF license—issued by the FCC the same day the Johnsons were authorized to purchase KANG.

As usual in such cases, the outcome of the competition hinged on the question of which station would get the best of the network franchises. Contrary to what could have been normally expected, both CBS and ABC quickly made up their minds that a floundering station like KANG, plus the magic of the Lyndon B. Johnson name, was a better proposition than the soundly operated, but nameless KWTX and threw their franchises to the LBJ Co.

At first, the luckless owners of KWTX attempted to fight back by bringing suit against the Johnsons under the federal antitrust laws, but nothing came of it, as was to be expected. Thereupon they threw in the sponge and agreed to give the LBJ Co. an interest of 29.05% in their company in return for the money-losing KANG which had served the Johnsons as a pawn in an adroit squeeze game and now had played out its role.

Says *Life* magazine: 'A man who is a stockholder and director of KWTX says: "There is no questioning the fact that Johnson was in on the negotiations for the merger. And he was the only one in on them."'

This, then, is another incident which clearly belies the fiction that Lyndon Johnson himself has no part in the broadcasting business.

On the strength of this and other pieces of evidence, *Life* unequivocally states: 'No one in recent years has had any dealings with KTBC without being aware that the driving force behind the operation was Lyndon Baines Johnson. There is every indication that Johnson, first as congressman, then as senator, was extremely active in the radio-TV enterprise while Lady Bird was nominally in full charge. A former KTBC employee recalls that during the 10 years he worked for the station, it was Lyndon himself who presided over meetings of department heads, and that he continued to do so even after becoming Vice President...'

And Haley notes in his book:

'...Ever since it became a public issue, he (Johnson) has claimed that he owned no interest in it (KTBC station). Yet on October 3, 1956, when it turned up that he had joined Mrs. Johnson in transfer of stocks to their daughters, J. D. Kellam, the station's manager, in an amendment to its ownership reports, explained to the FCC that this was done by Johnson and his wife "to avail themselves of the split gift provisions of the Internal Revenue Code." But if he was not one of the owners, how could he legally take advantage of the gift tax exemptions? Again in a restriction-of-stock agreement placed on file with the Commission, January 10, 1956, Claudia Taylor Johnson was joined by her husband as "stockholder"'.

All of which goes to show, with dazzling clarity, that President Johnson, when he once more formally proclaimed at his press conference of April 16, 1964, that he had no interest whatsoever in the Texas Broadcasting Corp., was being highly disingenuous, to say the least. And there would seem to be an excellent case for the FCC to use its authority and revoke KTBC's operating license on 'hidden ownership' grounds. Yes, but—

One final item will illustrate the point, redundantly. Back in 1957, a company called Midwest Video of Little Rock., Ark., organized an Austin subsidiary named Capital Cable for the purpose of cutting into the Johnson monopoly through the so-called community-antenna TV system. It is a long and involved story I can only touch upon here. The upshot of it is that after long manuvering, in which the Austin city council quite unashamedly played the role of a Johnson puppet, the LBJ Co., by the end of 1963, had both Capital Cable and another competitor called TV Cable, in a corner. First, TV Cable was swallowed up by Capital Cable and then the latter granted a 50% stock option to the LBJ Co., to be exercised within three years.

'Will Lyndon Johnson choose to exercise the option on Capital Cable—or, now that he is President of the United States, is he even concerned with such matters?' *Life* asked and then answered the most important part of its questions thus:

'An executive of Capital's parent firm, Midwest Video, has reported that two officers of his firm were summoned from Little Rock to the LBJ Ranch last December. Here, said the executive, while German Chancellor Ludwig Erhard was an official guest, the President took the two Midwest men—C. Hamilton Moses and George Morell—aside and, among other things, informed them that he intended to exercise the option, but that he might not get to it "until five minutes before it runs out."'

This episode proves that the 'irrevocable trust arrangement', under which Lady Bird ostensibly relinquished all control of her broadcasting business, is just as much of a fiction as is Lyndon B. Johnson's alleged lack of interest in the Texas Broadcasting Corp., alias LBJ Co.

The fact that *Life* adds, rather lamely, 'Moses and Morell have denied such a meeting took place,' corroborates, rather than disproves, the point. All witnesses who have been questioned by the reporters for *Life* as well as *Newsday* and others, in this matter, almost pathetically pleaded for anonymity, and for good reason.

Given the ruthless and vindictive nature of the most powerful man in the United States, any informant cited by name who gives the lie to Johnson's pious disclaimers and thus helps to expose him as the inveterate liar he is, has only the choice between a formal denial and political or financial suicide.

CHAPTER 7 - 'Just a Little Ranch'

JUST as false and insincere as Johnson's persistent disclaimers of ownership in or control over his broadcasting business, is his allegation, also made at the April 16, 1964 press conference, 'I own a little ranch land, something in excess of 2,000 acres...'

'It is possible, however, to trace at least 11,000 acres of ranch land in Llano, Gillespie and Blanco counties, in which the Johnsons have a substantial interest,' *Life* magazine states. And that isn't exactly 'a little,' even by Texas standards.

It was not until after he had become a Senator, in the manner already described, that Lyndon Johnson's 'land hunger' began to make itself felt.

First, in 1951, he bought 243.7 acres along the Pedernales River, the site of the old Johnson homestead and now of the LBJ Ranch, from his aunt, Mrs. Clarence Martin. Little by little, he added surrounding acreage to this ranch, which at present comprises some 414 acres.

Like KTBC in Austin, and in even more bewildering fashion, the LBJ Ranch has been the object of some fast juggling manuevers, the evident purpose of which was to cloak the ownership, save taxes and make the Senator from Texas appear as the poor but honest country boy he never was by any stretch of the imagination.

Newsday, in its issue of May 27, 1964, described this manipulation as follows:

'The now world-famous LBJ Ranch has had an interesting career of its own. It was first purchased by the then Sen. Johnson in 1951. He sold it to the LBJ Co., in 1954. From that time until December 1, 1963, the company paid taxes on the entire property. On that date, which was 10 days after Johnson became President, he repurchased 57.55 acres, including the ranch house.

'Up until the time he bought back the property, Johnson was a paying guest in what was assumed to be his own house. A man authorized to speak for Johnson on the matter told *Newsday* that until December 1, 1963, Johnson paid the LBJ Co. for room and board whenever he and his family stayed at the LBJ ranch'.

This bit of legerdemain is hard to beat.

Imagine the situation. Senator Lyndon B. Johnson, his wife 'Lady Bird' and their two daughters, Lynda and Luci, come down from Washington for some happy, relaxed days at the ranch.

The ranch belongs to the LBJ Co., in which the proud bearer of that name has no interest, financial or otherwise. Everything down there belongs to the missus and the kids, aside from a marginal interest reserved for top LBJ Co. officials.

Father not only must pay for his own room and board at the ancestral home, but his hard-hearted wife and children even make him pay for their lodging and food at the ranch which they own.

Why is the poor man treated so unfairly?

Evidently for tax purposes, for if the Senator and his family are paying guests at a ranch in Texas, on a much-needed vacation from his Washington chores and the home he must keep in that city, then this extra expense can be charged off to professional travel, professional entertainment or God knows what. And the extra money that's dropped into the till of the LBJ Co. for entertaining paying guests at the ranch won't make much difference, anyway, to Lady Bird and her two affluent daughters, who are big earners, with plenty of deductions available to them for 'charitable donations' and what not.

Why did the President, on December 1, 1963, repurchase the ranch? the *Newsday* reporter asked the authorized spokesman for the Johnson family. The answer was:

'He wanted to use it occasionally and have a homestead down there. I advised him that a President should own his own home instead of renting it, in keeping with his high office,' the spokesman said.

Indeed, indeed. Just think what a ghastly impression would have been made on a President de Gaulle or even a Chancellor Ludwig Erhard by a President of the United States so poor he didn't even own a house, but had to rent one!

Newsday went on to report: Over the years, all the things used on the ranch—farm equipment, automobiles, cattle feed, groceries, "etc."—have been bought and paid for by the company, while the ranch was generally regarded as Johnson's Texas home. Throughout this period, the LBJ Co. has used the ranch house to entertain guests of the corporation, including clients and advertising account executives doing business with the TV and Radio station. And the company has given its customers the "red runway" treatment by flying them directly into the ranch on Johnson's airstrip'.

One of the most noteworthy features of the LBJ Ranch, it should be interpolated here, is a 6,300-foot tarred landing strip for airplanes which can even accommodate jets. Another prominent feature is a large gourd-shaped swimming pool.

'The airstrip itself is an example of how intertwined the personal and corporate property are in fact, if not in legal terms,' *Newsday* continues. The President, in a published interview in January, referred to political charges that the government had footed the bill for the airstrip. Gazing out at the runway, he said: "Five thousand dollars worth of lights. The runway cost me $25,000 and I paid every cent of it. Paid for the lights, too. They're always saying how much money the government spent to put in my strip, and the government didn't spend a cent. Lyndon Johnson paid it, every bit out of his own pocket."'

That's honest, plain-spoken Lyndon B. Johnson for you. Only, in his eagerness to set the record straight and to hammer home that it wasn't the government's money that had been spent on that strip, but his very own, he made the mistake of forgetting the fine distinction he had always drawn between LBJ and the LBJ Co. As *Newsday* put it:

'It is clear that the President was not then making any distinctions between his pocket and that of the LBJ Co. In an interview last week, the family's authorized spokesman said: "The airstrip was built and paid for totally by the company and the company uses it extensively." The airstrip itself is on the part of the ranch owned by the company; the hangar is on the President's 57 acres. Johnson permits the company to continue its use of the hangar and ranchhouse just as it used them before he repurchased the 57 acres'. Here the unsurpassed duplicity of the whole arrangement is exposed in all its beauty. This is even better than Lyndon B. Johnson paying his wife and daughters for the privlege of entertaining them on their land and in their house—before he 'repurchased' the ranchhouse.

In the second article of its extraordinarily enlightening series (May 28, 1964) *Newsday* revealed that the LBJ Co. had been making extensive use of the practice of 'horsetrading' advertising time on its radio and television station in Austin, KTBC, 'as part payment for such items as land, cars, trucks, tractors and cattle feed—most of which are in heavy demand at the famous LBJ Ranch'.

While the practice of swapping advertising time for merchandise is not uncommon in the broadcasting industry, the Long Island paper notes, such bartering as a rule takes place for goods and services related to the operation of a radio or TV station such as automobiles for news coverage, photo equipment and advertising in newspapers and trade publications. By contrast:

'A recent check with Austin businessmen shows that much of what the corporation pays for or swaps for has been delivered directly to the LBJ Ranch. With a lot of livestock to feed on the LBJ Ranch and its other ranching operations, the company does a big business in fodder. It is not uncommon for a KTBC salesman to buy a couple of hundred pounds of Purina's Best while offering the dealer equal value in radio or TV time. Sometimes the deal is for cash, sometimes it involves a swap-out'.

From 1960 on, Lyndon B. Johnson went on a regular land-buying spree, much of the time in close association with the lawyer and real estate dealer A. W. Moursund whom he was to appoint trustee for his holdings after he had become President.

His first large purchase of land, outside of the LBJ Ranch, was the Scharnhorst Ranch in Blanco County, Texas. Its owner, Eddie Scharnhorst, had been borrowing money from the LBJ Co. for years. By 1960, Scharnhorst, then well into his 70s, decided he had had enough of the exacting life of a rancher and was entitled to peaceful retirement. So he sold out his 1,802 acres to the LBJ Co. for $30,250 cash and cancellation of the $23,750 he owed the Johnson family.

According to *Life*, Eddie Scharnhorst remarked recently: 'Him (Johnson) and Moursund, they're buying every ranch they can get hold of'. It sounds a bit like a grumble and it may well have been one, for three years after Scharnhorst had sold out to the LBJ Co., the value of his land had more than doubled, as is affirmed by the Moursund 'Trustee's Statement'.

It is made absolutely clear by a number of specific instances cited in the *Life* story that A. W. Moursund was acting, in those years, as purchasing agent for Lyndon B. Johnson. Thus, in April 1962, Moursund bought up 1,727 acres for $141,867 from a man named C. W. Voyles and, a day later, sold it to the LBJ Co. Again, shortly afterwards, Moursund bought 467 acres for $45,805.20 cash and, the next day, sold it to the LBJ Co.

His biggest purchase, in the names of himself and the LBJ Co., *Life* reports, was the acquisition of 4,561 acres from Texas Christian University in Llano County near Packsaddle Mountain. This deal involved $200,000 cash and a $300,000 note. One day later, the LBJ Co. sold its half-interest to Lyndon Baines Johnson himself.

According to *Newsday*, which also mentions this deal, giving a few additional details, this purchase took place in 1961. The paper noted that 'a real estate boom is under way' in the 'beautiful Highland Lakes country in Llano County, Tex.,' where this particular property is located.

In Moursund's 'Trustee's Statement of the Johnsons' Holdings,' which puts Lyndon B. Johnson's personal net worth at 'under $400,000', the President is credited with the ownership of 'slightly under 2,500 acres of farm land and ranch in Texas'. A footnote gives these additional details:

This property included the following:

1. Granite Knob Ranch—purchased 900 acres in 1960 at $30.00 per acre. This is close to the Lewis Place and could probably be sold today for somewhere in the same price range as the Lewis Place cost [i.e. at $65.00 per acre - see below. - J. J.]

2. Haywoord Ranch—purchased 1140 acres in 1961 at $110.00 per acre.

3. Lewis Ranch—purchased 415 acres in 1962 at $65.00 per acre.

4. LBJ Ranch—only 29 acres purchased in 1963. (The Haywood, Lewis and LBJ Ranches are about market value today in our judgment.)

Then—still in the context of the footnote—there follows this utterly unbelievable statement:

'Income from these properties has averaged $2,600.00 per year for the last four years'.

If Lyndon B. Johnson has been unable to earn more than $2,600 a year from the operation of four ranches totaling 2500 acres, then he must surely be rated the most incompetent farmer in Texas—a judgment oddly at variance with everything else known about that man, in particular his staggering wealth.

Again it must be emphasized here that if any ordinary Texas rancher were to file such an income tax declaration with the IRS, he would have a team of inspectors roaming over his farmland and combing his records in a matter of days. But Johnson—

In assessing the 'Financial Position of Mrs. Lyndon B. Johnson' and attributing to her, as has been mentioned before, a total net worth of 'slightly over $2.5 million', the Trustee's Statement lists, as far as farm and ranch land in Texas is concerned, the same acreage of 2500 and adds exactly the same footnote as above.

This shows that the Johnson couple hold each in his or her personal name—and apart from any real estate owned by the Texas

Broadcasting Corp., as a corporate entity, 2500 acres of farm and ranch land in Texas, or a total of 5,000 acres. Since they are credited each, as far as the LBJ Ranch is concerned, with 'only 29 acres purchased in 1963,' i.e. the roughly 58 acres which Johnson, after becoming President 'repurchased' from the LBJ Co. because he no longer could live in a 'rented house,' it is evident that the remaining 356 acres of he LBJ Ranch, which are still under 'corporate' control, must be added to these 5,000 acres, for a total of 5,356.

That, however, is not yet the end of the story of the Johnsons' land holdings. Additionally, Lady Bird is credited with 'approximately 3700 acres farmland in Alabama,' which, according to the Moursund statement was 'inherited and purchased many years ago at the rate of $8.00 per acre. The most any of the best part of it has ever been sold for was $40.00 per acre'.

During the 1964 election campaign, some Republican Congressmen took a party of inquisitive newsmen out to Mrs. Johnson's Alabama farm. They found it populated by a flock of Negro tenants living in conditions of abject misery, with leaking roofs, an almost total lack of utilities and shocking sanitary conditions. The total value of these 3700 acres is given as 'slightly over' $29,000, which even given the state of neglect in which it was found by the reporters, surely represents a large undervaluation.

Finally, the 'Trustee's Statement' credits the two daughters, Luci Baines and Lynda Bird Johnson, with unspecified real estate holdings worth approximately $30,000 each, or $60,000 together.

According to Moursund, then, the Johnson Family's land holdings represent an aggregate (book) value of $529,000. However, this accounting makes no mention of the Johnson's $200,000 home in Washington (presumably held in the name of the LBJ Co.), nor does it take into account any other urban, residential or resort property.

Yet the *Life* reporters' search of available records turned up real estate transactions involving 71 building lots in Llano County, 13 in Burnet County and 10 in Travis County (which includes Austin).

All told, *Life* magazine states, the Johnsons have accumulated over the years, total land holdings currently worth about $3.6 million, including:

(1) Eight ranches (three owned by the Johnsons outright; one in partnership with A. W. Moursund; plus four ranches and part of the LBJ Ranch property owned by the Texas Broadcasting Corp.) for a combined value of $1,250,000.

(2) Resort and residential property, either held in whole by Johnson interests or in partnership with Moursund; current market value: about $2,250,800.

(3) Underdeveloped Alabama land held by Lady Bird: about $100,000.

All of which is a far cry, indeed, from the 'little ranch land' Johnson admitted owning at his press conference.

CHAPTER 8 - Wheeler-Dealer's Merry-Go-Round

ONE of the most intriguing bits of information to be culled from *Life* magazine's informative account 'How LBJ's Family Amassed Its Fortune' is this item:

One large bank in the State of Texas had a vice president, 'one of whose major standing assignments was to make sure that Johnson interests did not, under whatever guise, acquire any stock in *that* bank'. (italicized in the original - J.J.)

So here you have a busy executive, normally with plenty of absorbing business on his hands, whose primary responsibility lies in keeping a tight watch, lest the United States Senator from his State makes off with his bank!

Texas banking law, it seems, has its peculiarities. One of them is the requirement that every bank must be an independent. No two parts of the same bank can even function in separate buildings, even in the same city, says *Life*, unless a physical connection, such as a tunnel, exists.

These rigid regulations make it comparatively difficult to acquire control of a Texas bank, but at the same time they enhance the attraction of bank stocks as an investment, despite their generally modest yield, because the local bank, in each community, represents its financial spine even more markedly than elsewhere. *Life* quotes one prominent Texas banker as saying:

'The small rural bank controls the lifeblood of the county. You give me control of a little bank in a ranch county and I'll make myself a million dollars'.

Lyndon B. Johnson would not be Lyndon B. Johnson if he had missed out on that opportunity.

Because his name has been for many years anathema to his fellow countrymen from Texas (as the Haley Book, in particular, impressively shows), Johnson had to employ 'guises' to worm his way into the regional banking business. A master of underhanded and oblique manouvering, he succeeded in that endeavour, too.

The principal 'conduit' used by Johnson for the purpose of infiltrating Texas banks has been a versatile outfit called the 'Brazos-Tenth Street Co'. of Austin, Texas.

'At last count,' reports *Life* 'Brazos-Tenth had acquired at least $1 million worth of shares in nine Texas banks'.

Who does Brazos-Tenth represent and what does that name stand for?

Originally, *Life* informs us, Brazos-Tenth was just a real estate developer's housekeeping device for an old stone building on the corner of Brazos and Tenth streets in downtown Austin, set up in 1955.

'Since then, it has grown into an energetic, diversified company whose activities are to a great degree interwoven with the Johnsons' interests.

'Because Brazos-Tenth is a private company, the names of its stockholders are not a matter of public record, but Attorney

Moursund says that no member of the Johnson family has a direct interest in the company'.

If there is any truth in that statement, then only through the use of the word 'direct', for there is plenty of evidence that, indirectly at least, Brazos-Tenth has been serving the Johnson interests in many ways and over a period of many years.

The first connection is an obvious one, for the old stone house at the intersection of Brazos and Tenth streets was bought and torn down by the LBJ Co., which then erected in this choice location, in 1959, the streamlined new KTBC Building.

Even more revealing is the conspicuous use of that old promoter's device of indirect financial control, interlocking directorates.

For one thing, it was none other than Donald Thomas, a chubby, shrewd-eyed individual who had served for many years as secretary to the LBJ Co., who became the new president of Brazos-Tenth Street Co., after the company's founder, E. H. Perry, had sold it, and its only asset, the corner property, in 1959. Besides, Perry, at the time, confided to an associate that the buyer was Lyndon B. Johnson.

On the other hand, A. W. Moursund, Johnson's unofficial purchasing agent and later his official trustee, has also acted repeatedly as an LBJ stooge in transactions involving the Brazos-Tenth Street Co. One such instance, relating to the Moore State Bank of Llano, Texas, is told by *Life* in these terms:

'Moore State, founded in 1922, is a substantial institution, the only bank in Llano County that survived the Great Depression. As of December 1963, Moore State reported undivided profits of $245,371.41, and for 35 years uninterruptedly it had paid the holders of its 2,000 shares a dividend of $5 a share every six months. But in August 1963 the local newspaper reported that A. W. Moursund had "purchased a portion of the stock at substantially more than book value."

'It wasn't until the stock listing was filed for 1964 that the new ownership was unveiled to some degree. Moursund owned a mere 20 shares, as did Donald Thomas of Brazos-Tenth and Texas Broadcasting. But Moursund's mother, Mary Stribling Moursund, held 749 shares and Brazos-Tenth had another 749, which clearly constituted control. Moursund was retained as legal counsel for the bank at a fee of $1,000 a month.

'Holders of the remaining 462 shares began to discover what this meant when they were told early this year that Moore State would quit paying the long-accustomed dividends. Under Texas law, bank dividends are payable at the discretion of the directors, and a stockholder has no recourse except in case of fraud.

'One stockholder in Moore State, who complained to Moursund, was told, "Any stockholder who is unhappy, I'll be glad to buy his stock." Moursund's offer, however, was pegged at the book value of the stock, which was substantially less than he himself had paid for the control stock. Some people did sell out. Others, resentful and stubborn, are still clinging to their shares'.

A raw deal, a typical Johnson deal for the small stockholders. He, with his 14 million dollars and an annual salary of $100,000 as President of the United States, plus another $100,000 for expenses, can afford to put off the division of the bank's $245,371 undivided profits for as long as he wishes, even if the small stockholder cannot. In the meantime, any of them are welcome to dispose of their stock into the hand of the Johnson trustee—at book value. It is an illuminating story.

In conclusion, let me cite one more example given in the *Life* story, which graphically illustrates the whirlwind-like wheeler-dealer tactics employed by Johnson & Co. in their real estate transactions:

'One multifold deal began on February 1, 1962, when the LBJ Co. sold a number of subdivision properties in Llano and Travis counties to the Brazos-Tenth Street Co. The deed was signed by J. C. Kellam, as president of the LBJ Co., and Donald Thomas as the same company's secretary.

'Before the sun set that day, Brazos-Tenth sold the packet, minus one lot, to Johnson himself. (At the time, Johnson was Vice President of the United States! - J. J.) Donald Thomas again signed the deed, *this time as president of Brazos-Tenth* (italicized in the original - II). On July 24, 1962, Johnson sold part of the package back to the LBJ Co., which on April 6, 1963, resold it to Johnson's staff member and present White House aide, Jack Valenti, who, shortly after Johnson became President, sold it back to LBJ Co'.

When *Life*'s reporters tried to find out from an Austin lawyer long familiar with some of Lyndon Johnson's business dealings, just what the meaning of these goings-on could be, the attorney, too, declared himself baffled:

'I admit I don't know what these complicated switches back and forth really mean,' he said. But I suspect there may be tax advantages somewhere'.

This seems to be, indeed, the only plausible explanation. And it adds to my conviction that some day not too far off, when Lyndon B. Johnson, no longer President of the United States, will have a lot of explaining to do, the Internal Revenue Service will also be standing in line to get its due.

That is the story, then, pieced together from a variety of reliable and well-informed sources, of how Lyndon B. Johnson became a multimillionaire. He is now a wheeler-dealer emeritus, though he may still try to get back into the old business when he bows out of the presidency.

In the meantime, let us have a close look at some of his old cronies and fellow wheeler-dealers and how he helped them to feather their nests, while still adding a feather, here and there, to his own.

CHAPTER 9 - Texas Billie

LONG, long ago, Texas was the land of enterprising pioneers and derring-do cowboys. Then it became the private preserve of the greediest and most ruthless type of oilmen in the world. And, in the wake of the great oil boom, Texas produced a new human species known as the wheeler-dealer. The very term is a Texas idiom that has conquered the American language the way Texas has conquered the Union.

Lyndon B. Johnson who managed to pyramid 25 years' salary as a Congressman and vice-president into a 14-million-plus-dollar fortune;

H. L. Hunt of Dallas, the billionaire oil tycoon, tax-dodger and rabble-rouser;

Clint Murchison, Jr., also of Dallas, heir to a multimillion dollar business empire (oil, shipping, banking, catering, manufacturing, book publishing, etc.) amassed by his father Clinton Williams Murchison;

The late oil magnates Hugh Roy Cullen of Houston Tex., and Sidney W. Richardson of Fort Worth, Tex., (a great friend of Eisenhower's as well as the late Clint W. Murchison);

Leonard F. McCollum of Houston, Tex., boss of the immensely successful Continental Oil Corporation (Conoco), top lobbyist of the oil industry and one of President Johnson's chief advisers on oil questions;

Bobby Baker, a kindred soul from a neighboring state—

They all are, or were, typical representatives of wheeler-dealerdom, Texas style.

The hallmark of the authentic wheeler-dealer is his ability to amass a multimillion dollar fortune in a minimum of time without ever doing anything flagrantly illegal, or at any rate, without ever getting on the wrong side of the law.

In this sense, the most notorious of contemporary Texas wheeler-dealers, Billie Sol Estes, was a flop. He got caught.

Getting caught is an unpleasant experience in Wheeler-DealerLand. Your bosom pals of yesteryear suddenly don't know you any more. The boss you have been working for, or to whom you have been paying tribute, advises that he has never set eyes on you, never heard of you before. Your power dissolves like magic and, from one day to the next, you may be stepping from a palace into a penitentiary.

Billie Sol Estes made the mistake of trying to go too far too fast. Safe wheeling-dealing takes time.

'I know I can get rich in 15 years,' Texas Billie once said, 'but I want to do it in two'.

He did it, too, but the giant business concern he built up in record time turned out to have been jerry-built; at the first sign of strain, it collapsed like a house of cards. And now he is doing 15 years.

In 1954, three years after the roly-poly Billie Sol Estes, then aged 26, had set himself up in business in the West Texas town of Pecos, he was named by the National Junior Chamber of

Commerce as one of America's ten most promising young men. And what a promise he was!

It is not possible to do more than outline here the principal phases of Estes' brief but meteoric career. To try to do the subject full justice would require the writing of a book at least twice the size of the present one, and to devote every page of it to Texas Billie and his soap bubble empire. Our main subject is, after all, Lyndon B. Johnson.

The magic word behind Billie's spectacular, if short-lived success was influence. At the height of his career, in 1961 and early 1962, Estes made a point of flying to Washington about once a month. Invariably, on the eve of every departure for the nation's capital, he made huge withdrawals from one or the other of his various bank accounts. On a single trip, he is reported to have taken with him $150,000 in cash, returning home nearly empty-handed.

Investigators of the McClellan Committee, which looked into Estes' tangled affairs after he had tumbled into bankruptcy, turned up check-stubs showing that Estes, in a single year (from April 1961 until the end of March, 1962) had taken out at least $673,581 in cash from his bank accounts—not counting a lot of checks he wrote out during the same time. Most, if not all, of that cash stayed in Washington.

The web of Estes' business interests and financial entanglements was even more complex and impenetrable than that of Bobby Baker.

More than two dozen different business firms were lumped together in 'Billie Sol Estes Enterprises, Inc.,' when the bubble burst in March, 1962.

Cotton, fertilizer and grain storage were the main ingredients of his multimillion-dollar business empire. The largest share of it was accounted for by three grain storage companies—United Elevators, Allied Storage and Lester-Stone—all of which made huge profits from Government contracts. In the single year of 1961, United Elevators alone was paid about four million dollars by the U.S. Government for storing huge quantities of the national grain surplus.

In order to make that kind of money from Government sources, one has to have connections in Washington. Billie Sol Estes had plenty of them, especially in the Department of Agriculture which handles the grain storage program. At least three top officials of that Department, including the Assistant Secretary, James T. Ralph and Deputy Administrator Emery E. Jacobs, were forced to resign as a result of the Estes scandal. Jerry R. Holleman, an assistant Secretary in the Department of Labor, also had to hand in his resignation after it had been disclosed that he once accepted a gift of $1,000 from Estes.

Some Texas politicians also paid dearly for their relationships with Billie Sol Estes. Rep. J. T. ('Slick') Rutherford lost his seat in the 1962 elections after he had been forced to admit publicly that he had helped Estes obtain cotton allotments from the Government. Senator W. Yarborough's image also suffered as a result of the established fact that he had interceded in Washington, on behalf of Estes, a couple of times. However, his intervention, in both cases, appears to have been half-hearted and, what is more important, failed to accomplish anything. This really lets Yarborough out, for the hallmark of a wheeler dealer's real connections in politics is success.

Who was the mysterious, but enormously effective, power in Washington that guaranteed Billie Sol Estes' success while the going was good? Was it Lyndon B. Johnson?

In the course of the 1964 presidential campaign, Sen. Barry Goldwater repeatedly charged that Billie Sol Estes, like Bobby Baker, had been a Johnson protégé.

In one speech (as reported in the *New York World Telegram and Sun* of September 24, 1964) Goldwater declared:

'The Billie Sol Estes case is more than just a scandal. It is more than a sordid picture of favoritism and fraud. It is a study in the operations and attitudes of some of the top officials of government—many of whom are still with us'.

After that opening shot, Sen. Goldwater, in the words of the *World-Telegram*, 'deposited Billie Sol, like an unwanted foundling, on Mr. Johnson's own doorstep. Reminding that the Texas wheeler-dealer in illegal cotton acreage allotments withdrew $40,000 in cash for a trip to Washington in 1962, he (Goldwater) said:

"The record shows that Estes spent about $6,000 of this for tickets to a $100-a-plate Democratic dinner and turned most of the tickets over to his friend, Cliff Carter, in the office of the then Vice-President, Lyndon Baines Johnson. We have never learned what happened to the other $34,000. Whose office, whose pocket got that?"

'Sen. Goldwater said that Agriculture Secretary Orville Freeman, instead of investigating the case when it broke, merely claimed it had been "ballooned out of proportion."

'Estes has since been convicted in Federal and State courts of fraud in connection with manipulation of cotton acreage allotments. Several second-echelon agriculture officials subsequently quit or were fired as a result of the case.

'Sen. Goldwater said Mr. Freeman ignored months of warnings from the FBI about Estes, even naming him to the National Cotton Advisory Board, while at the same time Lyndon Johnson's office was busily contacting him on behalf of Estes.

"'This isn't rumor; this isn't speculation," Senator Goldwater said, "This is on the record, tying the office of the man who now lives in the White House with Billie Sol Estes."

'The GOP presidential nominee said it is up to the President to expose wrongdoing in the government, "but the interim President whose office dealt with Billie Sol Estes does not press for exposure. His power is used for far different ends, and the White House has been turned into the whitewash house."'

The Whitewash House. Not bad a term. That's exactly what it has been ever since Lyndon B. Johnson moved in. And Coverup House. Covering up for his own misdeeds and those of his friends, has been a full-time occupation of Johnson's for as long as he has been President, and on half a dozen different fronts. The Billie Sol Estes front. The Bobby Baker front. The Walter Jenkins front. The LBJ Broadcasting Company front, And, most importantly, the Kennedy assassination front.

What positive evidence is there to tie Lyndon Johnson to Billie Sol Estes' crooked business dealings?

Not an awful lot, to be sure. Two Congressional Committees 'investigating' the case in what has become the traditional LBJ pattern have done their very best to blur the tracks and to dim the background to Billie's operations. A couple of 'suicides', eliminating key witnesses also helped a good deal. What remains is circumstantial evidence, yet it is strong.

In the first place, there is the proven connection between Billie Sol Estes and Johnson's administrative assistant, Cliff Carter. Besides the facts cited by Sen. Goldwater (see above), there is that tell-tale little note from Carter to Estes which somehow fell into the hands of LBJ's political foes:

Billie Sol:

Just a quick note to acknowledge your fine letter about Bill Mattox." I'll see that gets in the proper hands.

Cordial best for the New Year (signed) Cliff

Am moving say family to Washington this week so call on me in the Vice-President's office as we can serve you.

According to the same source, it is well established in the sworn testimony of witnesses before the Courts of Inquiry held in

Texas that Billie Sol did say that he knew Johnson, on many occasions. He did display a personally autographed photo of Johnson on his wall. He did say that he was telephoning Johnson, several times. He constantly invoked Lyndon Johnson's name in conversation, as witnesses have testified.

It is also a matter of record that Estes sent small gifts to Johnson and that these were acknowledged with thanks. On this score, *Newsday*, on February 14, 1964, published a special dispatch from Washington, ironically entitled 'Lower the Stereo, I'm Eating Melon', which ran as follows:

'Billie Sol Estes, the bankrupt Texas tycoon who bragged of being on a first-name basis with top government officials, never quite made it to the White House—but his cantaloupes did.

'Congressional investigators said yesterday that before the Estes scandal broke, the wheeling-dealing Estes sent crates of Texas melons to the then Vice President Lyndon B. Johnson, the late President Kennedy, Sen. Ralph Yarborough (D-Oklahoma [should be Texas, J. J.]) and Jack Cox, a Republican who made an unsuccessful bid for governor of Texas in 1962. Apparently all Estes got in return for his gesture were thank-you notes.

'The cantaloupe list came to light yesterday as House investigators culled the files of the former boy wonder whose $150,000,000 empire toppled under congressional federal, state and press scrutiny. Estes, who was fond of telling his Texas cronies about his influential Washington friends, saved the thank-you notes.

'Johnson, who more recently was on the gift list of former Senate aide Bobby Baker, acknowledged the Estes gift with notes of appreciation on August 3 and August 16, 1961. Johnson addressed Estes as "Dear friend" and once wrote, "Pecos cantaloupes are the best in the world and are old friends of mine." In each thank-you note, Johnson signed his full name'.

Perhaps the most damning piece of evidence against Johnson, in the Estes case, is the 'clearance' he got, in October 1964, from the House Intergovernmental Relations subcommittee which had been looking, or rather pretending to look, into the tangled affairs of the West Texas promoter.

Under the headline 'House Unit Clears Johnson and Others in Estes Case', *The New York Times* reported on October 12, 1964:

'A House subcommittee cleared President Johnson and other officials today of any wrongdoing in connection with Billie Sol Estes' grain storage dealings with the Federal Government'.

Let's stop here for a moment and ponder the implications of this paragraph. The Chief Executive of the most powerful nation in the world should be, like Caesar's wife, not only above reproach but beyond suspicion. For any President of the United States—or Vice-President, for that matter—to be 'cleared' by a congressional committee dominated by his own political henchmen of 'wrongdoing' in connection with the fraudulant manipulations of a convicted swindler is disgraceful per se.

The New York Times dispatch goes on to say:

'The investigators, however, severely criticized the Agriculture Department and other Federal agencies for failing to catch the Texas promoter as he used fraudulent manipulations to built up his now bankrupt multimillion-dollar empire in cotton, grain and fertilizer...

'The subcommittee suggested action to improve cooperation among Federal agencies, including a better exchange of information, and proposed closing a "possible loophole" in Federal laws.

'It said it had found no evidence of bribery, political influence or misconduct by Federal officials in Estes' grain storage licensing. The subcommittee chairman said there was no evidence that political figures owned interests in Estes' facilities.

'The House report followed by 10 days a Senate committee finding that absolved Secretary of Agriculture Orville L. Freeman and other farm officials of any deliberate complicity in Estes' schemes. The Senate panel, however, rebuked the Agriculture Department for slipshod procedures that it said had enabled Estes to acquire Federal cotton allotments illegally...'

Note the perfect parallelism in approach, investigative technique and even wording between this congressional disposal of the Estes case and the Warren Report, released only a few days earlier.

The Warren Commission too, 'found no evidence', or found 'no credible evidence' of anybody but Lee Harvey Oswald being implicated in the assassination, even though the testimony of literally hundreds of witnesses pointed towards a conspiracy. The evidence that had been staring the investigators in the face was not 'found', when their report was issued, because it had been swept under the rug and trampled upon by the investigators themselves—exactly as in the Estes case.

Again, the Warren Commission, felt that it too had to produce something for the million dollars the taxpayers had to shell out for its labors and so it criticized the insufficient liaison between the FBI and the Secret Service and their defective efforts in protective intelligence research—and promptly got tit for tat from FBI Chief J. Edgar Hoover ('perfect example of Monday morning quarterbacking').

This is the established cover-up technique, such as it has been perfected under the Johnson regime. Whether you look to the Estes scandal, or the Baker mess or the Kennedy murder—all intimately linked with each other—it is always the same picture: unwanted evidence is swept under the rug; inconvenient witnesses are given the brush-off or worse; a few minor officials are rebuked for 'slipshod' procedures; better liaison between government agencies is recommended—and those who have been running the show are 'cleared of wrongdoing'.

In the Estes case, the chairman of the subcommittee, Rep. H. L. Fountain, Democrat of North Carolina, laid it on as thick as circumstances would permit. His committee, he declared, had found 'no evidence that the then Vice-President (Johnson) or his staff participated in any way in the relationship between the

Federal Government or its agencies other than routinely referring to the Department of Agriculture correspondence, including complaints about activities in which Estes was involved'.

Obviously here some mythical 'complaints' were tagged on to the real correspondence that passed back and forth between Johnson's office and the Department of Agriculture to conceal the core of the matter: that Estes was in touch at all with the office of the Vice-President which was not concerned in the matter, as the Department of Agriculture was, in an administrative capacity. No amount of double-talk about 'routinely referring' (incidentally, this term is another favourite of the Warren Commission) can change the fact that Lyndon Johnson and his staff had no business at all with Billie Sol Estes —except shady business.

There was also 'no credible evidence,' Rep. Fountain went on to say, 'to support allegations that prominent political figures or members of their families secretly owned interests in Billie Sol Estes' grain storage facilities'.

This, again, is exactly the same investigative, or rather whitewash technique employed by the Warren Commission and the Bobby Baker probers.

How can you find 'credible evidence' involving 'prominent political figures' if you carefully refrain from putting those figures on the carpet? Sherlock Holmes himself couldn't have found evidence he wasn't looking for, especially if he had gone about it blindfold.

The abrupt downfall of the once high-riding Billie Sol Estes came about because he, just like Bobby Baker, overreached himself. He had so many irons in the fire that he was in constant need of financing. His bubble burst when a local newspaper reporter found out that tanks of anhydrous ammonia, a fertilizer, that he had used as mortgage collateral in obtaining loans from nationwide financing firms, were nonexistent.

Once he had been caught in one shady deal, Estes' creditors lost confidence in him and disaster quickly snowballed. He went into bankruptcy and, at the end of March, 1962, was arrested by the FBI. One year later he went on trial, in federal district court in El Paso, on multiple charges of mail fraud involving the swindling of about 100 individuals and a dozen major finance companies, in mortgage deals which involved $24 million. The jury found him guilty on four mail fraud counts and one conspiracy charge; he was declared innocent on nine other counts. He was sentenced to 8 years in prison and later drew additional prison sentences following other indictments in federal and state courts. He was last reported to be serving a 15 year stretch in Leavenworth federal penitentiary.

CHAPTER 10 - The Senator from Lobbyland

THE higher they go, a popular proverb holds, the harder they fall.

Not always. It all depends on where the climber, having lost his foothold, happens to land on his downward whirl. If he has provided himself with a mattress to cushion his fall, he may not only survive but get back on his feet unscathed.

Take the case of Bobby Baker. He had ascended to dizzy heights of power and wealth before he came a cropper in the fall of 1963. It could have been a fatal nose-dive, but it wasn't. The cushion was there, firmly in place, and it held.

'On any issue, I have at least ten Senators in the palm of my hand,' Baker used to boast in his heyday. There were more than that number standing by to catch him in their arms as he plunged. And the most important of them had, providentially, risen to the pinnacle of power by the time Bobby badly needed help.

They used to call him the 101st Senator, and that was no mean compliment. It signified that the hundred sages, coming in pairs from each State of the Union, recognized Bobby Baker as one of their own, even though he was nominally only a Senate employee.

In fact, Baker had for years been more powerful than all but a few of the Senate's members. he was really a sort of super-Senator, the sole representative in Washington of the key state in the Union, Lobbyland.

There is no need to dwell at length on the early antecedents of Robert Gene Baker. They are fairly well known, and highly unimportant. No psychiatrist has yet come forward to suggest that Bobby Baker's whirlwind career in the outer space of legality might have been the result of an unhappy childhood and defective upbringing.

Suffice it to say that the man who, more than anyone else, became the symbol of Washington life (politics cum sex plus corruption) was born in 1928 at Pickens, South Carolina, the son of a postman with eight children. At the tender age of 14, Bobby exchanged the peaceful life of the countryside for the hustle and bustle of Washington. It was not his own decision, though. Rather it was made for him through the play of local politics. In 1941, South Carolina's newly elected Senator Burnet Maybank wanted to do a political friend in Pickens a favor by offering his son a post as a Senate page. The boy wasn't interested and the friend suggested instead the son of a friend—Bobby Baker.

To the most competitive wrestling place in the world, the young man from Pickens brought only three major assets, but each of them was worth a million: a nimble mind, Southern charm, and a total lack of scruples. One can go far and high in Washington on a combination of these talents. Even minus the charm as the case of Lyndon Johnson shows.

Before very long, the newcomer from South Carolina had elbowed his way to the top of his class. As Chief Senate Page, he was in a position to make himself agreeable to, and to be noticed by, the Senators who count.

With a sure flair for the right connections, young Baker contrived to become the protégé of two powerful politicians who had simultaneously moved into the Senate, in 1949, on the Democratic ticket: Robert S. Kerr of Oklahoma and Lyndon B. Johnson of Texas.

Besides being both Southern Democrats, the aging Senator Kerr and the then still youthful Sen. Johnson were held together by a far more potent bond: their common allegiance to the oil industry, the greatest single force in U.S. politics as well as U.S. business.

As head of Kerr-McGee Oil Industries of Oklahoma City, Sen. Robert Kerr was one of America's leading oilmen in his own right. When he died on January 1, 1963, he left an estate of $20.8 million, including 449,882 shares of Kerr-McGee stock, valued at more than $14.4 million.

The extraordinarily warm relationship between oilman Kerr and Bobby Baker was brought out again and again, in various phases of the subsequent Baker investigation. Here are some highlights:

Sen. Kerr extended to Baker an almost unlimited line of credit at the Fidelity National Bank and Trust Company of Oklahoma City, which he controlled. According to the expert testimony given to the investigating committee, in January 1964, by government accountant Lorrin Drennan, Jr., Baker and his associates borrowed between January 1959 and November 1963 a total of $2,784,338 from 22 banks and Government agencies. Among the biggest items in the list were loans totaling $475,000 from Kerr's Fidelity National Bank and $471,000 from the First National Bank of Dallas, which is controlled by the Dallas Oil Magnates, in particular the Hunts and Murchisons (see below). On one occasion, Baker and his associates borrowed $175,000 from Fidelity National, on the advice of Sen. Kerr, to buy stock in another Oklahoma Bank, the Farmers and Merchants Bank of Tulsa.

Kerr also advanced cash to Bobby Baker on a number of occasions. The aggregate of these advances was in the neighborhood of $40,000, Cabell Phillips of *The New York Times* reported on November 2, 1963. The paper went on to say:

'In the summer of 1962, according to reliable information, Senator Kerr, who was then sick, sent for Mr. Baker and told him that he was to regard the advances as payment for services rendered rather than as loans and that he was to report the sums on his income tax as earnings...'

Baker did so report them in his income tax return for 1962, but Sen. Kerr, who as donor was obligated by law to report gifts of more than $3,000 to any individual in one year, did not. This was revealed to Mr. Phillips by Robert S. Kerr, Jr., the son and heir of the late Senator, who also disclaimed any knowledge of the transaction. In a telephone interview with *The New York Times* correspondent, Mr. Kerr also revealed that Baker, 'two weeks ago' had come to Oklahoma City to see him. That means he must have hurried there within a few days after his resignation from office.

'He asked me if I knew anything about dad having given him some money,' Mr. Kerr was quoted as saying. 'I told him I didn't know anything about it, and that it wasn't on any of the books. And knowing how dad kept records about things like this, I told him I doubted any such gift ever existed'.

This disclaimer put Bobby on the spot because a 'gift' reported to the Internal Revenue Service that is disavowed by the donor doesn't look so good in the eyes of the law.

And what 'services' did Bobby Baker render to the powerful senator from Oklahoma? Let's turn now to *Newsday*, which reported in its issue of November 9, 1963:

'The swashbuckling trail of Senate aide Robert G. (Bobby) Baker led back to the floor of the Senate yesterday with reports that he double-crossed the Senate majority for which he worked by helping to defeat the Kennedy administration's medicare bill.

'Backers of the bill charge Baker gave Democratic leaders wrong information about the number of senators lined up to support the measure. This wrong information, the backers say, led the majority leadership to call the bill to the floor. Once it got there the bill was defeated by a narrow 52-48 count. The defeat was a smashing victory for the late Sen. Robert F. Kerr (D-Okla.), who had led the fight against medicare and who, just weeks before, is reported to have given Baker $40,000 either as a gift with which to pay off debts or for "services rendered". Kerr frequently has been mentioned in the past as a Baker benefactor...'

Helping kill President Kennedy's medicare bill was certainly not the only service Bobby Baker performed for Senator Kerr. Bobby must have found other ways of ingratiating himself with the rugged old oil tycoon, at the time the richest member of the U.S. Senate. He also made himself most useful in preserving the oil industry's tax privleges, as will be detailed below. And he may have done other favors for old man Kerr.

Fred Black, a long-time Baker associate and one of those who, on Kerr's advice, borrowed money from the Senator's bank to buy stock in the Farmers and Merchants Bank, later told the Senate committee investigating Baker's affairs:

'Sen. Kerr told me... that outside of his sons, his wife, he never knew and loved a man so much as he did Bobby Baker... there wasn't anything in the world that Bobby Baker would ask him to do for him... that he would not do'.

Bobby Baker, eager as always to follow in the footsteps of his master, also became a great champion of the oil interests, though he operated less openly than did Johnson. He established a particularly close working relationship with the oil multi-millionaire Clint Murchison, Jr. of Dallas whose fiscal 'worth' is not much below the Hunt figure. This matter will be dealt with more exhaustively in a subsequent chapter.

One of the few solid disclosures of the Baker 'Investigation' has been that the enterprising young man, working for the

Government at an annual salary of $19,612, was able to amass a fortune of at least two million dollars.

It is not possible, of course, to estimate with any degree of accuracy how much of this wealth was contributed, directly or indirectly, by the grateful oil industry, any more than one can tell how big a share of LBJ's 14 million has come from the same source. There are too many highly-paid 'business consultants' about Washington who make it their special business to draw the veil of discretion over such relationships and transactions.

The hard fact of the matter, however, is that both Johnson and Baker served the oil interests faithfully and well over a period of many years and that they have, in turn, handsomely benefited from the oilmen's benevolence. In the words of *Time*: 'The relationship with Kerr was cemented first; before very long Kerr was tipping Baker to profitable stock investments, something that the tough rough oil millionaire did for few others. Next, Baker ingratiated himself with Johnson. Recalls a former Johnson staffer of Baker:

"'He was an unabashed lackey, a bootlicker. He'd think of all manner of excuses to come in the office and see Johnson, and he'd tell him about all the things he was doing for him, all the little ways he was helping him'" (*Time*, March 6, 1964).

This was, indeed, the basic secret of Bobby Baker's success: he was always helping people, doing things for them. Only people that count, to be sure; and things not available to them in the ordinary way.

He was a purveyor of committee-assignments and tax favors as well as of female charms on an exalted level. He was The Great Arranger, the sure-handed fixer, not a peddler, but a dealer in influence. If he ever had principle it must have been 'Live and Let Live—at Taxpayer's Expense'.

He knew how to make and keep Government officials, Congressmen, big Businessmen and the top brass happy and they, in turn, repaid his favors with commissions and rebates; with tax exemptions and favorable tax rulings; with Government contracts and business partnerships.

He was, to quote *Time* again 'a gentleman with innumerable friendships and connections' who... 'made it his unending business to know things—and what he didn't know about the Senate and its members probably was not worth the trouble. He knew who was against what bill and why. He knew who was drunk. He knew who was out of town. He knew who was sleeping with whom...'

He ought to have known, for he had a hand in it much of the time.

CHAPTER 11 - Bobby and LBJ: Like Rocket, Like Booster

THERE is nothing 'speculative' about the relationship between Lyndon B. Johnson and Bobby Baker. Neither myth nor rumor have a part in it. Not even the 'findings' of another Warren Report, were it to run to 54 volumes and two million words, could obscure the hard historical fact that these two gentlemen were, for years, one heart and one soul. Two peas of a pod. As thick as thieves.

They are very different personalities, to be sure. The tall and once lanky Johnson has always been a tough go-getter, Texas style, quick of temper and quick on the trigger. By contrast, the pudgy Baker, baby-faced but hawk-eyed, became, in spite of his rural origins, the smoothest of city slickers, Washington style.

If President Johnson, in the course of the 1964 campaign, mustered the nerve to state in a nation-wide television broadcast from the White House that Bobby Baker was not a particular friend of his, that he was merely an employee of the Senate and that he (Baker) had been there before he himself got there, that simply gives you the measure of the man.

In the picaresque Baker affair, as later again in the sordid Jenkins scandal, President Johnson made it perfectly clear that he is a friend in need only to the extent of his own interests. He can be exuberant in his praise of a fair-weather partnership, but when the going gets rough he'll throw his best-loved bosom pal to the wolves.

In *Newsday* of January 31, 1964, Thomas Collins reported from Washington: 'As the campaign train rolled through the vote-rich southern countryside one day back in 1960, Sen. Lyndon B. Johnson, the Democratic candidate for vice-president, turned to an aide and said: "That Bobby Baker is the greatest man who ever worked for me. You watch him. He's going to be governor of South Carolina some day."

'Today, says a man who rode the campaign train with Johnson and Robert G. (Bobby) Baker, "Lyndon has divorced Bobby completely. I don't think he'd say hello to him if he saw him coming down the hall."'

Campaign of 1960; campaign of 1964. A vice-presidential candidate on the make; a president 'in his own right' in the making. A world of difference.

'Such a falling out between two men in the high-pressure atmosphere of Washington politics is not unusual and in the case of Johnson and Baker is understandable,' *Newsday* went on to say. 'Johnson himself has been scorched through the gift of a stereo set and in the heat that has been turned on his former protégé. And the onetime shoulder-to-shoulder relationship that existed between the two men figures to be a key issue in the upcoming election campaign. The Republicans are not going to let the President forget that at one time, in the words of one observer, "They were so close they could read each other's minds."'

Although Bobby Baker by that time had fallen from grace and the President had broken off relations with his former partner, Johnson never lifted a finger to bring the publicly exposed rogue to justice. On the contrary, as Chief Executive he did everything in his power—and no president in this century has ever wielded greater power than Lyndon B. Johnson—to shield Bobby Baker from the law. The passive cover-up for his misdeeds which the Senate investigating committee was to produce as the only tangible result of its 20-months' labor, was directly inspired by the President, as will be detailed in a subsequent chapter.

Johnson, of course, was acting under inescapable compulsion when he moved heaven and earth to cover up for Baker. In shielding his former associate, he was protecting himself. There is no greater force in nature than the instinct of self-preservation—most notably among politicians.

Unfortunately for President Johnson, every phase and facet of his intimate relationship, of long standing, with Bobby Baker is in the record—in cold print and in colorful pictures. A few samples have already been given above. Let us review some more.

The first thing that strikes one in considering the Johnson-Baker relationship is the uncanny parallelism in their careers. Both came to Washington, the City of Unlimited Possibilities, as penniless young men; each became a multimillionaire while serving the Government.

Coming both from the rural South, they descended on the Federal capital within eight years of each other, in spite of a 19-

year difference in age. Naturally, LBJ got there first, though Bobby beat him to the Senate (as a page boy, not as a member) by seven years.

In the earliest stage of their Washington life, they both evinced the same ability to push their way to the top within the subordinate Congressional group to which they belonged. Johnson, who had arrived in Washington late in 1932 as a secretary to Rep. Kleberg, promptly set about conquering the leadership of his Congressional secretaries' group (the 'Little Congress'). Baker managed to become Chief Senate Page within two years of his arrival, as has been noted before.

Both were eager young beavers who latched on, unashamedly, to some of the most powerful figures of their time. Johnson to Representative Sam Rayburn and Senator Tom Connally; Baker to Senators Kerr and Johnson.

In 1951, the freshman Senator from Texas and his 'unabashed lackey and bootlicker' (see above) formed a mutual log-rolling society which lasted for twelve years. That year, the position of Senate Majority whip opened and Johnson had his eye on it, despite a conspicuous lack of seniority. Bobby proved helpful. In his own words, 'I kept leaking stories to the newspapers that Johnson had the inside track; that in a showdown he would have the votes'. In return, Senator Johnson moved to have young Baker named assistant Democratic Senate secretary.

A year later, the Eisenhower boom provisionally stripped both Johnson and Baker of the 'majority' prefix. To Johnson, however, the loss of the Senate majority by the Democrats, in the 1952 elections, also brought an unexpected windfall. For the then Democratic Floor Leader Ernest McFarland of Arizona was also swept away by the Eisenhower tide, losing his Senate seat to Republican Barry Goldwater. What happened next has been described by *Time* (March 6, 1964) in these terms:

'The day after the elections, Baker was summoned to the telephone from law class at American University. It was Lyndon Johnson calling from Texas. "He wanted to know what people in Washington were saying, how things looked up here," Baker once recalled. "I told him it looked like he was the leader. At the beginning of the next Congress he was."'

Two years later, the Democrats recaptured their majority in the Senate and now the time was ripe for another payoff to Bobby. On January 5, 1955, Senator Johnson took the lead in sponsoring Baker for the nomination as Secretary to the Democratic Majority in the Senate. Bobby got the job and used it for the next eight years, to ride herd over the Democratic members on behalf of his master, Lyndon B. Johnson. To quote again from *Time*'s cover story on Bobby Baker:

'As it happened, Johnson was one of the most effective—and most domineering—floor leaders in the Senate history. He set right out to bridle the Senate, and he used Baker as a bit. Recalls a Senate veteran: "Bobby was Lyndon's bluntest instrument in running the show the way he wanted." For being such, Baker was rewarded with equal measures of prestige and praise'.

In view of the fact that President Johnson subsequently chose to disavow his former protégé and even to assert that Bobby had never been a particular friend of his, some textual quotations are in order from authentic LBJ remarks about Bobby Baker.

On July 27, 1956, for instance, Johnson rose on the Senate floor to deliver a speech which included this gem: 'I know I should refer to him (Bobby Baker) formally as Secretary to the Majority, but my tongue even as my heart says "Bobby" instead... Always present, always alert, and more than anything else, always understanding and persuasive with his wise counsel. I say to all of you here tonight that there, indeed, is a young man of rare and real promise'.

As Congress wound up its 1957 session, Johnson used the occasion to heap more fulsome praise on his faithful henchman, as quoted in *Time*:

'The secretary to the majority is the most tireless and indefatigable man on this floor. Bobby Baker is a young man who already has gone much further in life than many others of far greater years. And it is my personal opinion that he is just getting started'.

In this appraisal, Johnson was right. His 'young man of rare and real promise' was then just getting started. And, before the promise turned sour, he had indeed gone much further in life.

In a speech made on the Senate floor on August 30, 1957, Johnson declared: 'He (Bobby Baker) is a man who truly serves his country, and I consider him one of my most trusted, most loyal and most competent friends'.

Less than a year later, on August 23, 1958, Johnson again used the Senate floor as a sounding board for a veritable paean in honor of his favourite:

'There have been few times in my life that I have ever seen a young man who combined so much wisdom and maturity with such youthful vigor and enthusiasm as Bobby Baker... He is a young man who has already gone very far and who is going much farther. I believe he will reach much greater heights'.

On the same day, Sen. Alan Bible, Democrat of Nevada, in a tribute to the then Senate Majority Leader Johnson also had some nice and pertinent things to say about Baker: '...Bobby Baker, the Secretary of the Majority, a young man who has that rare gift of getting things done with a minimum of time and a maximum of efficiency. I like to refer to Bobby Baker as Lyndon Junior, an accolade he well deserves'.

At the 1960 Democratic national convention in Los Angeles Bobby Baker was an active supporter of the then Senator Lyndon B. Johnson when the latter was battling with the front-running John F. Kennedy for the top place on the national ticket.

During the 1960 campaign, vice-presidential candidate Johnson used the occasion of a swing through the mountains of South Carolina, with Native son Bobby always at his elbow, to call on the proud father of his protégé and tell him that his son was 'my strong right arm, the last man I see at night, the first one I see in the morning'.

Not bad for one who, one campaign later, had ceased to exist even as a friend.

Newsday, in the above-cited article by Thomas Collins, gave these further details about the close personal relationship between LBJ and 'Lyndon Junior':

'Baker and his wife attended social functions with Johnson, were guests at the LBJ Ranch in Texas and exchanged gifts. Two of Baker's children, Lynda and Lyndon, were named after Johnson, for which, according to those who knew them, Johnson gave Baker two white-faced Hereford cattle, which are still at home on the range of the LBJ Ranch.

'Baker was always at Johnson's elbow, whispering to him in the Senate chamber, counting the house to see how many votes Johnson had on a bill, lighting his cigarette ("Bobby was a fast man with a lighter", said one Baker friend) and making certain that everything Johnson wanted, Johnson got'.

Not only is the record of Johnson's own statements there to attest to the close and cordial relationship between him and Bobby Baker, but a lot of pictures, too. One of the most eloquent may be found in the *Time* cover story already cited above repeatedly. The photo shows a smiling Baker being hugged by a grinning Johnson. *Time*'s legend: 'Bobby and Booster'.

CHAPTER 12 - A Case of MAGIC (How the 'F-80 Club' Took Care of Its Own)

THEY used to call it 'the mess in Washington'. Now it's The Great Society. It's the same thing, really.

Happily, The Great Society is a bipartisan institution. For every Democratic deep freeze, there is a Republican vicuna coat; for every 'Checkers' speech by Nixon, there is a Johnson broadcast explaining how innocently he came by that stereo set.

With only two political parties vying for popular favor, and both equally shot through with rogues and wheeler-dealers, there is a built-in guarantee that nothing will change in Washington, regardless of who wins.

The Bobby Baker affair provides a perfect example of how the system works. It involves about as many prominent Republicans as Democrats. No wonder the 'investigation' of this super-scandal never got anywhere.

As a matter of fact, it was a Republican Congressman, Rep. John W. Byrnes of Wisconsin, who helped the Democratic secretary of the Senate majority, Bobby Baker, get off the ground in his first known business adventure of major proportions, the MAGIC deal.

'MAGIC' stands for Mortgage Guarantee Insurance Corporation, a home-mortgage insurance company founded in

Milwaukee, Wisconsin, by a man named Max H. Karl who also became president of the firm.

Some time about the middle of 1959, Bobby Baker got wind of the fabulous profit potential inherent in this venture. A key element of the situation was this: Paul Rogan, an executive vice-president of MAGIC, was a good friend of Rep. John W. Byrnes who at the time was chairman of the Republican Policy Committee and a ranking member of House Ways and Means Committee which writes the tax laws.

Accordingly, when Rep. Byrnes interceded with the Internal Revenue Service on behalf of MAGIC, a favorable tax ruling was promptly issued. Then six months later, Paul Rogan offered Byrnes $2,300 worth of MAGIC stock, which the latter bought. Within a few months, this stock skyrocketed to $23,000, ten times its purchase value.

That's the way they do business in Washington.

When Bobby Baker heard of this cozy arrangement—by that time his office in the Senate Buildings Room F-80, had become the established terminal of the Congressional grapevine—he decided to get in on the ground floor, too.

In August 1959, he called the president of MAGIC, Mr. Karl, to express interest in the company's stock. The two men quickly came to terms. Baker obtained, for himself and a group of friends, 200 shares of MAGIC and 50 shares of an affiliate company, for $28,750.

By the time Baker got his shares, in March 1960, two stock splits had already occurred—the first 8 for 1 and the next 10 for 1, on the shares that had already been split. Before the year was out, the market value of Baker's 250 shares had soared to $400,000, like magic.

The first thing to be said about this transaction is that it was totally illegal. Under existing regulations, Mr. Karl was prohibited from selling any stock in his firm to out-of-town buyers before the Wisconsin stock had been registered with the Securities and Exchange Commission.

In his testimony before the Senate Rules Committee investigating Bobby Baker's extracurricular activities, Mr. Karl admitted, early in February 1964, that the legality of this sale was subject to question, Then, why did he do it? he was asked.

'I was impressed with his (Baker's) title', Karl candidly explained. He thought it would be good for MAGIC to have 'well known stockholders', he added and Baker 'knew a lot of people'.

No sooner had Bobby Baker made his killing in MAGIC stock than the good friend in Milwaukee put the bite on him. At the time, the company was seeking certain changes in federal regulations that would make its private mortgage-insurance business more competitive with Veterans Administration and FHA mortgage insurance.

And so Mr. Karl took pen in hand and wrote an appealing letter to his stockholder Bobby Baker pointing out that MAGIC's just cause had already received the friendly attention of some

Congressmen. Then, addressing himself directly to Baker, Karl added: 'You undoubtedly know many congressional leaders who share the same view'.

Sure enough Bobby did know Congressional leaders, none better than the Senate Majority leader, Lyndon B. Johnson. He got busy, and MAGIC stock pursued its skyward course.

Although the whole operation smells a mile away, Karl, in reply to a question put to him by Republican Senator Carl Curtis of Nebraska protested: 'I wasn't lobbying, sir. I'm not used to that term. I was just trying to keep them informed'.

Then what about his suggestion that Baker might know other 'congressional leaders'?

Karl: 'I was just expanding on a philosophy'.

To a direct question whether he had ever asked Baker to use his influence on MAGIC's behalf, the witness replied in righteous indignation: 'Definitely not. What he did was talk to some of his friends about the great possibility of the company'.

That's the way it always goes. There is no graft, no influence-peddling, no lobbying. Just a friend talking to a friend about a friend. And if one friend happens to be in Government and the other in business, that's purely coincidental. As is of course the phenomenal rise of the company's stock to ten times or more of its original value.

For Bobby Baker, until then a Government employee in the middle-income brackets, this magic deal was the first taste of Big Business. He liked the taste and came back for more of the same.

When he first made his deal with Karl, in August of 1959, Baker didn't even have the $28,750 required available in ready cash. Three months later, he wrote to Mr. Karl to ask him if he could arrange a loan for $16,000 with the stock (which had not yet been delivered to him at that time) as collateral.

Karl arranged the loan and signed the note. 'I try to be accommodating,' he explained to the investigation committee.

Baker paid $1,000 on the note after the first 90 days. It was renewed for two more 90-day periods and finally came due in June, 1960. By that time, Baker was able to pay off the loan by selling a few of his MAGIC shares which had skyrocketed in the meantime.

Bobby Baker's MAGIC scheme of quickly getting rich produced still another fruitful angle. A list of purchasers of MAGIC stock in the Washington area, as disclosed apparently by the Securities and Exchange Commission (as described in *The Christian Science Monitor* of December 19, 1963) turned out to be singularly revealing.

Of nine entries on this list, six gave their addresses as that of Mr. Baker, 'Room F-80, Senate Office Building'. One of these entries reads: 'John W. and Barbara Byrnes'. There is no other couple John W. and Barbara Byrnes than the above-named Republican Congressman from Wisconsin and his wife. This fact disposes of Mr. Karl's vigorous assertion, before the investigating committee, that he knew of no connections between Baker and Byrnes in assisting his firm.

Among the other purchasers on this list, a couple named Mr. Alfred S. and Mrs. Gertrude C. Novak deserve particular attention because their names recur frequently and disturbingly in the Bobby Baker saga.

The long acquaintance between the Novaks and Bobby Baker began, it seems, when the latter some time in 1957 was introduced to Gertrude who happened to be on the staff of the Senate Small Business Committee. This committee acts as a watchdog over the Small Business Administration in which Baker, as we shall see, was keenly interested.

Gertrude Novak, an attractive blonde, then introduced Baker to her husband Alfred, a Maryland builder, and they all became good friends.

'We thought of him (Bobby Baker) as a brother,' Mrs. Novak later explained in a press interview. 'We had complete faith in him'.

Brotherhood and faith notwithstanding, Baker exacted a big kickback from the couple for letting them in on the juicy MAGIC stock purchase deal.

One day in 1960, Mrs. Novak told the investigating committee, Baker urged the couple to buy as much stock in MAGIC as they could afford. He said he was out of funds himself, but that this was a real hot tip. The Novaks put in $12,000 and soon were happy to discover that they had struck a gold mine. Gratefully they turned over to Bobby Baker, as per arrangement, one half of the net profit they had made, i.e. $27,444.93, although he had put up no money for the deal. The other $27,444.93 they kept.

In view of this testimony, the question was naturally raised as to whether Baker had a similar arrangement with Rep. Byrnes and his wife and the other two (unidentified) members of his 'F-80 Club'?

Before long, Bobby Baker followed up his initial investment in MAGIC, and his lucrative kickback arrangements with selected friends, by buying more stock in this firm, on borrowed money. Among those he approached, was Robert F. Thompson of Dallas, executive vice-president of Tecon Corp. (Texas Construction Corporation) one of the innumerable affiliates of the Murchison oil empire. Like other Murchison interests this Dallas construction firm relies heavily on Government contracts. Among other things, it does nearly $90 million worth of work annually for the Army Corps of Engineers.

Clint Murchison, Jr., head of the combine, has been for years a close personal acquaintance of Lyndon B. Johnson, the oilmen's best friend. When Thompson, who first met Baker in 1957, was asked by a member of the investigating committee where the two had been introduced to each other, he candidly replied, 'I thought that it was in the office of Lyndon Johnson'.

When Thompson learned about the fantastic money-making possibilities of MAGIC, he was instantly all agog. At the oilmen's own First National Bank in Dallas, any representative of a Murchison firm is assured of an almost unlimited line of credit.

Thompson promptly got a $110,000 loan on a note. Bobby Baker who under his arrangement with Thompson was to share equally in the profits or losses of this operation, did not even have to co-sign the loan. He cleared $21,000 on this deal alone, without having to put up any money or assume any risk in writing.

This seemed a bit stiff to some members of the investigating committee who wanted to know from Thompson why Baker did not even have to co-sign the note for the loan.

'I just borrowed the money and had a gentleman's agreement with Bobby,' Thompson replied and added proudly, 'That's the way we do business in Texas'.

The way they do business in Washington is apparent from the fact that Baker, according to information furnished to the committee by Karl, eventually wound up with 9,274 shares of MAGIC with a value of around $200,000 (*Christian Science Monitor*, 30-1-64) without ever having had to disburse a cent of his own.

It is also apparent from the fact that Rep. John Byrnes, having been caught as a side prop in the Baker scandal, put on a great show of righteous contrition that was on a par with Richard Nixon's famous 'Checkers speech'.

Speaking on the floor of the House, on Nov. 21, 1963, Byrnes defended his purchase of MAGIC stock and declaimed, 'As far as I was concerned, the purchase had nothing to do with the tax matter'. He asserted he never knew until last week that he got the stock at a special low price reserved for those in the business.

'I swear before God and this House, that had I known of these facts, I would not have purchased the stock,' Byrnes exclaimed in what an AP dispatch described as 'a choked voice'.

As he came to the end, the dispatch also informed, 'Byrnes raised a hand to his eyes and brushed away tears'.

The total insincerity of this mawkish performance is self-evident on at least three counts.

In the first place, the most rudimentary of ethical standards should have prevented an influential legislator from buying stock, at any price, within a few months after interceding on behalf of that firm with the Internal Revenue Service.

Secondly, Byrnes' discovery that he had gotten his chunk of stock at a cut-rate price came very late in the day. With the value of his shares reaching, in a matter of months, a level at least ten times that of their original purchase price, he must have realized, before the year 1960 was out, that this was no normal appreciation, even for 'blue chips'.

And, of course, as a lawmaker and senior member of the Ways and Means Committee, Byrnes must have known that the scale of MAGIC stock to him, before the issue was registered with SEC, was downright illegal.

On the strength of Byrnes' touching display of crocodile tears, one of the sob sisters of the American press proclaimed him a 'Baker Victim'. In truth, his role in the Baker scandal was anything but that. The only real victims of Bobby's crooked dealings have been the American taxpayers.

CHAPTER 13 – Serv-U—Bobby

ONE good thing Bobby Baker had learned in the exercise of his official functions, was that automatic vending machines were a booming business—especially, if you knew how to get them installed in defense plants, NASA establishments and other places where the Government has a big say.

With the easily-earned cash from the MAGIC stock deals tingling in his pocket, and his good friend and protector Lyndon B. Johnson installed in the office that's just one heart-beat away from the presidency, Baker, in 1961, launched his biggest and most successful (for a while, anyway) business operation, a vending machine company called the 'Serv-U Corporation'.

When Serv-U was formed, in December 1961, as a Maryland corporation, Baker prudently kept in the background. As president he installed Eugene Hancock of Miami, a vending machine operator with considerable experience in this business. One of Bobby's brothers, Charles Baker, became a vice-president, and Bobby's wife, Dorothy, was made an assistant secretary of the corporation.

In passing, it may be noted that Mrs. Robert G. Baker has also moved for years in the Congressional circuit so dear to her husband's heart. When, in 1950, Bobby met and married Dorothy Comstock, a comely blonde from Springfield, Illinois, she was already working on Capitol Hill as a clerk of the Senate Internal

Security Subcommittee. Later she rose to the position of records manager for that Committee, an $11,750-a-year job.

It may be presumed that Mrs. Baker, in more than fifteen years of filing and supervising the information dug up by the staff of the Senate Internal Security Subcommittee, acquired a vast amount of experience in her job. She probably knew more about who's who and what's what inside the Government, and outside, than any other woman on Capitol Hill and it would be unnatural if she did not occasionally share the benefit of her knowledge with her husband. And since one of the latter's chief functions was to run a good Congressional intelligence system for Lyndon B. Johnson, this was indeed a marriage of convenience as well as (presumably) of love.

Even more interesting than the list of executives of Serv-U was the roster of the corporation's stockholders. It included Bobby Baker himself, of course, even though he at first denied that he was an owner, after the spotlight had fallen on his own complex affairs.

Frequently, the true facts of such a case do not come out until much later. Indeed, it was not until the middle of 1964, that the original array of major stockholders in Serv-U became known, after all of them had been bought out by Baker, leaving the latter in control of at least 84 percent of the total.

According to *The New York Times*, which gave details of these operations on June 17, 1964, in a major article entitled 'Baker Gains Control of Vending Concern', the original distribution of the stock was as follows:

Bobby Baker – 28.5%

Fred B. Black, Jr. – 28.5%

Edward Levinson – 13.5%

Benny Sigelbaum – 13.5%

Previously, Baker's law partner Ernest C. Tucker, who shared a downtown law office in Washington with Bobby, had told investigators that he had held as a trustee 28.5% of the stock of Serv-U for Baker and another 28.5% for Black.

The purpose of this arrangement is obvious. It was designed to cloak the ownership of the two principal stockholders, both of whom had reasons to hide their interests in Serv-U.

Now for a closer look at Bobby's associates in this—and other—business ventures.

Fred B. Black, Jr. was a Washington 'industrial consultant' and president of Blyco Inc., a public relations concern. One of his principal clients, at the time he met Bobby Baker, several years ago, was the North American Aviation Corp., Inc., which engaged him as a contact man with Government agencies. To put it bluntly, Black was North American Aviation's top lobbyist in Washington. He did a good job. NAA got the biggest slice of NASA's space exploration ventures.

There never was an ethics code in the world of lobbyists, nor do the normal rules concerning conflict of interests apply to them (or to the lawmakers on whom they feed). It is not surprising, therefore, that Black, after having become a major stockholder of Serv-U, should have fruitfully worked both sides of the street. As a lobbyist for North American Aviation, he obtained lucrative government contracts for that firm. As Bobby Baker's partner in Serv-U, he saw to it that this company's vending-machines were favored by plant managers of North American Aviation.

As a matter of fact, this company became Serv-U's principal customer and the source of its most lucrative contracts. Other aerospace industries they did major business with included the Northrop Technology Laboratories.

With such sponsors as these, its hardly surprising that Serv-U, starting from scratch on a shoestring, should have been able, by the end of 1961, to build a business that grossed more than $3.5 million in less than two years.

What is surprising, though, is that Black apparently thought he could conceal from the Government the vastness of his earnings. He made the same fundamental mistake as hundreds of other top-bracket earners, legitimate businessmen as well as gangsters; with things apparently going his way all the time, he did not consider the possibility that some day something might go disastrously wrong, with the result that the ensuing bad publicity would bring the Internal Revenue agents down on his trail.

Fate caught up with Bobby's business partner faster than with himself. Indicted on income tax evasion charges, a few weeks after the Baker scandal broke in the fall of 1963, Black, on June 18 1964, was given a 15-month-to-four-year prison sentence and fined $10,000, after having been convicted on three counts of evading

$91,000 in Federal income taxes over a three-year period beginning in 1956.

Baker's other two principal partners in Serv-U, Edward Levinson and Benny Sigelbaum, have both been publicly identified as prominent Las Vegas gambling figures.

Levinson is manager of the Hotel Fremont casino in Las Vegas and its largest stockholder (20 per cent). He also holds a 27.5% interest in the Horseshoe Club, another Las Vegas casino.

According to *The New York Times* (November 7, 1963), Edward Levinson 'has extensive associations with notorious underworld figures'. He is one of three brothers long prominent in gambling operations, first in Newport, Kentucky, later in Las Vegas. In Newport, he ran the Flamingo Club, which in 1961 was closed as an illegal gambling outfit, in association with his brothers Mike and Louis ('Sleep-Out-Louie') Levinson.

In the same article, the *NYT* pointed out that Baker and Levinson had been associated in other gambling ventures with the 'Nevada-based gambling operator, Clifford Jones... a former lieutenant governor of Nevada'. Jones, the paper further revealed, had once acted as a stooge for the Meyer Lansky gang, representing their interests in the Thunderbird Hotel, a notorious Las Vegas gambling outfit.

The Times, also mentioned reports 'that Las Vegas gambling money might be involved in some of Mr. Baker's operations'. We'll deal with this interesting matter again in another context (see Chapter 18). These are not the only indications that the spectrum of

Bobby Baker's business associations reached all the way from Capitol Hill to the fringes of the organized underworld, if not into its inner sanctum. The Baker investigation has also disclosed—most gingerly, to be sure—numerous points of contact between the versatile Bobby and the notorious labor racketeer Jimmy Hoffa.

Bobby's third major partner in Serv-U, Benjamin B. Sigelbaum, is a Miami real estate investor. According to *Newsday* (12-3-64) 'Fred Hanford, a retired FBI-agent, said Sigelbaum told the investigators he was a close friend of Las Vegas gambler Edward Levinson and had many real estate investments with him but no gambling interests. Sigelbaum, according to Hallford, said he had invested $60,000 to buy 13.5% of the stock in the Serv-U Co., the vending-machine outfit in which Baker has a major interest. Hallford said Sigelbaum also stated that Levinson advised him to buy stock in the Tulsa, Okla., bank in which Baker also had bought shares (see Chapter 10). Hallford and Sigelbaum stressed that he had never asked Baker for any favors nor had he done any for the former secretary to the Senate majority'.

That is, of course, a routine denial which all friends of Bobby Baker, including President Johnson, have 'stressed' again and again. If we are to believe these gentlemen, they all were linked to each other quite innocently and it was sheer coincidence that they all got fabulously rich in common and at the same time. *Honi soit qui mal y pense.*

Originally, a third Las Vegas gambler, Edward Torres, had also been a big stockholder in Serv-U, the subsequent Senate investigation brought out. On this score, an AP dispatch from Washington, dated Jan. 14, 1964, gave these details:

'L. P. McLendon special counsel to the Senate Rules Committee listed Mr. Baker's associates in the March, 1962 ventures as B. B. Sigelbaum and Edward Levinson, whom he identified as Las Vegas hotel operators (this disposes of Sigelbaum's denial that his association with Levinson did not include gambling interests —J. J), and Fred Black... Mr. McLendon placed in evidence a document from Serv-U files attesting that it had bought out Mr. Torres's interest in the company for $75,000. Mr. McLendon said the evidence indicated that Mr. Torres had bought the stock for $16.50 a share and sold to Serv-U last July 4 for $187.50 a share'.

Even the gentle McLendon of the placid Senate Rules Committee apparently had an uneasy feeling that behind a windfall of such colossal proportions, involving a more than an elevenfold appreciation of the gambler Torres' stock, in a matter of a few months, there might be a payoff of some sort.

'Don't you know there was something more than stock involved', he asked former Serv-U President Eugene Hancock, from whom he had elicited this information.

'No, I don't,' Hancock replied, innocently.

Asked by Sen. Hugh Scott whether he knew of Torres's 'association with gambling interests,' the witness answered:

'Now I know'. He had read about it in the newspaper, he explained.

In reply to another question replete with significance which Sen. Claiborn Pell put to him: 'In your opinion, did Mr. Baker ever use his office as secretary to the Senate Democratic majority to help the company,' Hancock exclaimed emphatically: "No sir'.

Did Senator Pell expect an emphatic 'Yes sir', perhaps?

Another key witness before the Committee, Edward M. Bostick, president of Melpar Inc. (more on this company in the next chapter) gave an even better performance. As he emerged from the committee's office, on Dec. 6, 1963, Mr. Bostick ran into a cluster of reporters. He turned them back saying 'Mr. Bostick is down there, down the hall'. When one of them asked, 'Mr. Bostick, may we quote you as denying that you are Mr. Bostick?' he candidly replied 'Yes'.

CHAPTER 14 - Sweet Tunes of Payola—And a Jarring Note

LET'S set the stage with a textual quotation from one of America's most notoriously sensationalist newspapers, *The Christian Science Monitor*. As an inveterate sensation-monger, I have always felt a strong affinity for this unabashed scandal sheet and have, on occasion, contributed to it. In its issue on January 16, 1964, *The Christian Science Monitor* carried a dispatch from its Washington correspondent Richard L. Strout which began thus:

'The scene is a room in the historic Capitol in Washington. The suite is that of the secretary of the Senate majority. It is the very center of one of the best-beloved architectural landmarks of American government.

'A brisk young man enters the office and is greeted warmly by the secretary. He is taken at once into the inner sanctum. For a minute or two the men inside converse cheerfully.

'Then the newcomer takes an envelope out of the bulging breast pocket of his coat and puts it on the desk. The man behind the desk takes the envelope and removes its contents. It is filled with $50 and $100 bills. He counts the bills carefully and his fingers seem to run lovingly over them.

'"He liked to count the money," explained Ralph L. Mill, former head of the Capitol Vending Company, who gave the above version of the meeting in testimony before the Senate Rules Committee'.

Ralph Hill, a vending machine operator and former pal of Bobby Baker's, was to become the latter's undoing. He set the stone in motion that has been rolling ever since—getting nowhere.

Hill was president of Capitol Vending Co., a vending machine company which was doing a flourishing business long before Bobby Baker cast his lynx eye on the possibilities inherent in this particular line of moneymaking.

Some time in 1961 Mr. Hill engaged in negotiations with Melpar Inc., an electronics firm in suburban Virginia and, as a subcontractor to North American Aviation, the recipient of many lucrative government contracts. Hill wanted to get his machines into the Melpar plant but ran into an unexpected obstacle.

At one of the earliest bargaining sessions, he was informed by Edward M. Bostick, president of Melpar, Inc., and Arthur C. Weid, executive vice-president that the vending-machine contract had already been promised to Baker (he was not yet in the vending machine business, but was eying it) who, it was understood, could hand it to whomever he wished.

In plain words, the setup was this: a big company working on government contracts, feeling indebted to an influential government official, favors the latter with a contract to supply vending-machines which he himself cannot as yet fill for lack of production facilities. But he 'owns' the contract and can pass it on to whoever has the machines—for a consideration.

At first, Hill told the Senate probers, Baker demanded a monthly fee of $1000 for giving his nod to Melpar officials to go ahead and do business with Capitol Vending Co. This, Ralph Hill thought, was a bit stiff and he bargained for better terms. Eventually, the two men settled for payments starting at $250 a month and going up to $650 a month. All told, Ralph Hill forked out $5,600 over a 17-month period. A modest sum, to be sure, compared to some of the other gravy Bobby Baker was tapping at the same time, but significant as a token of unabashed graft.

In gangster language, the kind of deal described above is called a 'shakedown' and the money that passed from hand to hand—always in cash—is known as a 'kickback'. In the more refined style of the Great Society in Washington, the operation is referred to as 'payola' which *The Christian Science Monitor*, in the above-cited article, defined as 'a kickback received for using his influence on behalf of business interests'.

On January 25, 1964, the scandal-mongering *Monitor* reverted to the subject with another piece by Richard L. Strout entitled 'Payola Sounds Irk U.S. Capitol' which began with these words:

'Is there a "payola atmosphere" in Washington?

'The Bobby Baker hearings again raise the question.

'President Johnson has himself entered the matter, saying he received a $585 hi-fi set from Mr. Baker. It was in the course of a normal exchange of gifts between friends, he said. The President volunteered this comment and did not submit to questions from the press. (See Chapter 24)

"'Payola" is the practice of giving hidden gifts, or kick-backs for favors received'.

After this promising start, the lurid Boston scandal sheet tears into 'Names and Figures' as follows:

'Here are the Washington figures involved in the Baker cases:

'Rep. John W. Byrnes (R) of Wisconsin, top Republican in the tax writing House Ways and Means Committee, helped Mr. Baker obtain a favorable federal tax ruling for Mortgage Guaranty Insurance Corporation of Milwaukee and thereafter was let in on an early purchase of stock giving him quick profits of $20,000...

'Rep. John L. McMillan (D) of South Carolina, chairman of the District of Columbia Committee, has long been close to Don B. Reynolds, local insurance man associated with Mr. Baker. In July, 1961, it was disclosed that Mr. Reynolds, who was then seeking an insurance contract for the district armory, purchased a $5,100 Cadillac for Mr. McMillan. Mr. McMillan said he had reimbursed Mr. Reynolds. (See Chapter 24)

'Walter Jenkins, presidential White House assistant, denies pressuring Mr. Reynolds to place $1200 in advertising with the Johnson TV station at Austin, Texas. Mr. Reynolds says Mr. Jenkins sought the advertising to show appreciation for the $200,000 life insurance business, which he, Mr. Reynolds, got in policies on Sen. Johnson's life.

'President Johnson, at an impromptu Thursday press conference, said that he had exchanged gifts with the Baker family and had received a $584 stereo phonograph from Mr. Baker: "He was asking for nothing and, so far as I know, expected nothing in return."

'Insurance man Reynolds previously testified that the hi-fi set was solicited for Senator Johnson by Mr. Baker (who also got a free hi-fi set).

'Mr. Reynolds testified that the invoice plainly showed it came from Mr. Reynolds...'

Here, the reader has been introduced, in the words of *The Christian Science Monitor*, to the rudiments of some of the juiciest scandals of the Baker affair: the hi-fi set 'solicited' for the then Senator Lyndon B. Johnson by his faithful henchman, Bobby Baker; the $1200 advertising deal for Johnson's TV station obtained 'under pressure'. Walter Jenkins' dubious personality and more than dubious role as manager of Lyndon B. Johnson's private business and later as presidential assistant etc. All these matters will be dealt with exhaustively in subsequent chapters of this book.

As I shall certainly be accused, right and left, of slandering the Leader of the Free World and other pillars of The Great Society, I intend to share this censure as fully as possible with other notoriously irresponsible opinion-makers, such as *The New York Times*, *The New York Herald Tribune* and *The Christian Science Monitor*, all of which have been and will be quoted extensively. A 'kickback' is due each and all of them—and to *Newsday*—and they'll get it. Let's hear what the *Monitor* has to say about some other 'Names and Figures' connected with Bobby Baker:

'William N. McLeod, Jr., former clerk of Mr. McMillan's House District Committee, got $1,500 from Mr. Reynolds. He was another participant in the meeting in Mr. Baker's office in 1960 at which Mr. Reynolds got the insurance bonding contract for the stadium.

'Mr. Reynolds testified that he paid $4000 to Mr. Baker in appreciation for this business. The money to Mr. McLeod, Mr. Reynolds testified, was also part payment for getting the stadium contract.

'Matthew McCloskey, Philadelphia builder, former treasurer of the Democratic national committee and just-resigned Ambassador to the Republic of Ireland, expressed his desire to bid on the stadium at the 1960 meeting in Mr. Baker's office. He got the contract for about $70,000 in July, 1960'.

The Christian Science Monitor, for all its sensationalism, is not the world's liveliest newspaper and the reader of the foregoing may get the impression that the Baker case is really a rather dull compilation of irregularities in business dealings without much color or human interest. I hope to correct that erroneous impression in dealing with McCloskey and that stadium deal in a subsequent chapter. But first, back to *The Monitor*: :

'Testimony has disclosed a lucrative Florida real estate deal in which Mr. Baker participated with Sen. George A. Smathers (D) of Florida. A statement from Senator Smathers said he cut Mr. Baker into the deal, and another staff member, because they were worthy young men with growing children. The Senate Rules Committee announces that it will not investigate fellow senators and dropped the Smathers angle'.

Indeed. They dropped the Smathers angle, as they dropped the Johnson angle, and the Kerr angle, and the Dirksen angle, and the Jordan angle, and maybe half a dozen other senatorial angles, because the U.S. Senate is the world's coziest club where you can commit any kind of outrage without getting so much as a dirty look from a fellow member. We won't drop the Smathers angle, though.

'James R. Hoffa, head of the Teamsters Union which is alleged to have put up money for one of Mr. Baker's far-flung enterprises, a Florida development, is also named,' Richard L. Strout's article in *The Christian Science Monitor* of 25-1-64 went on to report. 'Mr. Reynolds testified he asked Mr. Hoffa to take his own name off an underwriting contract at Mr. Hoffa's office here. Mr. Reynolds quoted Mr. Hoffa as telling him to relax "they [the McClellan Committee, then looking at Teamsters Union records] will never see your name. I have got two sets of books."

'Clinton Murchison, Jr., Texas oil magnate, is said to have participated in the Florida land speculation with the Teamsters Union, and other Baker-Reynolds dealings, either personally or through his Washington connection, Thomas Webb.

So far the rogues' gallery of the Baker case, presented by *The Christian Science Monitor*, in capsule form, to its eyebrow-raising readership: A President of the United States worth 14 million dollars, involved in petty kickback transactions; two Congressmen doing favors for, and getting favors from, a group of wheeler-dealers; a senator in a business partnership with Bobby Baker; a top official of the Democratic Party and former Ambassador wangling a huge business deal with the aid of a notorious influence peddler; a labor racketeer and an oil magnate joining hands in land speculation with Baker and his political friends; a top assistant to the President accused of having solicited favors for his boss from a businessman—and who, shortly afterwards, gets kicked out of the Government for grave homosexual offences (See Chapter 24). A representative, if incomplete, cross-section of The Great Society.

Unfortunately for all concerned, the key figure in this cozy set-up, Bobby Baker, shared not only the typical gangster's predilection for cash instead of checks, but also his propensity for double-crossing a weaker partner. If he hadn't overreached himself and cheated the long-suffering Ralph Hill out of the very deal for which he was paying tribute, month after month, Bobby would still be sitting ensconced in his plush Senate office suite, Lyndon Johnson would never have been on the hot seat, the sweet sounds of payola would still fill the scented air of Washington, and everybody would be happy. And I submit, President Kennedy would still be alive.

But Bobby was too crooked even for an environment where almost everything goes. After his own vending-machine venture, Serv-U, got under way, he tried to pressure Hill into selling out—on terms far more profitable to Bobby Baker than to the Capitol Vending Co.

Hill refused to comply, with the result that Baker went into action against him. Bobby still had the inside track with Melpar and was able to persuade this firm to break its contract with Capitol Vending Co. and put in Serv-U machines instead.

Pushed to the wall, Hill pleaded, cajoled and finally threatened to bring suit against Baker and his associates, unless Baker allowed the status quo to be restored. It was all in vain. Bobby, in that fateful year of 1963, was riding so high he felt he could do as he pleased.

The upshot of this struggle was that Hill, on September 9, 1963, sued Baker, Black and Tucker for $300,000 in damages and at the same time projected vital portions of the Bobby Baker story into the national limelight.

Even so, Bobby Baker and his friends might have escaped serious harm but for the intervention, at this juncture, of a man who has justly earned for himself the title of the 'Sherlock Holmes of Capital Hill'—John J. Williams, Republican Senator of Delaware.

The mild-mannered, soft-spoken Sen. Williams has long been a thorn in the flesh of wrong-doers in Government. Since 1949—three years after first coming to Washington—Williams has acted as a one-man investigating committee, with his eye particularly on tax-fixing. 'I don't know just how I first got into this investigation business,' He says, 'but when a constituent you respect spends two hours telling you about a suspected tax-fixing ring in Washington, you sit up and take notice'.

Williams went after the tax-fixers so vigorously that his disclosures in some 15 years of sleuthing resulted in indictments against more than 200 persons, mostly bribe-givers and bribe-takers; 125 of them were convicted.

Naturally, Sen. Williams takes greater delight in going for Democratic rather than Republican scalps, but it would be doing him an injustice to suggest that he would stop at the party line in his pursuit of crooked officials and politicians. 'He is an implacable Milquetoast who always gets his man' it has been said of him, and a holy terror to all those who benefit in one way or another from the 'mess in Washington'.

Williams' attention had already been drawn to the versatile Baker by the antics of Elly Rometsch (See Chapter 21) which preceded by a few weeks the exposure of Bobby's financial entanglements. But it was not until after Ralph Hill brought suit against his disloyal business partner that the Senator really swung into action. His disclosures on the floor of the Senate sparked the investigation by the Senate Rules Committee and caused Bobby Baker to resign from his post as secretary to the Senate Majority on October 9, 1963.

Although the ensuing proceedings followed the classic pattern of whitewash and cover-up, the investigation nevertheless turned up a number of clues that were pursued by various newspapers and in due course produced a fairly well-rounded picture of the Baker affair.

Senator Williams, while adding greatly to his national stature, did not enhance his popularity on Capitol Hill with his initiative in the Baker case and his continuing private investigation of the case. Too many of his colleagues in the Senate, and too many members of the House of Representatives, have been exposed by the countless ramifications of the Baker scandal as unworthy of the trust their constituents placed in them, to let Williams enjoy peace on Capitol Hill.

One day, as Sen. Williams, who happens to bear a striking resemblance to Daniel Webster, stood by the full-length portrait of that formidable orator which adorns a wall of the Senate Building, an aide remarked upon this eye-catching likeness.

Williams wistfully replied: 'I guess there are a lot of people around here who wish it was me hanging up there'.

CHAPTER 15 - A String of Murders - or a Rash of Suicides?

AMONG other striking similarities, the Bobby Baker and Billie Sol Estes affairs have a most disturbing element in common: through both of them runs, like a red thread, a multitude of mysterious deaths, involving business partners, witnesses and investigators.

By conservative count, at least six persons have died under highly suspicious circumstances so far, two of them in the course of the Estes investigation, and four during the Baker probe. Five of them are supposed to have committed suicide; the sixth died ostensibly in an accident. Let's take a closer look.

Billie Sol Estes' affairs had come under the scrutiny of the FBI as early as the beginning of 1961, after an unidentified Texan had given the Bureau detailed information on Estes' bank transactions. This has been confirmed in the report of the House subcommittee headed by Representative H. L. Fountain. At the time, however, the United States attorney in El Paso decided that there had been no apparent violation of Federal banking laws and the case was dropped. When Estes was finally arrested, more than a year later, his arrest, in the words of the subcommittee report, 'was based on confirmation of essentially the same information that had been submitted in 1961'.

After the FBI had first been alerted, the Department of Agriculture assigned one of its senior officials, Henry Marshall, Supervisor of Federal cotton allotments in Texas, to conduct a quiet investigation of Billie Sol Estes' cotton allotments. In his report, which was sent to Washington in the late spring of 1961, Marshall revealed the entire scheme of the Estes allotments to have been fraudulent and punishable by law.

Now, to quote again from the above-cited pamphlet *LBJ—A Political Biography*:

For whom was Marshall's revealing report intended? For Emery Jacobs, the Deputy Administrator who accepted over $1,400 in expensive clothing from Billie Sol Estes. In turn, Jacobs reported to Lyndon Baines Johnson's ostensible business manager, Walter Jenkins, and his aide, Arthur Perry, in personal letters written January 31, 1962, saying: "*Our motive*, of course, is to establish that this sale of laud was in fact a *bona fide sale* and not a device to purchase cotton allotments." [Italicized in the original].

'Jacob's letters to Johnson's office were written at the request of Undersecretary of Agriculture Charles S. Murphy, the official who was identified by the Department as "responsible for the appointment of Billie Sol Estes to the National Cotton Advisory Board."

'In view of the fact that Johnson has disclaimed any interest in Billie Sol Estes, we must wonder why the Undersecretary felt he had to explain to Johnson that the Department of Agriculture's motives were purely in Billie Sol Estes' interests'.

By the time Jacobs reported in this manner to the office of Vice-President Johnson, investigator Henry Marshall was no longer in a position to gainsay. On June 3, 1961 he had been found dead of gunshot wounds on his ranch in Texas. Marshall's death, at the time, was listed as a 'suicide' and he was quietly buried—as was his report.

After Billie Sol Estes' arrest, however, investigators of the McClellan Committee in May, 1962, decided to exhume not only the long-forgotten Marshall report, but also the body of its author. They then got the shock of their lives. Dr. Joseph Jachimczyk, the examining pathologist, declared flatly that there could be no question of suicide because the victim had been riddled by five bullets from a bolt-action rifle and that one shot had struck in the back!

Funeral Director Manley Jones also testified that Marshall's body had borne wounds caused by blows, indicating a struggle.

'There is no doubt in my mind that Henry Marshall was murdered,' he declared. The Texas rangers apparently agreed for they gave the press an artist's sketch of a man believed to have asked for directions to Marshall's ranch shortly before the murder, with this query to the public: 'Have you seen this man?' As far as is known, nobody came forward to say he had.

Nevertheless, the McClellan Committee preferred not to press its inquiry into this particular matter any further. Sen. McClellan closed the book on it with the sibylline remark: 'His (Marshall's) death concealed more than establishment of an act of murder would reveal'. And that was that.

Between Billie Sol Estes' arrest and the exhumation of Marshall's body, another corpse turned up. On April 4, 1962, the badly decomposed body of one of Estes' accountants, a man named George Krutilek, was found in an automobile in El Paso—the city where a Federal grand jury was looking into Estes' affairs. Krutilek would have been a prime source of information to them concerning Estes' complicated business deals and secret partnership. And now he was dead—of a heart attack, according to the official story!

But—there was a hose stuck in his car window, and it led straight to the exhaust pipe!

The unusually high incidence of carbon monoxide mortality in both the Estes and Baker cases has attracted the attention of several writers. Clyde Walters did a comprehensive piece on this subject in the *Amarillo Globe-Times* of March 26, 1964. And, according to J. Evetts Haley:

'The enforced inhalation of this painless killer, carbon monoxide, leaving its own traces in lungs and blood and hence almost certain immunity for the murderer, is a subtle approach that would have charmed such early imaginative practitioners of assassination as the ancient Medici. Again in a case connected with Estes, this gas was held to be the legally blameless killer of Harold Eugene Orr; the late president of the Superior Manufacturing Company of Amarillo. Orr and the Company had played a key role in Estes' finance frauds, and Orr was arrested with Estes and given a ten-year federal prison sentence.

'February 28, 1964, just before he was to begin serving his term, Harold Orr went out to his garage, ostensibly to change the exhaust pipe on his car. There a few hours later, with tools scattered about—again by report, tools unsuited for the purpose—Orr was found dead. The Justice of the Peace pronounced it accidental death by carbon monoxide. But the stubborn disbelievers keep popping up with their questions. Was Orr, faced with prison, about to talk? And what of Howard Pratt, Chicago office manager of Commercial Solvents, Billie Sol's fertilizer supplier, found in his car, dead of carbon monoxide?'

Now let us pass in review the four deaths—each more mysterious than the other—that have accompanied the rise and fall of Bobby Baker to date.

The first dead body in the case belonged to Alfred S. Novak, Baker's original partner in the plush Carousel Motel of Ocean City, Md., a curious establishment with a curious history to which we shall turn in the following chapter. On March 3, 1962, Novak, aged 43, was found unconscious by his wife, Gertrude, on the floor of their garage. his death was first listed as due to accidental carbon-monoxide poisoning, but later it was attributed to suicide.

What makes the Novak case look suspicious is the fact that his death, allegedly by monoxide poisoning, followed closely upon his discovery that he had been swindled out of his legitimate share in the Carousel by his good friend and partner, Bobby Baker (for details, see the following chapter).

Perhaps the most extraordinary aspect of the second mystery death is that the press paid no attention to its Bobby Baker angle, conspicuous through it was.

On December 2, 1963, an AP dispatch from Miami reported:

'Grant Stockdale, former Ambassador to Ireland, plunged to his death today from his offices on the 13th floor of the du Pont Building.

'The police said Mr. Stockdale, an intimate friend of President Kennedy, had committed suicide. No notes were found, however. Mr. Stockdale was 48 years old...'

Note that Stockdale, according to this dispatch, did not jump out of his office window, as suicides normally do. He 'plunged to his death', a conveniently ambiguous statement that is frequently used when a person dies by a fall from a window and the authorities just don't know for sure (or don't want to say) whether the victim had jumped or had been pushed out of the window.

With no eyewitnesses in the case, and no notes suggesting suicidal intent, how could the Miami police come out with a flat statement that Stockdale had committed suicide?

Or did the Associated Press lend an unquestioning note to a somewhat less affirmative police statement? The question must be raised because *The New York Herald Tribune* in a dispatch from Washington by Dom Bonafede, published on December 3, 1963, stated: 'Police said it was an apparent suicide'.

'Miami police investigators, however, were unable to find a suicide note or provide any motive,' the *Herald Tribune* dispatch went on to say.

No motive. But the unnatural death of a prominent personality has to be explained somehow to the public. And so we are promptly treated to a variety of 'explanations', one more implausible than the other.

The AP dispatch cited above hints strongly that Grant Stockdale—a very rich man—had run into financial troubles, but substantiates this suggestion with ridiculous assertions:

'In a recent newspaper interview, he (Stockdale) said that he had borne heavy expenses by serving as Ambassador...'

Stockdale's appointment as ambassador to Ireland, made by President Kennedy in March 1961, was a typical political payoff, such as follow traditionally all changes in the Administration. Stockdale was not a career diplomat. His principal qualifications for the job were his services to the Democratic Party, his great personal wealth and the fact that he was a practicing Roman Catholic. The latter circumstance, incidentally, makes the suicide version look even more improbable than it would otherwise be, for the Catholic Church strongly condemns suicides and inexorably relegates them to hell.

Ambassadorial appointments like that of Grant Stockdale are made primarily for two reasons: in order to reward a faithful party stalwart for substantial campaign contributions and because the nominee can afford to supplement his salary with personal income in order to meet the expenses of diplomatic high living. No rich man appointed to a political ambassadorship ever went broke in the service. The suggestion that the religious Stockdale, having ruined himself in the service of his country, saw no other way out than to commit the sin of sins is simply ludicrous.

Aware of it, apparently, the AP dispatch adds some other possible sources of financial despair:

'When he left Ireland to return to his real estate business in July, 1962, Mr. Stockdale said, he found that the market had declined badly. He also spoke of the great expense of a large family. He had two sons and three daughters'.

If Stockdale found in July, 1962, that business had declined so badly that he could no longer afford to raise a large family, why did he wait another 17 months to jump out the window? And, what other big real estate operator was wiped out by the alleged 'decline' of the market between early 1961 and mid-1962?

All this is just plainly absurd, and the most preposterous of all is the suicide motive Dom Bonafede managed to dig up: 'Miami friends said yesterday that Mr. Stockdale, who was in the real estate and investment business, was despondent over the death of President Kennedy. He is reported to have fallen on his knees and prayed when he heard the news...'

On the strength of this paragraph, the *Herald Tribune* actually published the Bonafede dispatch under this four-column headline: '"Despondent" Kennedy Friend Dies in Plunge'.

Hard-headed businessmen—and Stockdale was certainly hardheaded, as his record shows—don't kill themselves because a friend has been murdered, be it the President of the United States. Besides, relations between Kennedy and Stockdale had soured considerably, as we shall see.

All this is part and parcel of the official myth-making that goes on day after day in the United States to gloss over the conspicuous taints in The Great Society. It has been going on at a greatly accelerated pace since the assassination of President Kennedy.

The truth of the matter is that Grant Stockdale was also a wheeler-dealer and had found himself caught in the Bobby Baker web. If his death was suicide, the reason was that he feared exposure. More likely, Stockdale was murdered because he knew too much and somebody else feared exposure.

Dom Bonafede's dispatch indicates that Stockdale did not resign his ambassadorship of his own free will but was in effect fired by President Kennedy in May 1962, even though this was done with the usual diplomatic niceties:

'Prior to his resignation it was disclosed that he had borrowed $5,000 interest-free from Sidney Kessler, a New York and Miami builder, who was seeking an $8,000 commitment from the Federal Housing Administration. The petition was later approved.

'President Kennedy reportedly learned of the loan and demanded that Mr. Stockdale return the $5,000.

'In a trans-Atlantic telephone call to a Miami reporter, Mr. Stock-dale reportedly commented that the President was "afraid the loan could make it look like I was finagling around with the FHA"...'

So much for the allegedly warm relationship between Kennedy and Stockdale which caused the latter to kill himself out of 'despondency' after ten days of mourning over his assassinated friend.

Coyly, the *Herald Tribune* story touches on the background to Stockdale's latest and last entanglements:

'Mr. Stockdale's name also came up briefly as a part time associate of Eugene Hancock, a vending-machine operator, mentioned in the investigation of Bobby Baker...'

The New York Times of December 3, 1963, is more explicit: 'Grant Stockdale once had close business connections with vending machine concerns that are under investigation in the Robert G. Baker inquiry...

'In an interview published in the *Miami Herald* last October, shortly after the Senate authorized a study of Mr. Baker's dealings, Mr. Stockdale said:

"I hope I don't get cut up too bad. I haven't done anything wrong..."

'Mr. Stockdale's responses were to questions about the similarities between the Washington damage suit against Mr. Baker, which touched off the Baker case, and a 1961 damage suit against Mr. Stockdale and others in Miami.

'In April, 1961, just as Mr. Stockdale was leaving Miami to assume his duties as Ambassador to Ireland, he was served with papers in a $131,000 damage suit. The suit alleged that he had used "undue influence" to gain contracts for Automatic Vending Services, Inc., a Miami company in which he owned stock.

'Mr. Stockdale accused the complainant, the Pan-Am Tobacco Corporation, of trying to "get some publicity because I am a United States Ambassador." He denied the charges.

'Pan-Am contended in its suit that Mr. Stockdale had been instrumental in gaining for his company the vending service contract at Erodex, Inc., an aircraft engine maintenance company in Miami.

'Subsequently, Automatic Vending Services, Inc., won contracts totaling $500,000 a year at Patrick Air Force Base and the Air Force missile test center at Cape Kennedy...'

To recapitulate the many and striking similarities between the Stockdale and Baker cases:

Grant Stockdale is a big wheel in the Democratic Party and a person of considerable influence in Washington; Bobby Baker is also a big wheel in the Democratic Party—geared to one of the biggest—and exercises even greater influence in the capital.

Stockdale is also a major stockholder in a vending-machine company. This outfit garners, one after another, extremely lucrative contracts in Government installations and Government-controlled defense plants. And eventually it becomes the target of a damage suit by a competitor, charging the use of 'undue influence' in obtaining these contracts.

Two years later, Bobby Baker travels exactly the same road with all its way stations, as has already been described in previous chapters. Any thought that all this could be purely coincidental is now dispelled by this paragraph in the *Times* story:

'Mr. Stockdale, one business associate said, was then "harassed" by newsmen concerning his connection with Automatic Vending Services and its president, Eugene A. Hancock...'

There you have it, in a nutshell. Eugene A. Hancock is the president of Automatic Vending Services. One of his biggest assets is a prominent stockholder, Grant Stockdale, who has plenty of pull in Washington. Coincidentally, of course, profitable government contracts start tumbling out of Washington's cornucopia and into the lap of the Hancock-Stockdale enterprise.

Then, a couple of years later, the scene shifts. Hancock is now president of the Serv-U-Corporation, another automatic vending concern, with the very, very influential Bobby Baker as his principal stockholder (in fact, though not in name). Automatically, again, the cornucopia tilts and starts pouring out juicy government contracts.

And, exactly as before, the new venture leads to a large damage suit in which it is charged that these contracts were obtained through the misuse of influence in Washington.

Hancock is then the conspicuous connecting link between the affairs of Grant Stockdale and those of Bobby Baker. Yet after

Stockdale's 'suicide', the Senate committee investigating the Baker scandal blandly declared that there was no tie at all. Stockdale, a spokesman for the committee said, was not under investigation and there had been no plans for the committee to question him. And, indeed, the committee did not ask Hancock, as far as is known, any questions about Stockdale when it grilled him.

Just one more of those fabulous 'coincidences', you see, that abound in every phase and facet of the Johnson regime, and most strikingly in the Oswald story: at the precise moment that the Bobby Baker investigation gets under way, an earlier high-ranking influence peddler formerly associated with the same figurehead president, Hancock, a man hoping and praying that he won't 'get cut up too bad' in the process, mysteriously plunges to his death from a tall building. Yet, in the official view, there is no link, no connection.

Mystery befitting a B-grade thriller surrounds the third body in the Baker case, one that belonged, in life, to a beautiful woman.

Like other housewives in the crime-ridden Washington area, Mrs. Sheila Drennan made it a standing practice to keep the doors of her home in suburban Maryland not only closed, but locked. Yet one day, early in 1964, when her children came home from school, they were surprised to find the front door not only unlocked, but wide open. Their misgivings found horrible confirmation. On the floor of the bathroom, the children found the lifeless nude body of their 34-year-old mother. Nothing else had been touched and in the adjoining bedroom, the police found the woman's clothing and rings arrayed on the bed. Apparently, she was about to take a bath when sudden death overtook her.

What had happened? Did Mrs. Drennan slip in the bathroom and break her neck, or was she murdered? The medical authorities were as puzzled as the police. County Medical Examiner Dr. John Kehoe was unable to make a firm determination of the cause of death. He noted an internal neck injury but expressed the view that this could have been caused 'by a fall or a mugging'. He thought, therefore, that the woman's death could have been 'either accidental or homicide'. And, what has this all to do with the Baker case? Simply this: Sheila Drennan was the wife of Lorin H. Drennan, Jr., a government accountant who gave the Senate probers a detailed picture of Bobby Baker's financial entanglements, including the fact that he had borrowed a total of $1.7 million from various banks in four years. And that Lorin Drennan's testimony was followed, in a matter of days, by the mysterious death of his wife (See Chapter 16). If the 'accident' that befell Drennan's wife may possibly have been unconnected with the Baker affair—who will ever be able to tell for sure?—the 'accidental' death, a few months later, of Bobby's Girl Friday, Carole Tyler, was certainly not due to mere coincidence. However, her case is so complex and so important that we must deal with it separately in a subsequent chapter.

CHAPTER 16 - Bobby's White Elephant: The Carousel

IT has become fashionable to distinguish two aspects of the Baker scandal: its financial complex and its 'moral side'. The latter term coyly refers to the naked fact that the '101st Senator' used to operate, in and near Washington, a chain of cozy establishments where tired Congressmen and high Government officials could seek relaxation in the pleasant company of alluring 'party girls'.

The role played by these classy sirens in the Baker scheme of things has been bluntly described by Sen. Carl Curtis of Nebraska, the ranking Republican member of the Senate Rules Committee, in these terms:

'Party girls and entertaining were part of the business promotion apparatus. The facts are available if we pursue it. Individuals were induced to enter into certain business arrangements as part of the promotion. Girls were solicited on Government telephone lines, taken to the place, entertained the prospective customer and it is part and parcel of the transaction'.

While Sen. Curtis' syntax may not be flawless, his—and his Republican colleagues'—contributions to the understanding of Baker's modus operandi have been substantial. Even so, however, any discussion of the 'moral side' of the Baker mess must of necessity remain fragmentary because the Democratic majority has kept the lid firmly on its Profumistic odors.

Bobby Baker used to be a developer of existing schemes, rather than an innovator. He certainly did not invent the formula 'get-a-contract-with-a-girl'—a practice long followed by Washington lobbyists and Madison Avenue 'business consultants'. He merely refined and perfected the technique.

In order to be able to cater better to the needs of his political sponsors and business friends, who preferred their entertainment served with discretion, Baker set up a number of high-class *maisons de rendezvous*, staffed with ravishing creatures, including some choice imports from abroad. After the Baker scandal broke, three of these jet-age seraglios gained nationwide fame: the Townhouse, The Quorum Club and The Carousel Motel. Let us begin our exploration of the 'moral side' with a brief history of the last-named because it is also linked to two of those mysterious deaths that have been discussed in the preceding chapter.

Bobby Baker got his first taste of the lucrative and in many ways useful motel business when he bought stock in a Howard Johnson motel in North Carolina which happened to include among other influential stockholders the then Secretary of Commerce, Luther Hodges.

When the enterprising young man first decided, some time in 1960, to grace the Atlantic seashore outside Ocean City, Md. with a super-modern, plush, all-purpose motel, he thought he could do it for around $400,000. As he didn't have that kind of money at the time, nor even a major portion of it, he persuaded his old friends, the Novaks of Silver Spring, Md. to form a partnership with him.

Alfred S. Novak, a builder, and his brother Donald, a real estate promoter, were to be Baker's principal partners in this venture, but Alfred's wife, Gertrude, was also a tangible asset because of her employment by the Senate Small Business Committee.

Before very long, however, difficulties arose between the partners. The Novaks were appalled to see the actual construction costs of The Carousel rise far above the estimates. In part, this was due to faulty calculation, but in part also to the fact that Bobby Baker was constantly changing and expanding the original plans for the motel. He wanted a bigger restaurant and insisted on putting in a nightclub.

And so what had started out to be a $400,000 motel eventually developed into a $1,000,000 palace. The Novaks kept putting more money into the ever expanding enterprise, until their resources were strained to the limit. When urgent cash payments were due, Alfred Novak would send his wife, Gertrude, to Baker's office suite in the Senate Building. In testimony before the Rules Committee, Mrs. Novak was later to recount in graphic detail how she used to rush up to his office to pick up amounts ranging from $1000 to $13,300, always in cash. It was just like old payola, playing in reverse.

'We kept wondering where he was getting his money from,' Mrs. Novak related. Once she asked him. He smiled quizzically. 'I've got lots of friends,' he explained.

As construction costs soared, and with no end in sight, Mr. Novak became intensely worried. He withdrew more and more into himself and even refused to discuss his embarrassing venture with his wife. That's her story, anyway.

Then, on March 3, 1962, about four months before the date that had been set for the grand opening of The Carousel, Gertrude Novak found her husband lying inanimate on the floor of their garage. The door was closed and the car motor was running.

It looked like an open-and-shut case of suicide. Alfred Novak had been despondent over the runaway costs of his motel venture. His resources were giving out. Possibly he was facing bankruptcy. He saw no other way out of his predicament than to die by his own hand—and suicide by carbon-monoxide poisoning is such an easy death.

Gertrude Novak, however, didn't like the idea of her husband being listed as a suicide. From the life insurance viewpoint, it can be an embarrassment. And Mrs. Novak meant to collect the $45,000 in life insurance that was her due as long as her husband did not commit suicide. She was sure it had been an accident.

Accordingly, a death certificate was issued which listed 'cardio-respiratory failure' as the cause of Alfred Novak's demise, and Gertrude Novak, now in business with Bobby Baker in her own right, collected her $45,000 in life insurance. As chance would have it, the insurance agency from which she collected was headed by Don Reynolds, still at the time a good friend and business partner of Bobby Baker's, but later the star witness against him.

Two months after Novak's passing, the coroner listed the cause of death as suicide.

Accident or suicide? Nobody, it seems, ever entertained the thought of a possible third alternative—murder.

Why should there have been any thought of murder?

Foul play and shady dealing usually go together. And there was plenty of shady dealing in the Novak case.

In the first place, it is a matter of record that as the opening day for The Carousel approached, and as Alfred Novak worried himself sick over his financial troubles, Baker calmly suggested that he sell out.

Sell out? Who would buy a partnership in a faltering business venture?

Bobby was sympathetic. Well, maybe his pal wouldn't be able to get all his money back, in fact he stood to lose a good deal, but it was better to get something than nothing, wasn't it?

And who would the prospective buyer be?

Oh, Baker didn't know them too well, but it was a prosperous company, he could vouch for their solvency. Automatic vending machines was a great business these days.

And so Alfred Novak sold out to Serv-U corporation, taking a $100,000 loss on his investment in The Carousel. He never knew that Bobby Baker and Serv-U were one and the same thing. Or if he ever learned about it, death overtook him before he could speak his mind. Maybe it was the shock that killed him.

Nor was that all. There was something else Alfred Novak should have known, but never did. Even his wife didn't learn about it until a year and a half later, after the Baker hearings had got under way.

At the very moment that the Novaks were scouting around for an exit from the expensive motel business, the flamboyant Murchison brothers of Dallas, Clint Jr. and John, were interested in adding just such a flashy item to their far-flung business empire. In testimony before the Committee investigating Baker's affairs, Robert F. Thompson, vice-president of the Murchison-owned Tecon Corp. of Dallas (See Chapter 19) revealed in late January 1964 that he had offered to buy The Carousel for $1,500,000. Baker turned down the offer and never told his partners. In February, 1963, Baker sold the motel for $1,000,000 to his own Serv-U corporation, paying off Gertrude and Donald Novak on the basis of their shares. When Alfred's widow learned that she could have got half as much again if Tecon's offer had been accepted, she was understandably furious.

Newsday reported on January 30, 1964 that Mrs. Gertrude C. Novak, 'who still is a partner with Baker in two land deals in Maryland... huddled yesterday with lawyers to see if criminal or civil charges could be filed against the former Senate aide for his failure to reveal a $1,500,000 offer to buy the Carousel Motel in Ocean City, Md...'

The paper went on to quote a legal source as saying that the failure of Baker to reveal the sale offer might not be criminal but could be the source of a civil suit. Under the law, he said, any corporation officer has a duty to act in the best interest of the company, and its stockholders.

But Bobby Baker did not always fail to have the stockholders' interests at heart, especially if the stockholder happened to be that big silent partner in Serv-U, Mr. Robert G. Baker. In fact he was even prepared to overstep the limits of legality.

This matter also came to light in the course of the Baker hearings, on January 23, 1961. In March, 1962, it developed, the Carousel had been damaged by a heavy spring storm. Baker promptly turned the minor disaster into a major windfall, in two different ways. On the one hand, he deducted $27,200 for 'casualty losses' from his 1962 income tax. Whether that was legal, remains to be seen.

On the other hand, however, Baker availed himself of this opportunity to raise some handy cash on favorable terms in a transaction which Sen. Hugh Scott, Republican committee member, bluntly labeled 'a fraud'.

It was a typical Bobby Baker deal.

First, he went to the Small Business Administration, a federal agency, to apply for a $54,450 'disaster loan'. Such loans, made widely available by the SBA in the wake of the 1962 storms, were highly preferable to commercial loans, the interest rate being 3 percent for 20 years compared to 6 per cent for 15 years on commercial loans. Most importantly, the SBA did not require collateral in such cases. However, before giving Baker the loan he had applied for, the SBA wanted to make sure that he and his partners had invested $160,000 cash in the motel. That was to insure that the building, then far from completed, would be finished. While SBA administrators were satisfied that Baker and his partners had already put up $60,000, they wanted proof of the remaining $100,000 investment.

How Bobby Baker complied with this stipulation, was thus described in testimony before the Rules Committee:

Baker called W. H. Lasher, president of the American National Bank in suburban Maryland, and arranged to borrow $100,000 for 15 days. The loan was granted, but only as a non-withdrawable entry in Baker's bank account. The $100,000, under the terms of the loan, was obligated by Baker to the bank as collateral for the loan. The bank noted on his account that the money was not to be withdrawn. At the end of 15 days, on June 13, 1962, the account was closed, the $100,000 reverted to the bank and the loan was considered paid, except for about $200 in interest for the short term loan, which was charged to another Baker account in the bank.

Now, at the time the loan was granted, the bank had given Baker a deposit slip showing a $100,000 deposit. This deposit slip was then used by Baker to 'prove' to the SBA that he had invested the money in the motel as the SBA had demanded. The deposit slip did not indicate in any way that this amount was restricted, and that Baker did not really have access to this money. In a nutshell, the transaction meant that Baker had paid the bank $200 for giving him a deposit slip to be used under false pretenses.

When the Rules Committee took up this matter, Mr. Lasher was conveniently 'on vacation' and 'could not be reached'. A spokesman for the American National Bank tried to squirm out of the responsibility incurred by the bank by saying: 'Baker was quite well known at the bank by reason of being a customer of long standing. And there are many cases where a person can take a loan but the money would not be usable'. However, he added, only Mr. Lasher himself knew the exact details of the loan in this particular case, and he was not available at the moment.

Meredith H. Hoffmaster, the SBA official who had approved the loan, took a different view of the matter. He told the Committee that he had approved the loan because 'I was dealing with reputable businessmen', and there was no reason why he should not have accepted the deposit slip at its face value.

'I would not have authorized disbursement,' he added, 'if I had known the money was restricted'. He closed his statement by saying, wryly, 'I'm not accepting any more deposit slips'. When he heard all this, Senator Scott fairly exploded. He branded the affair 'a phony transaction', stated flatly that 'in my judgment it was a fraud and intended to be a fraud', and demanded a Justice Department investigation.

Fredric Suss, the SBA's general counsel, who had previously told the committee that the testimony given before it was the first information his agency had had that the $100,000 in question was restricted, concurred:

'We certainly intend to discuss this with the Department of Justice to get their advice', he told newsmen at the close of that hearing. Later in the afternoon, he disclosed to reporters that he had already met with Justice Department officials to discuss the case. He would not go into details but remarked that it was a federal crime to misrepresent information willfully when seeking a federal loan—an offense punishable by a maximum of a $10,000 fine and five years in jail. It made no difference whether the government was injured or not, he added, meaning that the question of culpability in the case would not depend on whether the SBA loan to the Carousel Motel was being repaid—which it was.

Bobby Baker was now really in a fix. Until then, nothing had turned up in the hearings that could be definitely construed as being not only improper—as practically all of his transactions were—but downright illegal. In this particular case, however, he had clearly committed a federal offense, and he could have gone to jail for it.

It is in the light of this threat to Bobby's well-being that one has to review the strange misfortune that was shortly to befall the key witness in the case. For it was Lorin H. Drennan, Jr., one of two accountants on loan to the committee from the General Accounting Office, (the other was Edward T. Hugler), who had developed the evidence of that phony transaction and had placed it before the committee.

In any federal court action to grow out of this case, Mr. Drennan would again have been the chief witness against Baker and his evidence to the effect that the $100,000 bank loan described above was, as Sen. Scott put it, 'a fraud and intended to be a fraud', might have gone a long way towards convicting the defendant. Could it be that Sheila Drennan died after surprising a prowler who was looking for some files her husband kept at home?

CHAPTER 17 - The Dignity of Senator Dirksen

The Bobby Baker scandal was a bipartisan mess such as Washington had never seen before. Although he was secretary to the Democratic Majority in the Senate, Baker's affiliations in Congress cut across party lines with sovereign nonchalance. Above all, he saw to it that the men at the top—in both parties—were his bedfellows, for better or for worse.

That is the fundamental reason why the 'investigation' of the Baker scandal by the Senate Rules Committee never really got off the ground and never allowed the public as much as a peep at what was really going on. On both sides of the political fence, the leadership in Congress was deeply involved with Baker and determined to keep a firm lid on this Pandora's Box. Against so formidable an alliance, the small forces of good government in Congress—also bipartisan—could not prevail.

Some of the most heated and most futile battles erupted in the Senate over the question of whether the inquiry should be broadened to encompass the improper business activities and the party-going of Senators, or should be strictly limited to the Baker case.

A few days before the assassination of President Kennedy provided a convenient stoplight for the reluctant Baker investigation just initiated by the Rules Committee, Sen. Clifford P. Case, Republican of New Jersey, proposed a resolution requiring senators to make regular public disclosures of their financial holdings. The outcry that followed shook the hallowed chamber even more than the trumpets of Jericho would have done.

The loudest dissent from this revolutionary proposal was registered by the Senate Minority leader, Everett McKinley Dirksen, Republican of Illinois, on November 19, 1963.

After several other senators had followed Sen. Case's lead and offered proposals for public disclosure of their financial interests, Dirksen angrily took the floor to declaim: 'The dignity and self-respect of the Senate demand that they be rejected'.

Of himself, Sen. Dirksen said that 'the senator from Illinois has not reduced himself to a Class B citizen yet'.

He told those who wished to disclose their assets, sarcastically: 'Why not? Nobody's stopping you'.

Dirksen went further to declare that he had not asked key Senate Republican employees to report all their outside interests, as Senate Democratic leader Mike Mansfield had required his party's key employees to do the day before.

In his near-30-years of congressional experience, Dirksen said, he had 'never found this necessary', and he indicated that he did not think it necessary now.

Dirksen's self-revealing stand in the matter drew a prompt and tart reply from *Newsday* in an editorial entitled 'What's Dignity to Do With It?' which was published on November 21, 1963. Referring to Dirksen's rejection of the public disclosure proposals and his pompously silly 'Class B citizen' remark, the paper wrote:

'On both counts the senator from Illinois is badly off base. Public servants have an obligation to assure those who elect them that their hands are clean, and that their financial transactions do not involve conflict of interest. Full disclosure does not make them into Class B citizens.

'Bobby Baker's warm and close association with so many members of the Senate, his intricate financial transactions, and his wheeling and dealing have raised a serious question. It needs to be answered, but it can be answered only if the members of the Senate are willing to have applied to them the same rules that now affect members of the executive branch...'

A few days earlier, on November 4, 1963, *The Christian Science Monitor*, in a dispatch from Washington, said:

'How extensively the Senate Rules Committee investigates the Bobby Baker case is likely to depend, in the last analysis, on how vigorously the newspapers and news media keep up the pressure.

'The disposition of the rules committee, as disclosed thus far, is to conduct a limited inquiry, probably pass a resolution condemning unethical and conflict-of-interest practices, and let it go at that. The Senate closes ranks in times of stress...

'The question which troubles Washington is whether it ever will be shown, on investigation, that somehow Senator "X" had some of his expenses cared for by lobbyist "Y", not for an immediate *quid pro quo*, but for an eventual favorable vote on some piece of legislation...

'The impression among news offices in Washington, where some of the best investigators in the press corps have been assigned to this case, is that the list of names of individuals who have had close associations with Mr. Baker, not illegal but violating usual conflict-of-interest standards, does include senators...'

Several months later, on March 4, 1964, *The Christian Science Monitor* noted: 'Senators buy and sell stock, engage in land speculation, and own businesses and radio-television companies— the very interests they are supposed to regulate. Businessmen are not thought to be trustees for the public good; senators are. Yet Mr. Baker could look about him and see members of Congress willing to conflict their interests...'

That is the heart of the matter. Only, the *Monitor* put its finger on it too gently. For one thing, the Boston paper forgot to mention oil and natural gas which some of the business senators are supposed to regulate while at the same time they are themselves big operators or stockholders in the field.

For another thing, the political partners Baker could see, looking about him, were not just plain members of Congress, but the very leaders of that august institution. He had the Senate Majority leader in his right pocket and the Senate Minority leader in his left. And all his inside pockets were stuffed with Class B senators and representatives, some of them so small they fitted into his vest pockets.

How does Dirksen fit into this picture? Here is how:

In the 15 months or so the Carousel Motel operated under the secret management of Senate Majority secretary Robert G. Baker, the luxury seaside resort was billed by Bobby Baker himself as the 'Washington hideaway for the advise and consent set'. (*New York Herald Tribune*, April 1, 1964).

And, who was to be found among the most assiduous guests at that fashionable snuggery but the self-righteous senator and Class A citizen from Illinois, Ev. Dirksen?

The matter was first brought to light by Drew Pearson in his column of March 25, 1964 'Dirksen was a frequent guest at Baker's plush Carousel motel at Ocean...'

Then, on April 1, 1964, *The New York Herald Tribune* published an even more sensational story under the six-column headline: 'Baker Motel Guest: Sen. Dirksen'.

The story, by Dom Bonafede of the Washington Bureau, said in part:

'Stanley L. Sommer, a Washington management representative and public relations consultant, acknowledged yesterday that he was host to Sen. Everett Dirksen, R., Ill., over the Labor Day weekend last year at the Maryland motel owned by Bobby Baker...

'Mr. Sommer told *The New York Herald Tribune* that the Senate minority leader, Mrs. Dirksen and her sister spent the holiday as his guests at the Carousel Motel, the Ocean City, Md. resort billed by Mr. Baker as the "Washington hideaway for the advise and consent set."

'Mr. Sommer said he maintains the year-around a large room at the motel for the pleasure of his "clients and political friends". The quarters, equipped with a kitchen, cost him about $2,000 annually and are included as part of his business and entertainment expenses, he said.

'Included among the firms he represents, he said, are U.S. Freight Forwarders Co., Northrup Aviation Corp., Dayco Rubber Co., a missile producer and a movable wall manufacturer. Several of the firms are engaged in government contract work.

'Both Sen. Dirksen and Mr. Sommer reported they are longtime friends going back to the time Mr. Sommer was employed by the Senate Appropriations Committee and that the sojourn at the Carousel was the result of a friendly gesture...

'Mr. Sommer said there was nothing unusual in his maintaining a room for friends and clients at the Carousel, inasmuch as "some people in our business have hospitality rooms..."'

Sounds very innocent, doesn't it? A senator—one of the most influential among the advise and consent set—happens to be a long-time friend of a professional lobbyist angling for government contracts for his business sponsors. The lobbyist—forgive me, the management representative—keeps the year round an expensive "hospitality room" in a swanky motel owned by the King of Lobbyists for the pleasure of his clients and political friends. The place has quite a reputation for lavish catering, nightclubbing, and parties attended by exceedingly attractive damsels. Oh, to be sure, when the Senator was invited down there, on that particular occasion, he brought his wife and sister-in-law along.

Question: Did Sen. Dirksen, who, we already know, was 'a frequent guest' at Carousel, always go there accompanied by his wife?

And, what happens next? Dom Bonafede reports:

'He (Sommer's) conceded that Morris Forgash, head of Freight Forwarders, sometimes kept his yacht *Natimor* in Washington to entertain clients and politicos.

'"Sen. Dirksen was never on the yacht", he said, "but there have been many Senators on it..."'

Enter a yacht and a yachtful of Senators. The point is made that Dirksen did not follow the example of his 'many' colleagues and set foot on the yacht (maybe he suffers from seasickness—J.J.). Since the yacht appears in a story about Dirksen at the Carousel Motel, however, one can presume that when Mr. Forgash brought his *Natimor* to Washington to 'entertain clients and politicos,' he sometimes anchored not too far away from the pleasant seaside resort where the Senator from Illinois happened to be a frequent guest. Let's listen to Bonafede again:

'He (Sommer) noted that the freight forwarding business was extremely competitive and that the yacht was used for public relations purposes, "like handing out tickets for the World Series or a championship fight."

'"This is a status thing," he said. "You invite a customer and have them meet a Senator—a big thing, you understand!..."'

How nicely put that is, and how descriptive it is of the inner workings of The Great Society. In darkest Africa, they would call it corruption in high places; in Washington, they call it a 'status thing'.

'He (Sommer) spoke candidly about Sen. Dirksen's stay at the Carousel,' the *Herald Tribune* story went on to say.

'"He said he was going down there, and all I did was let him use the room. Other people have used it, too," he added.

"Sen. Dirksen is the last guy who ought to be embarrassed by this. He is a straightforward man. He was always nice to me and has invited me to his home for parties."'

While Sen. Dirksen and the two ladies occupied Sommer's year-round hospitality rooms at the Carousel, we learn Sommer stayed at a rented cottage nearby. He just popped in to say hello, the lobbyist contended, and popped right out again because the Senator wasn't feeling well and was resting.

'I never asked him (Dirksen) for a doggone thing in all the years I've known him,' Sommer assured the reporter.

No, they never ask for a doggone thing. It just so happens that after a while some doggone thing very much in the minds of the party-giver or motel host concerned happens to materialize all by itself. As *The Christian Science Monitor* remarked, it isn't a matter of an immediate *quid pro quo* but of an 'eventual favorable vote on some piece of legislation' that follows upon the heels of senatorial expenses cared for by a lobbyist. But here, of course, we are talking about Senator 'X' and Lobbyist 'Y'.

Sen. Dirksen may have been 'a big thing' at The Carousel—to use the words of his good friend Sommer—but he wasn't the star attraction. This was Lyndon B. Johnson.

When the million-dollar, 45-unit motel was finally ready for business, in July 1962, Bobby Baker decided to have the gala of galas for its 'grand opening'. With the help of a chartered fleet of seven Capital Transit buses, all air-conditioned and all equipped with a bar, he brought 200 VIPs out from Washington for the celebration. Champagne was served during the trip and again on arrival.

Vice-President Lyndon B. Johnson and Lady Bird headed the party. The inevitable Perle B. Mesta also came along.

In mid-April 1964, Sen. Williams, in a Senate speech, revealed that equipment and staff from the Senate restaurant had been improperly used for the occasion.

'The senate restaurant records show,' Mr. Williams declared that, to a large extent, the facilities of the restaurant were used. For instance, the chef of the Senate restaurant and several of the management were sent to Ocean City for the weekend to take care of Mr. Baker's guests who would be at tending the opening of the Carousel.

'With them they carried food, table linens, serving trays, a considerable number of cooking utensils, warming pans, pots, pans etc. All this property of the Senate restaurant was loaded in cars and transported to Ocean City, Md., for use at the grand opening of Mr. Baker's motel. To what extent the food furnished was prepared by the Senate restaurant or to what extent Mr. Baker paid for these services I do not know'.

Reporters who tried to find out from the restaurant manager, Robert F. Sonntag, were quickly given the brush-off. Mr. Sonntag was too 'busy' to see them, an office spokesman declared.

Freeloading Bobby Baker not only put the facilities of the Senate restaurant to his own use, but he also gypped the bus company which had carried his guests to the 'Carousel' housewarming party. This was revealed on April 22, 1964, when Rep. Oliver P. Bolton, Republican of Ohio, read into the Congressional Record a statement saying that Baker had never paid the $1,324 he owed the D. C. Transit System, Inc. for the charter of the six buses that had carried several hundred persons to the opening of the Carousel Motel. Mr. Bolton stated he had learned from officials of the bus company that the bill had been sent to Bobby Baker, but had never been paid.

According to the same source, however, Baker had thought up another way of repaying the bus company for services rendered, for subsequently, according to Rep. Bolton, many letters were sent out by the D. C. Committee for Balanced Transportation, soliciting donations to a $100-a-plate dinner in honor of O. Roy Chalk, head of D. C. Transit. Among those listed on the letterhead were Robert G. Baker, Thomas Webb, and 'others who have been actively engaged in pursuing transit legislation in the House and Senate'. Legislative 'quid pro commercial pro' as usual.

CHAPTER 18 - Thank God, The Marines Are Coming!

WHEN the leader of The Great Society decided, on April 25, 1965, on the spur of the moment, to land some 30,000 Marines in the Dominican Republic, he certainly knew what he was doing.

Although democracy was hardly at stake, a fat Baker dossier was. Imagine those secret Dominican archives falling into the hands of the Commies! There would be the devil to pay both at home and abroad. Unthinkable! And so President Johnson made up his mind to tear up another scrap of paper, give the boot to the Alliance for Progress and occupy the Dominican Republic before it was too late. He did so in such haste that he found no time to consult even his closest advisers, let alone the O.A.S.

For years the Dominican Republic, like Cuba before Castro and other Caribbean paradises, had been a haven for American gambling syndicates. It had also been a favorite hunting ground for U.S. gangsters and racketeers of all stripes.

In *The New York Times* of December 20, 1963 (European Edition), Tad Szulc, the paper's leading expert on Latin American affairs, gave these interesting details about some of the operations involved:

'South Carolina's senior Democratic Senator, Olin D. Johnston, intervened with President Joaquin Balaguer of the Dominican Republic in 1961 in an effort to assist "a very close friend" in protecting a $200,000 investment in gambling concessions there.

'A letter on behalf of his friend's slot-machine and bingo concessions in Santo Domingo was written by Mr. Johnston to President Balaguer on the stationery of the United States Senate in June, 1961.

'The intervention on behalf of Bernard Allen, a professional gambling operator, was apparently successful. Senator Johnston wrote President Balaguer again in September, 1961, to thank him for helping Mr. Allen, a United States citizen...

'Senator Johnston's two letters were obtained by *The New York Times* from secret archives in the Dominican capital. Both the Senate Foreign Relations Committee and the Department of Justice have been aware of these letters for nearly a year.

'Senator Johnston, interviewed at his office, said he clearly remembered writing the letter on Mr. Allen's behalf.

"Just like I would for any American, I wrote a letter for him," he said. "He didn't want his property confiscated and I interceded..."

In the Dominican files were copies of President Balaguer's replies to Senator Johnston assuring him that there was no desire to cause "undue damage" to Mr. Allen, whose corporation had signed a contract for gambling concessions with the Dominican Government while Generalissimo Trujillo was still alive in 1960.

'In his first letter Senator Johnston reminded President Balaguer that "the operation of this business was through the personal orders of your beloved late chief, Generalissimo Rafael Leonidas Trujillo Molina"...'

Let's stop here for a moment to savor the contents and tone of this exchange of letters. The bloodiest tyrant in all the Americas, 'Generalissimo' Trujillo, has 'through personal orders' granted a gambling concession to an American professional gambler, in consideration of a 40 per cent cut in the operation (as Tad Szulc reports in a subsequent paragraph). Less than a month after the unspeakable Trujillo has been assassinated, a U.S. Senator writes a fawning letter to his successor in which he refers to the dead tyrant as 'your beloved late chief' and asks that the gambler's $200,000 investment in the Dominican gambling industry be respected, as it was. Ex-President Balaguer confirmed the correspondence in a telephone interview with the *Times*. Tad Szulc then went on to write:

'Senator Johnston's correspondence with President Balaguer was indicative of the friendships and associations that the Dominican dictatorship enjoyed in the United States.

'Earlier inspections of the Dominican archives revealed that the Trujillo regime had regarded other United States Congressmen as being favorably disposed toward the Dominican Republic in sugar quota and other matters.

'Among those cultivated by Trujillo officials and business associates in Washington was Robert G. Baker, former Secretary to the Senate Democratic majority, whose financial affairs are now under investigation by a Senate committee.

'Mr. Baker himself displayed an interest in other gambling concessions in the Dominican Republic this year. However, no apparent relationship was found between the activities of Mr. Baker and those of Mr. Allen two years earlier'.

It should be interpolated here that if Mr. Szulc was unable to find an 'apparent relationship' between the activities of Mr. Allen and Mr. Baker, this certainly does not rule out the possibility that there was a secret relationship. Bobby Baker was a master of disguise and he always took care to conceal his operations under various covers and smokescreens, as has already been demonstrated by numerous examples.

Moreover, the two men operated on different levels. While Allen was a professional gambler, Baker was a professional politician and influence-peddler. Obviously, therefore, he would not have entered into any kind of overt or easily detectable relationship with a person like Allen.

And there was another tie-in, as related by Mr. Szulc:

'Like Senator Johnston, Mr. Baker is from South Carolina. It was Senator Johnston who formally nominated Mr. Baker for the post of secretary to the majority at a caucus of Democratic Senators in January, 1955.

'Mr. Allen, who is known as "Bucky" to his friends, has been operating amusement parks in South Carolina for nearly 30 years. He maintained this activity after his entry in gambling in the Dominican Republic.

'Reached by telephone in Miami, Fla., Mr. Allen said that Senator Johnston had been a good friend for 30 years. But he refused to say whether the Senator had written letters in his behalf'.

Note that the gambler and the senator have been 'good friends' for exactly the same span of time—30 years—that Allen has been operating amusement parks, a highly profitable business, in Johnston's political preserve, South Carolina. Johnston, incidentally, has served in the Senate since 1944. He had been chairman of the Post Office and Civil Service Committee and also of Judiciary and Agriculture subcommittees.

Note further that 'Bucky' and 'Bobby' were obviously twin protégés—despite the difference in age—of the powerful senator from their homestate, South Carolina.

'He (Allen) would not discuss whether Senator Johnston assisted him in obtaining the 1960 contract with Generalissimo Trujillo, as was recently alleged in Santo Domingo by Dominican officials,' Mr. Szulc went on to report.

Here we get a glimpse of some of the dark secrets that may still be hidden in those ominous Dominican archives the enterprising *New York Times* reporter managed to penetrate ever so slightly. How sensitive the matter is may also be inferred from Allen's irritable reaction to Mr. Szulc's next move:

'When he was apprised that copies of Senator Johnston's letter had been obtained by *The New York Times*, Mr. Allen said: "If you imply that there was some bribery with Trujillo, that's simply not true"...

'Mr. Allen said at one point, "You are trying to malign the Senator, Mr. Johnston..."'

Now for a look at the 'other gambling concessions in the Dominican Republic,' in which Bobby Baker himself displayed an interest.

It was again *The New York Times* that produced the most extensive information on this subject in an article entitled 'Baker Assisted Nevada Gambler in Business Deal' by Wallace Turner which was published on November 7, 1963. Here are the most important paragraphs from this article:

'Robert G. Baker has acted as an intermediary on behalf of a prominent Las Vegas gambler who has extensive associations with notorious underworld figures, it developed yesterday...

'For weeks officials not directly connected with the Baker investigation have said privately that he had been involved in the entry of Las Vegas gamblers into other business activities that, unlike gambling, are legal in all states.

'Yesterday an executive of one of the nation's major and most respected business concerns—Pan-American World Airways—complained that Mr. Baker had involved him and his company with three Nevada gamblers, and that now Pan-American was connected with the Baker case.

'The facts, as described to *The New York Times* yesterday by John Gates, president of Intercontinental Hotels, Inc., a subsidiary of Pan-American for the operation of hotels along the airline's routes were these:

'Last June Mr. Baker approached Samuel Pryor, a vice-president of Pan-American, and asked that a business appointment be made for Mr. Baker and a friend to see Mr. Gates. The interview was to concern discussions of bidding on gambling concessions on Pan-American-operated hotels in Curacao, Netherlands West Indies, and the Dominican Republic.

"There are casinos in these places and we don't want anything to do with running them," Mr. Gates said in a conversation yesterday. "We just want someone else to take care of that, and keep us out of it. Gambling is just a headache for us in those places."'

We have already met, in a preceding chapter, some of the characters Baker was anxious to launch into the Dominican Republic gambling business, in particular the brothers Levinson. Edward Levinson, a major stockholder in two big gambling joints in Las Vegas, was the man Baker brought to see Mr. Gates.

At their first meeting, in June 1963, Baker, according to the *Times*, outlined the purpose of the talks.

'"Baker told me that this friend of his, Mr. Levinson, was interested in the gambling business, and had this hotel in Las Vegas and that it was very successful, and that they wondered if there was any opportunity for him in our two hotels in Santo Domingo and Curacao," Mr. Gates said.

'These hotels have been open for some years with casinos attached to them.

'Mr. Gates said he had explained that the right of selection of management of the casino in the Curacao hotel was vested in the hotel's owners. Pan-American operates the hotel and has the right of approval of the casino management. At Santo Domingo, Mr. Gates said, Pan-American can select the casino operation directly.

'Mr. Gates told Mr. Baker and Mr. Levinson that the Curacao hotel owners were about to open their casino operation for bidding in September.

'Mr. Gates also told them that he had received an indication of interest from another Nevada-based gambling operator, Clifford Jones.

'The next meeting requested by Mr. Baker came in July, Mr. Gates said, and this time the group was made up of Mr. Baker, Mr. Levinson, Mr. Jones and Jacob Kozloff, Mr. Jones' partner in four small casinos scattered across the Caribbean.

'Mr. Jones is a former lieutenant governor of Nevada... In the years that the Batista regime encouraged gambling casino operations in Havana, Mr. Jones was interested in one of them...

'The Jones-Kozloff combination controls casinos in Aruba; in the Netherlands Antilles; in the Dutch-controlled part of St.-Martin, an island partly controlled also by the French; in Surinam in Dutch Guiana; and in a new Government-owned hotel in Quito, Ecuador...

'Mr. Jones explained (in a telephone conversation with *The New York Times*) that he had known Mr. Baker for many years, and that, "I asked him to set up the meeting with Gates for me."

'Not until much later, Mr. Jones said, did he discover that Mr. Baker had first taken his other friend, Mr. Levinson to meet the Pan-American officials...'

Ponder this for a moment. It is June, 1963. Kennedy is still President, Johnson is Vice-President. Bobby Baker, Johnson's protégé, is secretary to the Democratic Senate majority and officiates, in practice, as the 101st senator, one of the most influential of the lot.

And this same Bobby Baker acts, at the same time, as go-between for a bunch of notorious Las Vegas gamblers, double-crossing one pal in favor of another because the latter is already a partner of his own in another venture (Serv-U Corporation). That's the way they do business in gangland. For the U.S. Senate to serve as the staging-ground for such operations is quite something.

The injured Jones apparently decided that, under the circumstances, 'if you can't lick 'em, join 'em' was preferable to an old-style gangland vendetta for we already know that he and his partner Kozloff attended the second meeting between Levinson-Baker and the Pan-American executive, in July.

'There was a third meeting between the gamblers and Mr. Gates,' the *Times* went on to say. 'This time, late in July or early in August, Mr. Baker did not attend. From this meeting, Mr. Gates said yesterday, there came a formal bid from Mr. Jones and Mr. Kozloff to take over the Pan-American-controlled casino in Santo Domingo.

"I don't know whether Mr. Levinson had an interest in this or not," Mr. Gates said'.

These developments would seem to indicate that between the second and the third meeting with Mr. Gates, the Jones-Kozloff combine had somehow prevailed over the Levinson-Baker combine. The *Times* then lifts another corner of the curtain that screens these goings-on from public view:

'Mr. Jones said in the telephone interview that Mr. Levinson had no part in the proposal, which is now being considered by Pan-American.

'"You know that as a Nevada license holder, he (Mr. Levinson) can't have any outside gambling interest," Mr. Jones explained'.

That is, to say the least, a curious statement, coming from that source. For, even though Jones ostensibly no longer operates now as a gambler in Nevada, the *Times* notes in another paragraph, he still holds stock in the Thunderbird Hotel of Las Vegas, one of the leading hotel-casino operations in that gamblers' haven. Moreover:

'Mr. Jones was once a central figure in a concealed-interest case pressed by Nevada authorities about 10 years ago. At that time it was alleged by state officials that Mr. Jones held interests in the Thunderbird Hotel as an agent for George Sadlo, an intimate of Meyer Lansky and his brother, the notorious gamblers. Mr. Sadlo could not have been licensed himself. The Nevada Supreme Court ruled against the state officials in this case'.

Whatever reasons may have prompted the Nevada Supreme Court to take such an attitude in this case, it is clear that some kind of association existed between Jones, a former lieutenant governor, and the Lansky stooge, George Sadlo. Incidentally, the *Times* is being excessively charitable in here describing Meyer Lansky and his brother as 'notorious gamblers'. They are notorious mobsters. So here you have another prime example of how power politics, Big Business and outright gangsterism mix freely in The Great Society. This is brought out even more clearly in a UPI Dispatch from 'Washington, November 7, 1963, where one reads that 'Baker was quoted as having told Sam Pryor, a Pan-American vice-president, that "for political reasons" he wanted to introduce Cliff Jones, a former Nevada lieutenant governor, and Edward Levinson, a Las Vegas hotel owner'.

To revert to *The New York Times* once more:

'Another involvement of Nevada personalities in the Baker case arose over the role of Senator Howard W. Cannon, Nevada Democrat, a member of the Senate Rules Committee that is conducting the investigation of the Baker affair.

'*Newsweek* magazine said in its current issue that "Baker found an ardent champion in the committee: Senator Howard Cannon."

'The magazine quoted the Senator as having said, when various aspects of Mr. Baker's operations were brought up, "I don't see anything wrong with that," and "there's nothing illegal about making an investment like that." Senator Cannon was pictured as opposing the Baker investigation'.

Here then, we are introduced to another one of the ten or more Senators Bobby Baker himself boasted he had in the palm of his hand any time, as he did: Senator Cannon of Nevada, and this one, to add a supreme touch of farce to the Baker non-investigation is a member of the committee ostensibly conducting that inquiry.

Senator Cannon's warm feelings for Bobby Baker were also brought out by Wallace Turner of the *Times*. While the senator, in a telephone interview, denied having made the statements attributed to him by *Newsweek*, or that he opposed the Baker investigation, 'Senator Cannon whose home is in Las Vegas, said that he had been friendly with Mr. Baker but had never travelled to Las Vegas with the former Senate employee. He denied that Mr. Baker had ever asked him for favors, or that Mr. Baker had ever asked him to do favors for Las Vegas gamblers'.

Such inane denials are, of course, routine in The Great Society, from the boss down. Besides, there have always been some senators from Nevada who didn't need much prodding to interceed in favor of their state's leading industry, gambling. On this score, the *Times* has Sen. Cannon as saying that he knew Mr. Levinson: "He runs a big hotel in Las Vegas and I flatter myself that I know every one of the hotel operators in Las Vegas."'

One could hardly put it more cynically, though it was not of course meant to sound that way.

Since we're on the interesting subject of the Baker-Cannon relationship, and since the good senator himself, in his interview with the *Times*, in early November 1963, had somewhat imprudently stated that he had never travelled to Las Vegas with Baker, it is pertinent to add here that in April, 1963, Baker chartered an airplane to fly a planeload of politicians and lobbyists to Las Vegas where they were to take part in a fund-raising dinner for Sen. Cannon. On this subject, *Newsday*, on November 16, 1963, reported:

'The air junket took place last April, when more than 80 congressional staff members and lobbyists took a Riddle Airlines DC-7 plane to Las Vegas for a fund-raising dinner for Sen. Howard W. Cannon (D-Nev), a candidate for re-election next year and a member of the Senate's aviation subcommittee. According to reports, the $16,000 bill for the plane was never paid. In fact, a source close to the airlines company said yesterday no bill was even rendered until last month. He said it had been considered "doubtful" when the flight was arranged that payments would ever be forthcoming.

'But Stanley L. Sommers (See Chapter 17) who shares office space in Washington with J. H. (Slim) Carmichael, board chairman of Riddle, said yesterday that about two months ago Jack Anderson, a new board member of the airlines and a newspaper associate of columnist Drew Pearson, presented the $16,000 bill to Baker. There was no explanation of why the bill was presented to Baker and airline officials denied it was. But Jack Conlon, administrative aide to Cannon, confirmed last night it had been. He could give no reason for the bill being presented to Baker but he said it had not been presented until after the first stories about conflict of interest had appeared about Baker. Conlon theorized that the bill had been presented to Baker as a means of embarrassing Cannon.

'Sommers is known to be a good friend of Baker's. He is, for instance, a public relations man who represents the Northrup Corp. an aircraft manufacturing firm...' (one of the firms Baker's Serv-U did business with, as has been noted before).

If all this sounds bewilderingly intricate, don't blame the author. I didn't make up the Bobby Baker case; he did. Complexity and obscurity are the very essence of this affair.

Let us try to distil, from the above quotation, a few pertinent facts.

Sen. Cannon was technically right in saying he didn't travel to Las Vegas with Baker. He was there, and Bobby was coming, with a planeload of cronies, all eager to help raise funds for the senator, without asking for anything in return, of course.

That trip was arranged by Baker, that's for sure. We have both Sommers' and Conlon's testimony for it, and he got stuck with the bill, even though he never paid it. The point of course is this: When the junket took place, in April 1963, Riddle Airlines were not in a hurry to collect because both Cannon and Baker were influential contacts. They might even repay their debts of gratitude in a coin even more acceptable than cash. Remember, Cannon is a member of the Senate's aviation subcommittee.

Then, in September, Bobby hit the skids and Riddle Airlines got panicky. A Baker out of the Senate and under investigation could be of no further use to them. So, belatedly, he was presented with the bill.

As for Conlon's 'theory' that the bill had been presented to Baker as a means of embarrassing Cannon, that is nonsense, of course. Certainly Jack Anderson, associate of Drew Pearson, a great Johnson fan, would do nothing to embarrass Sen. Cannon, one of the chief architects of the cover-up in the Baker case. The truth is far simpler: Baker got the bill because he organized the trip.

In testimony before the Rules Committee, John Gates of Pan-American, on February 27, 1964, confirmed all he had told *The New York Times* three months earlier about Bobby Baker and his gambling friends.

In addition, Gates, according to *Newsday* (28-2-64) testified that 'when news of the Baker investigation broke last fall, the hotel owners decided not to award any casino contracts, but the bid from Jones and Kozloff is still being considered. Shortly after the meetings with Baker, Gates said it was learned that Levinson's brother, Louis Levinson, had previous run-ins with the law. Edward Levinson was told he could not bid for casino operations if his brother was to be included in the deal. Gates said that decision by the hotel prompted Edward to withdraw his participation with

Jones and Kozloff. Gates said Edward Levinson himself had been checked and was known to be an operator of clean and honest gambling games...'

There is at least one more link between Baker and the Dominican situation. On this score, *Newsday* reported on March 4, 1964:

'In yesterday's session [of the Senate Rules Committee], former Dominican Republic cabinet minister Diego Bardas, a New York importer and exporter, told probers that in 1961 while he was facing charges of underselling cement in the United States, Baker introduced him to a U.S. customs official. Bardas maintained that this was not an exercise of influence by Baker and had no bearing on the dismissal of the charges. [Really, who'd think of such a thing—J. J.]. Bardas also said that in 1957, when similar underselling charges were being contemplated against him, he hired Baker's law partner, Ernst Tucker. When Tucker sent him a bill for $2,000, Bardas said. "I called Bobby and he told me to forget about it."'

At this point, some political background concerning the Dominican Republic has to be filled in. From 1930 until his assassination in May 1961, Trujillo and his family ruled the country. That means that Diego Bardas must have been a Trujillo cabinet minister. It is also clear from the context that he was on very intimate terms with Baker whom he called 'Bobby' and who told him on the phone to forget about a bill his own law firm had sent him.

Baker, his whole story shows, was not one to forget easily about money owing him (though he was rather inclined to forget easily bills he was supposed to pay, as we've just seen). It seems most unlikely, therefore, that he would drop the fee his law firm had earned for services rendered in having criminal charges quashed, unless there had been some other form of *quid pro quo*.

In order to conceive the nature of that *quid pro quo* one has to refer back to the Tad Szulc article previously quoted in this chapter, in particular the sentence: 'Among those cultivated by Trujillo officials and business associates in Washington was Robert G. Baker'.

The picture, then, is perfectly clear and well-rounded. Bobby Baker was the Washington contact man of the Trujillo clique. He used his influence on their behalf even to the point of interfering with the normal course of justice (Diego Bardas case). In return, he had the inside track on gambling operations in that country. That's why they all came to see him: Jones and Kozloff, and the Levinson brothers.

At one stage in the proceedings, however, there developed an unforeseen and annoying contretemps. On December 20, 1962, the first honest and free elections in the history of the Dominican Republic were held. They resulted in the election (by a 62 per cent vote) of Juan Bosch, a scholar, social reformer and foe of the Trujillo clique.

Bosch is no Castro, far from it. He did, however, favor a minimum of reforms, including an end to the U.S.-operated gambling industry in the Dominican Republic. That's why the powerful gambling interests turned against him, just as they vented their fury on Castro after the latter had abolished the gambling concessions of the Batista regime, (among the losers: Meyer Lansky and his mob).

In September 1963, the Bosch Government was overthrown by the same military and reactionary forces that had for so long supported the Trujillo dictatorship, even though some members of the new junta that took power after the Bosch ouster were personal foes of the late 'Generalissimo'.

Bobby Baker and his gambling cronies evidently had a hunch of what was coming for as early as June of the same year they started preparing for D-Day in Santo Domingo, when the green light would again go up for gambling and organized prostitution, which usually go together.

The popular uprising of April 24, 1965, threw another crimp into these schemes. The 'rebels', as they were called by the ruling junta, while they were in reality, supporters of the constitution and of the deposed president Juan Bosch, quickly gained the upper hand. There was a clear and present danger that they might seize the compromising secret archives of the Dominican Republic and the fat Bobby Baker files contained in them.

That was if not the principal at least one of the compelling reasons why President Johnson instantly swung into action. As usual he was protecting himself by protecting his creature, Bobby.

These are the tawdry realities behind the stately façade of U.S. foreign policy. Those are the forces that set the U.S. Marines in motion, all pious verbiage to the contrary notwithstanding.

CHAPTER 19 - Of Murchisons and 'Finders' Fees'

At the other end of Hispaniola, in 'Doc' Duvalier's perennial dictatorship of Haiti, Bobby Baker also engaged in plenty of fruitful wheeling and dealing. Here, we find him in business again with the oil-rich Murchison family of Dallas, Texas.

In a preceding chapter, I have already quoted the revealing remark by the Murchison executive Robert E. Thompson of Dallas that he 'thought' he had met Bobby Baker in the office of Lyndon Johnson.

As a matter of fact, Clint Murchison has always been a great LBJ fan and LBJ has always been a great pal to the Murchisons. Lyndon Johnson, in whatever official capacity he might be acting at the time, consistently kept a careful watch on the depletion allowance, the mainstay of all fortunes made in oil; and the Murchisons just as consistently kept oiling Johnson's political machine.

Into this mutually profitable scheme of things, Bobby Baker fitted snugly. There never was in the U.S. Senate—except of course for Bobby's two mentors, Johnson and Kerr—a more eager defender of the depletion allowance than Baker. Since he was practically in control of the Democratic Senate campaign fund, he was in a position to prod reluctant senators with the approved club-and-carrot treatment.

Senator Frank Moss of Utah, for one, revealed in the course of the Baker investigation that he was approached, some time in

1959, by a 'representative' of the Baker-controlled Senate campaign fund who offered him a substantial campaign contribution on the condition that Moss join in support of the oil depletion allowance. Moss says he declined the offer because of the 'string' attached to it.

Once one has made a multi-million dollar fortune in oil, thanks to the practically complete tax exemption inherent in the depletion allowance, it becomes profitable to branch out into other business enterprises. None of the Texas oil magnates can match the acumen and diversity of the Murchisons in this respect. They have invaded just about every conceivable form of business, including book publishing.

Early in 1959, the Murchisons cast their eyes on the money-making possibilities in Doc Duvalier's dark-skinned realm. There were plenty of cattle there waiting for consumers mainly because most Haitians are too desperately poor to buy meat. Why not set up a packing plant and export Haitian meat to the United States, the Murchisons wondered.

Until then, there had never been any exports of Haitian meat to the United States and Puerto Rico because Haiti lacked modern facilities and no single cut of beef produced there would have gotten by the stern eye of U.S. sanitary officials.

The first thing to do, then, to get an Haitian-American meat import business started was to build a packing plant that would meet the minimum requirements of U.S. sanitary standards. For this purpose, the Haitian-American Meat and Provision Company,

S.A. (Hampco) was formed in Port-au-Prince, Haiti, in the spring of 1959, with Gordon B. Duval, a New York banker, as president and Marshall F. Dancy, also of New York, as vice-president.

At the time, a dispatch from Port-au-Prince to *The New York Times* of March 8, 1959, reported that Clint W. Murchison, Jr., the Texas industrialist and financier, was also interested in the project of building a slaughter house and packing plant in the Haitian capital. In fact, Murchison controlled the operation, as the Baker inquiry subsequently established.

When the $500,000 Hampco plant opened for business, late in 1959, it was a great day for Haiti. President Duvalier—who had a personal finger in every worthwhile pie in the country—attended the festivities and heaped praise on this new milestone towards progress.

Although Duvalier is a physician of sorts, he has done little to improve sanitary conditions in his part of the disease-ridden island. His government also did practically nothing to control illegal slaughtering in the primitive abattoirs of Haiti and the peddling of infected meat products. Nor did this situation change much after the Hampco plant had been opened.

Hampco had originally hoped to capture the local meat market as well, but the natives neither cared for, nor could they afford to buy hygienic meat so this part of the operation proved a flop. In order to make money, the company had to get in on the profitable U.S. market, especially in Puerto Rico. This required a certificate of inspection that could be issued only after officials of the U. S.

Department of Agriculture had visited the plant and inspected its production to make sure that they met United States health standards.

What happened then has been described in *The New York Times* of November 13, 1963, in these terms:

'Dr. Edward A. Murphy, chief staff officer for procedures and requirements in meat inspection of the Department of Agriculture, said today that the department "found difficulties" in a first investigation early in 1961, and the certificate was held up. The investigation was made by Donald W. Born, the embassy's commercial attaché, who received instructions from the Agriculture Department.

'After the first refusal, Dr. Murphy related, there was a good deal of correspondence and telephoning by Mr. Duval.

"He was all over the place," Dr. Murphy said. "He was in Washington many times. He called me on the telephone and was over to the State Department."

'On May 15, Mr. Dancy, the company vice-president, called on David R. Thompson, the United States charge in Port-au-Prince. Mr. Dancy was accompanied by Samuel Ferber, who was connected with the Hampco plant.

'Mr. Dancy expressed the hope that a re-inspection could be made as soon as possible, and Mr. Thompson assured him that the embassy had made such a recommendation to the Department of Agriculture shortly after Mr. Ferber's last visit to the embassy.

'On the second inspection, the plant met the prescribed standards and the certificate was granted...'

It will be noted that nothing is said in this story about any improvements having been made in hygienic conditions at the Hampco plant between the first and the second inspections. As far as one can tell from this dispatch, nothing really changed, other than that the health officers yielded to pressure put on them by the power behind Hampco, the Murchison family, and by their contacts in Washington.

While Dr. Murphy told the *Times*, 'I certainly don't remember Baker's name being connected with the project,' the opening paragraphs of the dispatch, by E. W. Kenworthy of the Washington bureau, make it clear that there was a connection:

'The Justice Department is investigating a connection between Robert G. Baker and an American-owned packing plant in Haiti that was seeking approval in 1961 to export meat to the United States and Puerto Rico.

'Specifically, according to informants here, the Justice Department is looking into reports that the former secretary to the Senate Democratic majority entered into a deal to use its influence to speed clearance for the meat products in return for a promised commission on the imports if he were successful.

'The Department of Justice refused to comment on reports that such commissions were paid and that the Government had evidence of them. Nor would Justice Department officials comment on reports that the commission involved a payment of one-cent-per-pound on all imports into the United States and Puerto Rico.

'Other officials stated, however, that payment of the commission was shared by Mr. Baker and another man, whom they declined to name...'

Such discretion in mid-November 1963 is understandable. The Baker investigation was just then getting off to a slow start and the big question on everybody's mind—everyone, that is, who had an inkling of who and what was involved—was: What will happen if the whole truth comes out?

No sooner had the certificate of inspection been granted to the Hampco plant than a flood of Haitian meat started pouring into the United States and Puerto Rico: 1,609,886 pounds in the fiscal year ending June 30, 1962 and 2,703,968 pounds in the next fiscal year. Exports to Puerto Rico alone ran at the rate of about 40,500 pounds weekly.

Bobby Baker's influence had not only brought about a reversal of the U.S. officials' views on hygienic standards at the Hampco plant, but it also clinched a big import deal with the right people in Puerto Rico, as the facts established by the Senate Rules Committee show.

The right people, in this case, were one Señor Andreas Lopez Curet of San Juan, P. R., and Señor Jose A. Benitez, also of San Juan. Lopez is president of the Borinquen Meat Packing Company, Inc. and of the Borinquen Beef Products Company, both of San Juan. Benitez, a former Democratic national committeeman from

Puerto Rico, was Deputy High Commissioner for the Pacific Trust Territories at the time he went into business with Bobby Baker in 1961.

As a high Department of Interior official assigned to watch over the welfare of this country's trust islands in the Pacific, Benitez should normally have been stationed at Saipan. However, he found Washington more to his liking and therefore managed to devise an administrative technique that kept him most of the time in the capital rather than in his lonely Pacific domain.

When the first news stories concerning a Haitian meat deal connection between Benitez and Baker cropped up, late in 1963, Assistant Interior Secretary John Carver put the Puerto Rican on the carpet. Questioned about his alleged partnership with Bobby Baker, Benitez at first denied it.

'Benitez told me he was in partnership with only one man— the President of the United States,' Carver was quoted in a UPI dispatch from Washington, dated February 28, 1964, as telling reporters.

If this admission staggers you, wait for the end of the quote, for Benitez didn't want to be taken too literally:

'He said the partnership was to sell democracy to the people of the trust territories'.

Without going here into the question of how badly the aborigines of the Pacific islands need democracy, American style, the facts of the case show that Benitez was so busy selling Haitian meat to his countrymen that he flopped as a salesman of democracy.

On February 20, 1964, Benitez testified before the Rules Committee. He proved surprisingly outspoken, candidly admitting that he had headed straight for his 'good friend' Bobby Baker when he needed someone to clinch a meat export deal.

According to an UPI dispatch from Washington (20-2-64), Benitez told the Senate Rules committee that 'Baker came through as expected...

'Mr. Benitez said the former Senate Democratic secretary helped a Puerto Rican meat importer [Lopez—J.J.] get the output of a new slaughterhouse in Haiti in early 1961 [i.e. before the certificate of inspection had been granted—J. J.].

'As a result, Mr. Benitez said, he, Baker and two other associates of the Senate aide shared a one-cent-per-pound "finder's fee" on every pound of meat shipped from Haiti to Puerto Rico...'

This was probably the first occasion a student of graft and corruption, American, Oriental or otherwise, could find an unabashed piece of baksheesh referred to euphemistically as a 'finder's fee'.

Who were the two other Baker associates who shared the 'finder's fee' with him and Benitez?

We find the answer in the following excerpts from a Washington dispatch published in the February 5, 1964 issue of *Newsday*:

'Meanwhile the committee made public yesterday testimony taken from Thomas D. Webb, Jr. and Webb's partner Francis Law. Both men told probers that despite their business links with Baker, Baker had never used his influence to help in any transaction as far as they knew. They detailed a complicated meat import deal in which Baker received commissions from both the seller and the buyer.

'Law explained the deal worked like this: the Haitian-American Meat and Provision Corp. (Hampco) had been built by the Murchison family of Texas in association with Allen & Co. of New York. A Puerto Rican distributor, who wanted to buy meat met Webb and Law through Baker. It was arranged that the buyer, a man named Lopez, would pay a fee of one-cent-per-pound to Baker who gave half to Webb and Law and one quarter to Jose A. Benitez, former Democratic national committeeman from Puerto Rico.

'Webb said Baker made $4,264.46 from the deal in 1962 and $1,200 in 1963 on the fee payments. Law claimed Baker owed him and Webb more than $2,000 from the venture. When Lopez stopped importing from Hampco, Webb and Law located a new buyer, William Kentor of Chicago, who paid only a half-cent-per-pound fee to Baker, Webb and Law. Webb said that arrangement was still in effect. Hampco, Webb said, previously had agreed to pay Baker 10 per cent if its net profits up to $30,000 yearly maximum for services rendered. Webb said he did not know what those services were but he denied Baker used influence to win

Department of Agriculture approval for Hampco to export meat to this country. Webb said he had no idea how much Hampco had paid directly to Baker'.

This testimony shows that Baker did indeed get a kickback on the transaction from both sides: from the seller, Hampco, for services rendered (and the facts stated above clearly show, in spite of Webb's routine denial, that his 'services' to the company consisted in getting Dept. of Agriculture approval for a meat packing plant that failed to meet standard hygienic requirements), as well as from the buyers, first Lopez, then Kentor.

In a subsequent *Newsday* article, published on February 21, 1964, Baker's associate in this deal, Thomas D. Webb, Jr., is identified as 'a contract man for Murchison', which rounds out the picture.

After Benitez, in his testimony before the Committee, had admitted sharing in Bobby Baker's 'finder's fee', he was questioned again by his boss at the Interior Dept., Assistant Secretary John Carver. The upshot of that interview was that Benitez handed in his resignation, which was not announced, however, until several days later. About this second interview, UPI reported in the afore-cited dispatch of February 28, 1964:

'Carver said that in explanation Benitez said the deal was arranged before he took office and further that the checks from Baker were in the name of his wife who handled the family financial affairs. According to Carver, Benitez was technically correct in his initial disavowal. "We didn't consider it a basis for disciplinary action," he added'.

As a matter of fact, in making public Benitez' resignation on Feb. 28, Secretary of the Interior Steward Udall also announced that the former official had been immediately rehired as a $65 to $75 a day consultant to the department, which is hardly a sign of stern official disapproval in a case of blatant graft.

While the Hampco transaction still presents many obscure and confusing aspects, it's gist is perfectly clear. Sen. Curtis, one of the three Republican members on the investigating committee, was undoubtedly right when he suggested that the whole arrangement was a cover to mask a payoff to Baker from the Murchison family for his assistance on legislation (in particular the depletion allowance).

Baker has been involved with the Murchisons in many ways, several of which have already been described in preceding chapters. Many other examples can be cited.

For instance, Sen. Williams on January 26, 1965, put in The Congressional Record detailed information about two government contracts with the Sweet Water Development Corporation of Dallas, for development of a water desalinization project.

Sen. Williams showed in his statement that the Sweet Water Development Corp. is controlled by the Texas Construction Co. (Tecon) and thus represents a link in the Murchison combine. He identified Robert F. Thompson, a high Tecon official, as president of Sweet Water and said that other Murchison associates were partners or officers in the firm, which was chartered in March, 1961.

Williams told the Senate that the Interior Department's Office of Saline Water had entered into two cost-plus-fixed fee contracts with Sweet Water for development of a water desalinization process. He then quoted from what he termed 'a highly critical' audit report of the first contract and said that, among other things, it questioned the amount of legal fees paid by Sweet Water.

Mr. Williams then quoted from a letter that had come into his possession. It was sent to the Internal Revenue Service by the law firm of Rep. Emmanuel Geller (D) of New York and indicated that the latter had shared with Baker $10,000 in legal fees received from Sweet Water.

'Upon receipt of payment from the client for the legal services rendered,' the letter said in part, 'we sent our check in the sum of $2,500, representing 25 per cent of our fee, to Tucker & Baker, the forwarding attorneys'.

In other words: A Murchison company, no sooner formed, gets a lucrative government contract that gives it the right to charge off legal fees to the taxpayers. Next thing, the firm enters into legal arrangements that involve the payment of an outrageously high lawyer's fee, of which Bobby Baker and his law partner get $2,500, while the remaining $7,500 go to the law firm of an influential Congressman. Funny business as usual.

Here is another example:

According to an UPI dispatch from Sacramento, California, dated November 8, 1963, 'Gov. Edmund G. Brown disclosed today that Robert G. Baker made a special trip to California last May in an effort to protect a race track monopoly in San Diego... Governor Brown said Mr. Baker had spoken to him in opposition to legislation requiring competitive bidding for a lease at the Del Mar race track.

'The track is owned by the 22d District Agricultural Association, a public agency, and since 1936 has been leased to a charitable organization headed by the wealthy Murchison family of Texas.

'The Governor said Mr. Baker had been accompanied on the trip by Clint Murchison, Jr. Governor Brown said he believed that Mr. Baker was intervening on behalf of the Murchisons because of the financial support the family had given the Democratic party...'

Despite all this, the Rules Committee never questioned Clint Murchison, or even his good friend Lyndon B, Johnson, for that matter.

CHAPTER 20 - Sex and the Solons

'I PERSONALLY know of a Senator who keeps two call girls on his payroll. I know because I've been at parties where they've been'.

This amazing statement was made, on October 30, 1963, in the House of Representatives by Rep. Steed, Democrat of Oklahoma. It almost brought the Senate down, but not with laughter. In fact the solons were so aroused by Steed's outspoken accusation that they threatened parliamentary warfare against the House unless Steed were made to withdraw his charge.

Newsday, on October 31, published a number of additional details of the matter which to my knowledge have not appeared anywhere else:

'A miffed member of the House of Representatives charged yesterday that a member of the Senate had a couple of call girls on his payroll. How did he know? The girls told him so.

"I just discovered today that sex is more interesting to people than government," Rep. Tom Steed (D-Okla.) said, explaining how he happened to mix the report of call girls into his campaign to keep the Senate from limiting the mailing privileges of House members.

'The Oklahoman declined to identify the senator with the Polly Adler approach yesterday and said he would continue to keep the name to himself, even if a Senate committee should ask. None has.

'Steed said he met the damsels-for-dollars in the course of his own partying. "I stumbled into the wrong pew one night," he said cryptically.

'Steed said, however, that before leaving the pew he talked with a couple of the girls and that what they told him was unlike anything any senator ever wrote in newsletters to voters. "It became obvious what they were in the course of the conversation, and they told me whose payroll they were on", Steed said...

'If the senators want to reform things around here they ought to start with Senate," he said...'

The bombshell dropped by Rep. Steed, at the end of October, turned out to have a delayed-action fuse. Nothing more was heard (publicly) of the matter, until almost a month later. Then the bomb went off with a bang that rocked both hallowed chambers of the Capitol.

According to an AP dispatch from Washington, dated November 27, 1963, 'Irate Senators demanded yesterday that Rep. Tom Steed, D., Okla., name the Senator whom the Oklahoma Congressman charged kept "two call girls on his payroll."

Once again the dignity of Senator Dirksen (See Chapter 17) exploded into righteous fury.

'This is an insult to every member of the Senate and to every woman working on the Senate side of the Capitol,' the Republican leader declaimed.

'Rep. Steed apologized for the remark in a letter made public yesterday,' the AP dispatch reported, 'but the letter stopped short of withdrawing the statement'.

In a letter addressed to Senator Carl Hayden, chairman of the Senate Appropriations Committee, Rep. Steed, who himself is chairman of the House Appropriations subcommittee, wrote:

'This will advise that I have carefully checked the current published list of Senate employees. All those on your list that I personally know are men and women of highest integrity and moral character. Any remarks I have made which reflected on the character and integrity of these employees is sincerely regretted'.

It will be noted that there is no real conflict between this apology and Steed's earlier charge. 'Technically,' as they like to say in cover-conscious Washington, Rep. Steed undoubtedly was wrong. No Senator would be so stupid as to keep call girls on his official payroll. But he might very well do so on the side. Certainly Steed's above-quoted confidences to the *Newsday* reporter were detailed and specific enough and his candid admission that he met the girls by 'stumbling into the wrong pew' in the course of his own partying adds credibility to the incident.

In the weeks between the day Steed dropped his offensive remark and the publication of his apology, there had been a lot of hush-hush conferences on the subject between leading members of the Senate and the House. Strong pressure was brought to bear on Steed to withdraw his charges. The strongest was applied when the

Senate voted 88-2 to send an appropriations bill already passed by the House back to conference committee.

Before the vote, an indignant Senator Hubert H. Humphrey had urged his colleagues to 'send this conference report whizzing back to the House' because of what he, too, termed 'an insult' to Senators and their women employees.

Faced with the prospect that the $163.2 million appropriation to pay annual operating costs for the House and Senate might be held up indefinitely because of the Senator's collective indignation, influential House members prevailed on Steed to accept the face-saving compromise formula of his letter of apology to Sen. Hayden.

The pompous stuffed shirts and glib-tongued nonentities who abound in the U.S. Senate can be very hardboiled in their financial transactions (at least a dozen of them are outright wheeler-dealers), but they get very touchy where their morals are concerned. For the Senator, in nine out of ten cases, has a wife that keeps a sharp eye on hubby; and in ten out of ten cases he has a lot of constituents who are against sin.

Moreover, at the time Rep. Steed made his sensational call-girl charge, the Senate's sensibilities had already been touched on the raw by the Elly Rometsch affair which will be detailed in the following chapter.

One thing is certain: regardless of who 'the Senator with the Polly Adler approach' might be, and how extensive his call girl operation may have been, there is no doubt whatsoever that the

'101st Senator', Bobby Baker, was very active in the field. To him, a house may not have been a home, but the places of entertainment he kept for the advise-and-consent set assuredly were maisons.

The New York Times, on March 22, 1964, published a dispatch from Phoenix, Arizona by Tom Wicker that began with this paragraph:

'"Call girls and Bobby Baker and motels" have become the symbols of Washington under President Johnson, Senator Barry Goldwater charged today...'

And *The New York Herald Tribune*, in an article on the 'Secret Rules of Inquiry' governing the Baker investigation, reported on November 10, 1963:

'It is an open Washington secret that when the "sex angle" was introduced into the Baker case by revelations that a beautiful German model had been sent home after reported (and denied) affairs with Washington politicians, it scared almost as many people in Washington as when the Russian missiles in Cuba pushed the U.S. to the brink of nuclear war'.

Indeed, the power elite in Washington was so scared that it resorted to extreme measures to safeguard the reputations of those high-placed politicos most directly involved in the Baker scandal—both sides of it.

Newsweek, in its issue of March 30, 1964, described the situation in these terms:

'"Party girls... political contributions... abortions..." Pennsylvania's Republican Sen. Hugh Scott was talking about some still undeveloped aspects of the Bobby Baker affair. He charged that investigators had been ordered to skip the juiciest part of the story.

"I've been doing so much skipping lately," he quoted one gumshoe for the Democratic-ruled Rules Committee, "I feel like a kid playing hopscotch."

'Scott insisted that the six Democrats had been reluctant in digging up Baker's past and were under outside pressure—obviously the White House'.

With such auguries in mind, one can easily gauge the value of a statement like the one the Rules Committee's special counsel, L. P. McLendon put out on May 19, 1964: 'Committee investigators found no more than a scintilla of evidence and even that from an unreliable witness, that Baker or any other officer or employee had used call girls or other immoral women for promoting their outside business and financial activities'.

Let's have a look at the 'scintilla'.

CHAPTER 21 - Adventures of Elly Rometsch

SHE is, without question, one of the most ravishing creatures on earth: a 27-year-old brunette with the face of a madonna and the figure of a Venus, plus real brains. Too bad Hollywood never discovered her. Bobby Baker did, though.

If her dark, probing eyes are disturbing, so is her past. For Elly hails from East Germany. When a beautiful young woman, who has grown up under a Communist regime, suddenly goes west, there is always grounds for watchfulness. When she goes west and, in no time at all, reaches Washington, D. C., there is grounds for suspicion. Or there ought to be.

Yet, when Elly Rometsch turned up in Washington in April 1961, and promptly proceeded to penetrate the inner circles of the power elite, hardly an eyebrow was raised. Not until the Profumo affair had sent reverberations around the world, did anybody in Washington feel that a siren just out of a Communist country might not offer the most suitable companionship for top U.S. government officials, senators, generals and admirals, all loaded with defense secrets.

It is not that Elly did not have legitimate business in Washington, at any rate ostensibly. As the wife of Luftwaffe Staff Sergeant, Rolf Rometsch, she evidently had to go along when her husband was assigned to the logistics division of the German Embassy's military staff.

When Rolf married Elly in 1958, her father Franz Fimmel, her mother and all the rest of her family, were still living in East Germany. Why and how the young girl alone had managed to reach the Federal Republic, nobody has bothered to explain.

Normally, all persons whose closest relatives are living in Communist-controlled countries are considered potential security risks in the West because of the possibility that they might be pressured into intelligence activities through threats against their families.

A minimum precaution, in such cases, is to keep such persons away from all military installations and personnel. Under the circumstances, it must seem extraordinary that Air Force Sergeant Rolf Rometsch was permitted to marry this girl fresh out of East Germany, while other members of her family were still living in that country. Subsequently, after Elly had hit Washington, her parents and brothers were evacuated to an estate at Oberberge, near Schwelm, in the Ruhr district, where they made a modest living as tenant farmers.

After Elly had acquired worldwide renown of a kind in Washington, and had been bundled back to Germany, post haste, she was investigated by the MAD, Germany's military counter-intelligence services, which cleared her, as well as her husband—then about to divorce his all too famous wife—of all suspicions of espionage. Quite possibly there never were any real grounds for such suspicion, but Elly's origins, her unusually strong sex appeal, her husband's position with the Bundeswehr, his assignment to the

German military mission in Washington, and finally the young woman's multiple contacts with high U.S. officials and military men should certainly have been sufficient grounds for caution.

Where and how Bobby Baker got hold of this heady import from the East, is one of Washington's best-kept secrets. Uncontested is the fact that Elly became a close friend of Baker's Girl Friday, Carole Tyler, and that she assiduously frequented the various places of relaxation and entertainment Bobby had set up for his influential friends in politics and business, in particular the Quorum Club.

The Quorum Club, located in the Carroll Arms Hotel in Washington, just across the street from the new Senate Office Building, was organized in 1961—the year Elly came to town—by Bobby Baker and some friends as a private luncheon club and watering place for Congressmen, Congressional staff aides and lobbyists. Baker was the club's secretary at the time he was catapulted into the limelight by his financial shenanigans.

The 'exclusive' nature of this cozy Capitol Hill snuggery is apparent from its high cost to members. There was an initiation fee of $200 (according to other reports, $100) and annual dues of $50. A highball there costs $1.20. Membership is limited to 200.

It is a discreet place, identified only by the bronze letter 'Q' on the door. As one enters, one is confronted, on the opposite wall, by a gilded wooden triangle with an eye carved on it. It is presumably meant to convey a silent warning.

The Club consists of a suite of three fairly large connecting rooms. One is a cocktail lounge with a small bar in black-tufted leather, with a brass rail. The most conspicuous feature of this room, apart from an impressive array of bottles, is a big golden donkey head on the wall next to the bar counter. It is not a trophy, even though Dick the Great, alias Richard M. Nixon, once used these charming premises as a campaign office.

In the room adjoining the cocktail lounge, one finds a long leather sofa, two low cocktail tables, stools with red leather tops and a player piano. On the wall hangs an inspiring picture: a life-size nude reclining on a *lit d'amour*.

The third room is equipped with dining tables for four, On the walls are pictures of pheasants and a medieval pikestaff. An investigator might think that it was a suitable emblem.

On a table in the bar, three telephones, two black and one red, are arrayed. A U.S. Government Telephone Directory lies next to the red phone in the foreground. Doubtless it was a very hot line.

Though strictly 'for members only', the Quorum Club, once the spotlight had been turned on it in the wake of the Baker scandal, was thrown open on October 31, 1963 for a guided inspection tour by the press. The purpose of this visit was, as a UPI dispatch from Washington put it, 'to get the word around that everything is strictly on the up and up'.

Was it really? The day before newsmen were shown around the harmless-looking Quorum Club by manager William

Pickford, *Newsday* published some piquant details about goings-on there:

'(Senator) Williams....paid a call on the young, pretty West German woman who used to be the sleep-in baby sitter at the home of Mrs. Ellen Rometsch, 27, the beauteous deported model who is now back in Germany. What she told Williams at her apartment isn't known, but she told reporters that she moved out of the Rometsch house because: "Elly was doing things for money and I can't see it."

'The baby sitter, Ingrid Luttert, 24, a good looking brunette, told newsmen: "I know a lot I wish I didn't know." Among the things she said she knew was that Mrs. Rometsch used to work at the swank Quorum Club, a lobbyist hangout that Baker had a financial interest in. According to Miss Luttert, Ellen Rometsch was a hostess with a wardrobe she could probably carry in her evening purse—a skin tight costume and black mesh stockings.

'Mrs. Rometsch, who recently was divorced by the West German Air Force sergeant who brought her to Washington in 1961, left her home at all hours of the day and night, Miss Luttert said...'

In the light of this testimony by a girl close to the scene of action, the following excerpt from *LBJ—A Political Biography* deserves attention:

'Elly Rometsch, bored with the ordinary life of an ordinary wife, found the Quorum Club and its "Bobby Baker Set" a wonderful way to spend the day. Too bad that her husband was not a member... he might have enjoyed it too. Certainly he would have enjoyed the parties at Carole Tyler's place, which his wife frequently attended with the rest of the Quorum Club crew, all at Bobby Gene Baker's expense.

'From her base at the Quorum Club, Elly went off to bed with the power elite of the capital city, driven by strong and exotic desires that eventually brought her to the attention of the FBI. Under ordinary circumstances, the FBI will overlook a girl's good times, but it frowns on sexy imports like Elly when they seem to "specialize" in top government and defense figures. Elly was deported back to Germany where her husband later divorced her for "conduct contrary to matrimonial rules."' (This entire paragraph appears in heavy print in the original —J.J.)

Time magazine had this to say on the subject (March 6, 1964):

'Ellen Rometsch, a party girl of peculiar tastes, was sent back home to West Germany last summer after the FBI began investigating her sex habits. "Elly" is remembered as a sometime hostess at the Quorum Club, a Washington watering spot for lobbyists and Congressmen that Baker helped organize. Though Baker, as well as other men about Washington, probably breathed a sigh of relief when Elly left, he apparently had no part in getting her deported. She was subsequently divorced by her West German army sergeant husband on grounds of "conduct contrary to matrimonial rules."'

Perhaps the most enlightening story about Elly's adventures in Washington appeared on October 18, 1964, in the mass circulation

German illustrated weekly *Der Stern* of Hamburg. A complete and textual quote is in order:

'She wouldn't even wrap a towel around herself, the way Christine Keeler did. Naked, she took bubbling champagne baths for the pleasure of topflight American military men who took turns going to bed and sharing top defense secrets with her.

'The young woman, about whom such scandalous reports are current in America, is today busy milking cows in Westphalia. Elly Rometsch (28) the bogey-woman of Republicans in their election campaign against President Johnson, now helps feed the cattle and cart beet around on her parents' farm near Hasslinghausen.

'A year ago, Elly Rometsch was deported as an "undesirable person" and a risk to American security from the USA to Germany. At the time she would not comment on why this happened. However, Elly is not going to take lying down the latest charges that have been made against her in America. This is why she granted an interview to *Der Stern*:

Q. - 'Mrs. Rometsch, if all that's being said about you in America is true, you must have led quite a life over there. I suppose you have seen the papers. There is, for instance, what the Republican Congressman H. R. Gross has been saying about you: that you once took a champagne bath, completely naked, before the eyes of high-ranking Defense Department officials. An admiral, a general and a NASA official are supposed to have been among the entranced spectators'.

A. - 'That's a lot of stuff and nonsense. I've never bathed in the nude in champagne. Just because I am far away from America, and unable to defend myself, these ugly things are being said about me. Believe me, there's not a word of truth in it'.

Q. - 'However, the charges made by Rep. Gross are very specific. He talks about a sort-of call girl ring operated by the former secretary of the President, Bobby Baker. He is supposed to be the one who organized the wild champagne parties. You do know him, don't you?'

A. - 'I have never belonged to a call girl ring either in Washington or elsewhere. And I was married at that time'.

Q. - 'Sure, you went to Washington with your husband who had been assigned to a military unit there. And he had to leave the States together with you when the initial charges were made against you. After that, you promptly divorced, didn't you?'

A. - 'That's correct. However, the grounds for divorce were not what you seem to assume., i.e. That I led a loose life in Washington'.

Q. - 'But, isn't it true that you were acquainted with Bobby Baker who is supposed to have made illicit transactions with prominent Democratic politicians?'

A. - 'I was friend with Miss Tyler, his secretary. It was through her that I met Mr. Baker. But in all those 2-and-a-half years in Washington, I saw him only six or seven times. And always at big parties, where nothing illicit happened'.

Q. - 'What about Rep. Gross' suggestion that you may have been spying on American rocket secrets?'

A. - 'That's nonsense. You know, I was reared in the Soviet zone and came to the West in 1955. That's all there is to those nonsensical suggestions that I was a spy'.

Q. - 'Maybe so. But Rep. Gross has some valid arguments as well. He thinks it strange that you didn't marry your husband, until after it had become known that he was assigned to the-German military mission in Washington'.

A. - 'But that isn't true either. Rolf and I got married in 1958. At that time he hadn't yet joined the army. Shortly after our marriage he joined the Bundeswehr and it was not until 1961 that he was sent to Washington. At that time we had been married for three years and had a son two years old. The allegation, therefore, that I married him for espionage purposes is pure nonsense. The FBI and military counter-intelligence have confirmed this'.

Q. - 'Then, how do you explain these recurrent charges against you?'

A. - 'I can only say again and again: all this is being played up for election purposes and I am just a helpless victim, unable to defend myself. All the charges against me have long since been refuted'.

Nobody will blame Elly Rometsch for trying to save her reputation. Nor her husband for behaving like a perfect gentleman and doing his best to clear his wife's name—just before he divorced her.

In a trans-Atlantic telephone interview with the New York Journal-American (October 29, 1963), Sgt. Rolf Rometsch thus described the relationship between his wife and Bobby Baker:

'They were friendly together. They would have a drink together. But there was nothing more between them... All these things that are being said about my wife are not true. My wife told me she did not have relations with anyone...'

One simple question: would any wife tell her trusting husband that she did have sexual relations with other men?

Indeed, Rolf Rometsch's reply to a query by the *Journal American* whether he believed his wife's denial, was very weak:

'I've to—I think so'.

Then came this admission: 'My chief at the (West German) embassy told me I had to go back to Germany because of my wife's behavior...'

Further on, the paper reported: '...She was considered a security risk, a spokesman at the West German Embassy in Washington said, because of her high living.

'It was because of this risk—not any security violations, that the--- pair were sent away...'

'But Elly had boasted of her connections, it seems, and intelligence agents believed her...'

And now we are getting to the core of the matter.

CHAPTER 22 - Guess Who?

THE way that the American press reported the Elly Rometsch affair, and the related 'moral' aspects of the Baker scandal, would be highly amusing but for one disturbing consideration: in this, as in the Oswald case, virtually the entire press shirked its duty to tell the truth without fear or favor. It yielded to strong official pressure, and kept its peace.

Yet, there are times when muckraking becomes a public duty.

Let the powers that be proclaim that to expose them is unpatriotic. Let their cohorts wave the flag in your face and shout themselves hoarse, 'Rally around the President, boys'. Let those who live and rule by fraud and deception call it treason: the truth shall prevail.

When the Rometsch couple were whisked out of the United States, on August 21, 1963, not a word about it appeared in the press. Yet Elly had been the darling of Washington society for two and a half years and must have been missed by some of her 'set'.

Some papers, then, undoubtedly knew that she had been deported. Some editors must have been wondering why. Why didn't they send out their reporters to find out?

The deep secrecy of the Rometsch ouster was maintained for weeks even after the Baker scandal broke. When her story was at last out in the open, an immediate hush was imposed from above. It was probably President Kennedy's most fateful mistake that he yielded to the pressure of the party regulars and used his great personal influence to persuade the press not to name the names of any of the 'top government officials' involved.

Everybody who is anybody in the Washington press corps was aware of the facts and the names and the dates and even some of the juicier details of Elly's extramarital ventures. And they all knew also that the list of unmentionable names was topped by that of the then Vice-President, Lyndon B. Johnson.

In their attempt to keep the public informed without contravening Kennedy's no-names-edict, some papers performed miracles of between-the-lines disclosures. But none, as far as I know, ever broke the ban on naming names.

Newsday has to be credited with a unique performance. It went right to the brink of indiscretion, teetering for a while on the verge before pulling back. In its issue of October 29, 1963, the paper ran an almost full-page story entitled 'Baker Scandal Quiz Opens Today', which began with these words:

'Already liberally spiced with sex, scandal and intrigue, the tantalizing case of Robert G. (Bobby) Baker comes under official scrutiny today. And what everyone wants to know is: Who is going to get caught?...'

Who, indeed? Attentive readers of *Newsday* were at least allowed a good guess. For, topping this article were five pictures of interested personalities with the following legends:

1. Rep. H. R. Gross—Demands Facts
2. Sen. Everett Jordan—Pledges Open Inquiry
3. Sen. John J. Williams—Lead-Off Witness

4. Robert G. Baker—On Senate Grill

5. Vice-President Johnson—Feels No Taint

In the text of the story underneath, *Newsday* explained about Rep. Gross 'demanding facts'. The Congressman, the day before, had asked this question, in a brief speech in the House:

'Among other things I want to know, Mr. Speaker, are the circumstances under which a young German woman was hastily deported from this country a few weeks ago following an FBI investigation.

'Members of the Congress and the public are entitled to know whether there was any element of security violation concerned in this speedy and hitherto unpublicized deportation'.

About the man in Picture No. 2, Sen. Benjamin Everett Jordan, Democrat of North Carolina, who as chairman of the Senate Rules Committee was to conduct the inquiry into Bobby Baker's extracurricular activities, *Newsday* had this to say:

'...reports are that some ranking Washington officials have their fingers crossed in hopes that their own names will not figure in the revelations. Because of these reports, an inordinately sensitive watch is being kept on the hearings the Senate Rules Committee is opening today.

'The witnesses will be heard behind closed doors before their testimony is opened to public scrutiny. The Senate traditionally is reluctant to embarrass any member and some observers fear that the closed testimony will offer suitable opportunity for a whitewash. Others feel there have been so many revelations in the

Baker case that public pressure will demand that all testimony be brought out. Committee Chairman Sen. B. Everett Jordan (D-N.C.) has promised that the investigation will be a "searching" one'. (How 'searching' it turned out to be, the reader of this book will appreciate.)

Why Sen. Williams' picture was shown, is also explained adequately: 'It was Williams' personal investigation of Baker's activities that led to Baker's resignation from his Senate post earlier this month and the hearings beginning today. The committee itself is making no independent investigation until it hears from Williams...'

Bobby Baker's inclusion in this portrait gallery was a matter of course and requires no further explanation.

But, what about the Picture No. 5? Johnson was not involved either as investigator, witness or committee member. Why was his portrait included? And why the statement that he 'feels no taint'?

The only mention of the Vice-President comes in this paragraph which is well worth pondering:

'Baker, now 36, was a protégé of Vice-President Johnson's, who got to know him when Johnson served as Senate majority leader. A report, from those who claim "inside information", is that the Justice Department started an investigation of Baker as a means of embarrassing Johnson and eliminating him from the Democratic ticket next year. To counteract this rumor, White House officials were free with "background" statements yesterday that "there is absolutely no question about dropping Johnson"'.

In other words: Robert Kennedy (of whom it is well-known that he had strenuously opposed Johnson's selection as his brother's running mate in 1960) wanted Johnson off the ticket in 1964 and thought the Baker case would automatically eliminate LBJ. But John F. Kennedy still hadn't made up his mind and so he kept up appearances. Three weeks later, Johnson was President and less than a year later Robert Kennedy was out of the Government and out of the running, too.

'Despite Jordan's promise,' *Newsday* went on to say, 'there are still questions as to precisely how "searching" the committee investigation will be. The latest revelation in the case, and one which could turn into the juiciest the government has seen in years, is that a West German party girl, wife of a West German sergeant who was stationed at the embassy here, "entertained" high-ranking members of the government at a motel partially owned by Baker in Ocean City, Md...'

How many 'high-ranking' members of the Kennedy Administration, one is inclined to ask, were Bobby Baker pals and frequent guests at his Carousel?

In a follow-up story, published the next day, *Newsday* wrote: 'While rumors about Baker and his relationship with a frisky frau, who was bounced from the United States allegedly for her hanky-panky with top government officials, buzzed from the Potomac to the Ruhr?

Again, how many 'top government officials' are there? There is not much room at the top.

An UPI dispatch from Washington, dated October 28, 1963, started with this paragraph: 'A Senate investigator is expected to unfold at a closed hearing tomorrow a Profumo-like story of a German beauty's relations with prominent Washington figures...'

Why 'Profumo-like'? Was that a barb aimed at Defense Secretary McNamara? Or, did the case seem 'Profumo-like', because some other big wheel with access to defense secrets was involved?

The dispatch went on: '...Williams would not discuss the case with reporters, but one published report said that the woman, who has returned to Germany, had friends both in Congress and the Kennedy administration...

'She had attracted the attention of the FBI because of the expensive clothes she wore and the high standard of living she and her husband maintained in the country club section of nearby Arlington, Va. The woman also had a habit of dropping the names of prominent persons, according to reports.

'*The Washington Post,* which reported the woman's measurements as 35-25-34, said that the case involved "a spicy tale of political intrigue and high-level bedroom antics." The newspaper added, 'The importantly placed politicos with whom she is alleged to have cavorted in the more than two years she partied here were for the most part unaware she had a husband—or, for that matter, a small child—back at the chic Arlington home which investigators said hardly could have been maintained on the pay of a German army enlisted man'.

The New York Journal-American also smelled Profumistic odors. In its issue of October 23, 1963, the paper reported: 'A West German party girl was thrown out of Washington because of her Congressional capers, the Bonn Government confirmed today... The action came after the FBI notified Bonn of the girl's activities, which paralleled the Profumo-Keeler affair in London...'

In order to qualify as a 'Profumo-type' affair, or one that 'parallels the Profumo-Keeler affair,' there had to be these prerequisites:

    a) A Cabinet member with access to top defense secrets;

    b) He had to have an intimate relationship with a siren who also happened to be a security risk; and

    c) He had to be on friendly terms with the purveyor of the girl's charms (no offense intended to the memory of the late Dr. Ward).

Once more: how many men on the Kennedy team would fill that bill on all points?

In *The New York Times* of November 1, 1963, James Reston wrote:

'There is a mess in Washington again, and very little evidence that either the White House or the Congress is going to do very much to clean it up...'

After discussing first the case of Navy Secretary Korth (See Chapter 25), Mr. Reston turned to the Bobby Baker case: '...this city has been full of ugly rumors about illicit relations between

Baker's girl friends and prominent Senators and officials in the Administration.

'Every vigilant newspaper office in Washington has a list of names of those implicated with Baker and his lobbying friends and his girls. And the gossip feeds on itself to such an extent that it has already poisoned the atmosphere of the whole Government...'

The most outspoken comment about the Elly Rometsch side of the Baker affair appeared in the December 1963 issue of the German satirical monthly *Pardon*. It carried a composite photo that shows President Kennedy and Vice-President Johnson engaged in a conversation, not face to face, but back to back.

Says Johnson: 'I guess I better make another trip to Germany'.

Says Kennedy: 'To see whom—Erhard or Frau Rometsch?'

When that issue of the magazine was 'put to bed', Lyndon B, Johnson was still Vice-President. When it appeared on the newsstands, he was President of the United States.

CHAPTER 23 - The Short, Sweet Life of Carole Tyler

NEXT to Bobby himself, nobody knew more about Baker's intricate affairs than his pretty 'Girl Friday', Nancy Carole Tyler, a sultry brunette.

Bright and well-educated, while also endowed with a lithe, shapely figure and comely features, Miss Tyler was to Bobby Baker a confidante and a secretary, as well as a good friend. Most importantly, however, she served him, as Elly Rometsch did, as a high-class courtesan whose job it was to help Bobby win lucrative contracts and to keep his influential political sponsors happy.

The most precise testimony on this score has come from Rolf Rometsch as he sought to defend his wife's honor by explaining that what she was supposed to have been doing was actually done by Carole Tyler. In the above-quoted telephone interview with *The New York Journal American* (October 29, 1963), Sgt. Rometsch said:

'Elly told me she had no relations with anyone... She said this "society girl" had relations with high officials,' he continued, referring to an unnamed girl his wife knew in Washington. 'Elly had nothing to do with the relations this girl had'.

The reference is clearly to Miss Tyler and besides, the *Journal American*, a few paragraphs later, states: 'Apparently she [Elly Rometsch, as quoted by her husband] meant Mr. Baker's secretary, Carole Tyler'.

Whether Carole was also Bobby's own mistress, or only his decoy is a matter of scant importance. That she went nightclubbing with him is certain. *Newsday* reported on November 20, 1963:

'Mrs. Novak said last night the Senate investigators also questioned her about Baker's relationship with Carol Tyler, Baker's former secretary who has lived in a Washington town house owned by the former Senate official. In the interview, Mrs. Novak said she had seen Baker and Miss Tyler together in nightclubs and had been shocked. Baker is married and the father of five children'.

Not much is known about Carole's origins and antecedents. She was born in 1939 at Lenoir City, Tennessee, the daughter of Mr. and Mrs. Dave C. Tyler.

At the age of 18, she won a regional beauty contest and became 'Miss Loudon County, 1957'. Ever since, the papers referred to her as a 'former beauty queen', but that was hardly her outstanding achievement. Little notice was taken in the press, by contrast, of the fact that the attractive, talented young girl had also been a student at the University of Tennessee.

In 1960, if not earlier, she turned up in Washington and became friendly with Bobby Baker. The next year, he installed her in a sumptuous town house, conveniently located near the Capitol, which he had acquired for $28,800. The history of this luxurious snuggery, built in a modernistic style but bathed in a byzantine atmosphere is as revealing as any other part of the Bobby Baker 'epic'.

The house consists of four bedrooms (which of itself seems odd as the ostensible occupants were to be two unmarried young ladies), equipped with lavender wall-to-wall carpeting and French wallpaper, and a family room paneled in Philippine mahogany. The $6,615 furnishings, while Carole Tyler lived there, included $1,120 in draperies and a $250 dishwasher.

As it was part of a cooperative housing project constructed with FHA funds, this townhouse was subject to owner-occupancy regulations. In order to get around this stipulation which required that the house should be occupied by the owner himself, or by a member of his family, Baker, in his purchase application, stated falsely that the occupant would be his 'cousin, N. C. Tyler'.

After Miss Tyler had moved into the townhouse, early in 1962, she was joined there by a friend, Mary Alice Martin, who happened to be a secretary in Sen. George A. Smathers' office. A curious arrangement, to say the least, for Bobby's townhouse was soon to acquire a very special reputation. For more than a year and a half Washington buzzed with rumors about the sophisticated parties at the town house which were attended by several other young beauties besides the ostensible occupants of the house and the inevitable Elly Rometsch. On the male side, high government officials with defense contracts on their hands, influential Congressmen and lobbyists predominated among the invited guests.

After the Baker scandal had blossomed into full bloom, C. William Taylor, president of River Park Mutual Homes, the cooperative where the townhouse is located, wrote to Baker on November 14, 1963, reminding him of the owner-occupancy stipulation and asking him to sell the townhouse.

Now, according to *Newsday* (January 25, 1964) this happened:

'Baker called him November 21, [the day before the Kennedy assassination—J.J.], Taylor said, apparently believing Taylor's letter had been inspired by newspaper stories suggesting lurid parties in the townhouse. On the phone, Taylor said, Baker launched a defense of the girls and the townhouse. Taylor had made a memorandum of the telephone conversation and the committee placed it in the record over Taylor's objection'.

From this memorandum, the paper cited the following:

'Baker denied there had been any immoral activity in the house "and went on to advise that one of the three girls had been examined by a gynecologist and been pronounced a virgin."'

It will be noted, first, that only two girls, N. C. Tyler and Mary Alice Martin, were supposed to be living in the place. Where did the third girl come from? The reference cannot be to Elly Rometsch who was living with her husband at the time.

'There is something in there that might do harm to an innocent young lady,' *Newsday* quoted Taylor as saying in reference to the line in the memo about only one of the girls being examined. Taylor said he did not know when the examination took place or who the gynecologist was.

Whether or not Carole Tyler is supposed to have been the officially-approved virgin, the way she responded to the Rules

Committee's probing in the matter was certainly not that of an innocent young lady defending her honor.

One day apart, Carole Tyler and her boss appeared before the investigating Committee late in February 1964, to stage identical shows of constitutionally permitted non-cooperation. Bobby Baker, who was questioned repeatedly (on February 19 and 25), not only refused to answer any of the more than 100 questions asked of him, but he also declined to turn over to the committee the records they had requested by subpoena.

Flanked by his celebrated lawyer, Edward Bennett Williams, Baker imperturbably invoked the protection of the First, Fourth, Fifth and Sixth Amendments to the Constitution and added: 'I specifically invoke the privilege against self-incrimination'.

He explained his refusal to turn over his records by saying:

'I am presently being investigated by... the Federal Bureau of Investigation and the Internal Revenue Service. To force production of these records (here) would be to do indirectly for these agencies what they cannot lawfully do directly'.

Baker's admission in this context that he was also being investigated by the FBI is significant. Though he was a great tightrope artist in walking the hairline of legality, he undoubtedly overstepped the limits here and there.

While the large majority of the questions vainly asked of him by the committee dealt with his tangled business affairs, some of those he also faced without blinking in stony silence also implicitly revealed a good deal about his wheeling and dealing in sex.

Had he provided entertainment facilities for persons doing business with the Government, Baker was asked, 'and by entertainment facilities I refer to personnel, including party girls?'

Did he 'recall or wish to state how many people you have referred to a Puerto Rican doctor for the performance of abortions?'

It is almost one hundred per cent certain that the investigators in each and all of the queries they put before Baker in a vain attempt to elicit some kind of positive response knew exactly that the only truthful answer would be an unqualified 'yes'.

In the case of the Puerto Rican doctor, for instance, Don Reynolds had already disclosed to the committee that he once called Baker on behalf of a client who, in turn, knew a friend interested in an abortion. Reynolds testified that Baker supplied him with a Capitol telephone number which he passed along to his client.

Perhaps the most 'loaded' question—one loaded with political dynamite—was this:

'Did you have any association with a man now serving a prison sentence for white slavery?'

In the absence of a reply from Baker, it may be of interest to quote what *LBJ—A Political Biography* has to say on this score:

'As the story went, a convicted procurer named Fabianich who had received a one-year sentence for operating a ring of teenage call girls (one was only 16 years old) was suddenly pulled out of his cell just blocks from the Capitol for an interview with some high-level "investigators", who quizzed him about his connections with the Capitol Hill activities being uncovered by the Senate committee. The results of this "exam" were not revealed, but Fabianich must have failed it, because he shortly found himself being bundled up for shipment to the Federal pen at Leavenworth, Kansas—an unprecedented move in the case of a one-year sentence, but useful for placing him far away from the Senate investigation'.

When Carole Tyler, on February 26, 1964, succeeded her boss on the witness stand, the committee at least got an eyeful—although their ears only filled with silence. Dressed in a striking two-piece white suit and bright blue coat, and wearing long black gloves, Carole demonstrated by her appearance alone that unlike Baker, who had asked that television cameras be removed from the hearing room, she didn't mind at all being the focus of nationwide ogling. She was wearing heavy TV-make-up, her doe eyes were agleam with mischievous pleasure, her chestnut hair glowed in an upswept coiffure and her wide mouth was full of promise—to say nothing.

Called to the stand, Carole swore to tell the truth, the whole truth and nothing but the truth, so help her God, gave her full name—and clammed up. She wouldn't even give her present address, which was no longer that of the by now famous townhouse.

In reply to the more than 20 questions the committee asked her, she recited as many times, in a monotonous, slightly pouting voice what her lawyer, Myron G. Ehrich, had put down for her on a light blue index card which she gingerly held between the thumb and index-finger of her kid-gloved hands:

'I decline to answer on the ground that this investigation is unrelated to any legislative purpose and is an invalid invasion of my right of privacy; and I decline to answer on the further ground that my answer might tend to incriminate me'.

At one point in the proceedings, the committee counsel, 73-year-old Maj. L. P. McLendon, became so irritated by this long and repetitious recital that he suggested she should shorten her routine to saying: 'My answer is the same as before'. But her lawyer would have none of that shortcut. 'I think it would be more effective if she read it in full every time'. And so they both stood firmly on her constitutional right to invoke the Protective Amendments which she chanted like a litany.

Carole was a little more eloquent in a statement she distributed to the press which read in part:

'I resent the worldwide intimations...that I have indulged in improper conduct, to say the least,' and denied any 'legal or moral wrongdoing'.

Nobody would want to besmirch the reputation of a very pleasant young lady, especially one who has since died under tragic circumstances, but the search for the truth in the Baker case nevertheless demands a corrective here.

According to an AP dispatch from Washington, dated December 4, 1964, 'A Senate investigator testified today that a

Puerto Rico mortgage banker had told him of "several days of partying" in New Orleans last year with Robert G. Baker and two beautiful women companions, one of them a controversial West German beauty. The banker, Paul Aguirre of San Juan, invoked the Fifth Amendment to the Constitution and refused to answer any questions about his associations with Mr. Baker and the women— Mr. Baker's Capitol secretary, Nancy Carole Tyler and Mrs. Ellen Rometsch of West Germany...

'Unable to get answers from Mr. Aguirre about his business and social dealings with Mr. Baker, the Senate Rules Committee called to its witness stand Samuel J. Scott, a staff investigator who said he had questioned Mr. Aguirre in Puerto Rico last February 26.

'Mr. Scott said Mr. Aguirre had answered all of his questions fully at that time, but told him he would deny in any public hearing that he was involved in partying.

'"My wife is expecting a denial and she'll get it," he quoted Mr. Aguirre as having said...'

Aguirre's caution is understandable. What is the wrath of a frustrated Senate committee compared to the fury of a woman scorned? At the same time, however, this admission by the Puerto Rican banker shows that his "partying" in New Orleans was not as innocent as this currently popular euphemism would seem to suggest.

The dispatch went on to say: 'Mr. Aguirre refused to answer 66 questions in all. One was whether he had lent $60,000 to Mr. Baker.

'Senator John Sherman Cooper, Republican of Kentucky, reading from a report of the February investigation, asked Mr. Aguirre:

'"Isn't it true you told the investigator you went to New Orleans in May, 1963 to look at a trailer site, that you met Robert G. Baker there and that Baker brought two women with him?"

"The women were then identified by Sen. Cooper as Miss Tyler and Mrs. Rometsch.

'Mr. Aguirre declined to answer any of the questions on the advice of his attorney, Myron G. Ehrlich.

'"You're asking him about meeting women in New Orleans," Mr. Ehrlich said. "For a married man, meeting women in New Orleans could tend to incriminate himself. He'd better have a good explanation when he gets home."'

Sen. Cooper also asked whether the party had not moved on to Houston after leaving New Orleans.

The set-up, then, is perfectly clear. Bobby Baker, in the spring of 1963, was in need of a $60,000 loan. He was always in need of ready cash at short notice because he was constantly juggling tens of thousands of dollars in a maze of interlocking business ventures.

Here was this affluent Puerto Rican banker, one of Baker's many contacts on that island. Aguirre liked the company of attractive young women and he could lay the cash on the line. So this meeting in New Orleans, pleasure capital of the South, was arranged. Aguirre brought the money and Baker brought the women. In several days of 'partying', the deal was concluded. Then the group adjourned to new hunting grounds, in Texas.

This incident alone, which is on record in the Senate files, disposes of all the virtuous denials by Carole Tyler and Elly Rometsch and makes the roles these beautiful young women played in the Baker scheme of things quite clear.

Not only was Carole Tyler always ready and willing to perform as a hostess for Baker whenever a bit of partying was needed to swing a business deal or to make a love-starved politico happy, but she also had intimate knowledge of his intricate financial affairs. She was a real confidante to him and he did not hesitate to let her in on his most secretive and even his shadiest deals.

Among other evidence to that effect, there is the fact that Ralph Hill, when he realized that he was being pushed to the wall by his double-crossing business friend, Bobby Baker, tried to get Carole Tyler to intercede in his behalf. Hill's testimony on this matter, before the Rules Committee, was reported by *The Christian Science Monitor* (January 15, 1964) in these terms:

'Accompanied by a witness, Mr. Hill testified that he went to the three-story, four-bedroom townhouse owned but never occupied by Mr. Baker, which was used by Miss Tyler, a one-time Tennessee beauty queen, and another woman, her companion, a former secretary on the staff of Senator Smathers...

'Mr. Hill said he understood Miss Tyler had "tremendous" influence over Mr. Baker. He said that he told her on his visit of his plan to sue.

'"Miss Tyler said this would bring out everything about Bobby Baker," Mr. Hill testified. "She asked me to give her a week's notice." He said there were several people in the house at the time, including Scott I. Peek, former administrative assistant to Senator Smathers, who brought Miss Tyler's roommate into the house while he called.

'The testimony regarding Miss Tyler was brought out by Sen. Hugh Scott (R) of Pennsylvania. The Senate Rules Committee which is conducting the hearings, reportedly decided, at a closed door meeting December 12, not to go into the role of after-office parties and unusual relationships in its investigation, unless they were relevant to the inquiry.

'Some consider Mr. Baker's connection with high Democratic officials as relevant to the inquiry, however, and Republicans are not likely to let it drop...'

One of the 'unusual relationships' the Committee has most steadfastly refused to explore (Chairman Jordan: 'We're not investigating Senators') concerned the association between Bobby Baker and Sen. George A. Smathers of Florida, on at least three different levels.

In the first place, Baker was associated with Sen. Smathers in two Florida land ventures from which the former realized about $4,000 in both 1961 and 1962, as Milton H. Haupt, a former

Internal Revenue expert who prepared Baker's income tax returns, testified before the Rules Committee on January 13, 1964. According to Haupt, Baker owned one-fifth of the investment in these land ventures held by Senator Smathers.

Secondly, Sen. Smathers' administrative assistant, Scott I. Peek, was also a business associate of Bobby Baker's in several ventures.

And thirdly, Sen. Smathers' secretary, Mary Alice Martin, lived in Bobby Baker's townhouse, together with Carole Tyler, as has been noted before. In the eyes of the committee, apparently, all this was just another string of coincidences, not worth considering.

Obviously, then, Carole Tyler was a woman with a thousand secrets, many of which would have been a source of grave concern to people in high places. It is in the light of this incontrovertible fact that one has to view the ostensible "accident" that was to close her lips forever, a year after her silent performance before the Rules Committee.

Ostensibly, this is what happened: Carole Tyler, having moved out of the townhouse (which Baker sold in March 1964 to a Washington newspaperman) took up residence at the Carousel Motel, also owned by her boss. She kept out of the public eye as much as she could.

In the first week of May, 1965, a man named Robert H. Davis, a 13-year-old pilot for a West Virginia coal company, arrived at the motel where he stayed for several days. Davis, a resident of

Huntington, W.Va., had flown to Ocean City, Md. in his own plane, a single-engine red and white Waco biplane.

No sooner had Davis met Miss Tyler at the hotel than he invited her for a sightseeing trip in his plane over Ocean City airport and surroundings. Carole accepted and on May 9 they took off together. Carole was riding in the front and Davis in the back of the dual control plane.

All of a sudden and for no visible reason whatsoever—the flying weather couldn't have been finer—the plane plunged into the sea, about 1,000 feet offshore. Rescue boats reaching the scene shortly after the crash could find no signs of survivors. The Coast Guard eventually located the wreckage in murky water about 23 feet deep. Divers recovered the bodies of Tyler and Davis.

Officials of the Civil Aeronautics Board's Bureau of Safety promptly arrived on the scene to direct the salvaging of the plane. They hired a commercial barge with a crane to bring the Waco to the surface rather than to drag it ashore with a winch, because, as a CAB official indicated, the plane might be damaged by a sand bar between the spot where it was found and the beach. This indicates that the CAB thought it was a peculiar accident and wanted to make sure that its cause could be determined.

Judging by the circumstances, it seems reasonably certain that this crash was no accident at all, but a subtly arranged maneuver designed to close forever the lips of an extremely knowledgeable and therefore dangerous witness in the Baker case.

But what of Davis? Does this mean he was a suicide pilot?

Even dismissing this hypothesis as unlikely, two possible explanations come to mind.

For one thing, the plane could have been sabotaged by third persons, unbeknownst to Davis. The precautions taken by the CAB to keep the wreckage as intact as possible suggest that this possibility was not discarded *a priori* by investigators.

On the other hand, Davis, an experienced pilot, may have been hired to dump the girl into the sea and make it look like an accident. This theory is borne out by the fact that Davis, according to the *New York World Telegram and Sun* of May 10, 1965, was stunt-flying when the plane fell into the sea. To engage in stunt-flying seems hardly normal for a professional pilot who takes a girl he has just met out on a sightseeing trip. Women enjoy that sort of thing from the ground, not while riding in the passenger seat.

If this assumption is correct, then evidently something went wrong. Perhaps there was a struggle between Tyler and Davis with the result that the plane went irretrievably out of control and crashed, killing them both.

Who will ever know for sure what happened in the sky over Bobby's Carousel that day?

One thing is certain, though. If it was an accident, it came in as handy as the death, on November 22, 1963, of a President who knew too much about the Baker case and who was determined to clean out the Augean stables in Washington.

CHAPTER 24 - Sing No More, Don Reynolds!

'Is Don Reynolds there?'

The voice at the other end of the wire sounded impatient and urgent. The call went from office to office, from number to number in Washington. It was only hours since the reins of government had passed from the dead hands of John F. Kennedy into the strong, nervous ones of Lyndon B. Johnson.

Don Reynolds was finally located. The caller identified himself as George Reedy, long-time administrative assistant to Lyndon B. Johnson. He had talked to Don Reynolds before, but this time it was on behalf of President Johnson and therefore the warning he had to convey was couched in stronger and more authoritative terms: it would be better for Reynolds if he were to 'refrain from making any more statements' about the Baker case.

Reynolds understood, but he couldn't help himself. He was trapped by his earlier confessions made to Senator John J. Williams who had interviewed him at length on a number of occasions after the scandal broke. Williams already knew too much. The whole pattern was beginning to unfold. The implacable Senator kept probing and Reynolds, willy-nilly, continued to 'sing'. It was too late to shut him up *ex officio*.

What he had told Williams so far was peanuts compared to what was to come: a detailed story of how the man who had just become President of the United States had not only accepted but demanded kickbacks from a professional lobbyist while exercising the high functions of Senate Majority leader and Vice-President.

In his sworn testimony, which the Senate Rules Committee released on January 21, 1964, Reynolds declared that he had:

a) given to Lyndon B. Johnson a $580 stereophonic record player in 1959 at the request of Bobby Baker; and

b) had purchased $1,208 worth of advertising time—of no commercial value to him—on television station KTBC in Austin, which was owned by the LBJ Company. This was in 1961, after Johnson had become Vice-President.

Both these transactions were connected with the 'privilege' granted to Don B. Reynolds Associates, Inc., of writing $200,000 in insurance on Mr. Johnson's life over a period of several years, beginning in 1957. The applicant, Reynolds testified, was Lady Bird and the beneficiary was the LBJ Company.

What made the 'privilege' come Don Reynolds' way? Very simple: he had a vice-president named Robert G. Baker, who, during their association earned about $15,000 from this partnership.

Reynolds testified that his helpful partner had steered him to a number of interesting insurance prospects, including besides LBJ, the then Ambassador to Ireland Matthew McCloskey (see below).

As usual, Bobby Baker was working both sides of the street. He got for Don Reynolds, and also by the same token for himself, lucrative and prestige-bringing insurance contracts like the one he was allowed to write on the life of LBJ, then turned around and prodded his partner to return part of the profits in the form of gifts and kickbacks to the insured.

But Baker was not the only man putting the bite on the insurance agent. According to Reynolds' testimony, he was 'pressured' by Walter Jenkins, a long-time Johnson aide and treasurer of the LBJ Company, to buy the $1,200 worth of advertising on the television station of the Johnson family.

At an 'impromptu' news conference at the White House, on January 23rd, 1964, President Johnson acknowledged that he had accepted the gift of a $585 stereo set in 1959, but claimed that it had come not from Reynolds but from Bobby Baker with whom he had frequently exchanged gifts in the past.

'Baker expected nothing in return just as I expected nothing from gifts I gave him,' Johnson added.

If you believe that, you might as well believe that Bobby never expected anything from anybody for little presents or favors rendered and that the two-million-dollar fortune he amassed in a few years just fell into his lap like manna from heaven. And much the same goes for the man who, to quote Miller again, 'arrived in Washington with one suit' to become the richest President in the history of the United States.

The day before, Senator Williams, in a statement to the press, had declared that he saw no difference between public officials accepting a stereo player, a mink or vicuna coat, a deep freeze or an Oriental rug, thus covering about the whole range of the bipartisan mess in Washington since the last war.

"Whenever anyone gives a public official an article of such value", the Senator asserted, "he is expecting something in return". Which is, after all, no more than an expression of common sense.

"Any public official who accepts such gifts is not so naïve as to be unable to recognize that point," Sen. Williams added. No, Johnson was never naïve, you can depend on that.

As for the President's assertion that the stereo set had been a gift from Baker, rather than from Reynolds, that statement is belied by the details of the transaction which the latter has been able to put into the record.

According to Reynolds' sworn testimony, the incident of the phonograph occurred when he was drawing up a renewal on the life insurance policies written by him in favor of Lady Bird and her children (the LBJ Company). He said Baker told him Senator Johnson 'would like to have a stereo set' and asked what kind Reynolds could obtain at the best rate. He then gave Baker a Magnavox catalog which Bobby took out 'for Mrs. Johnson to make a selection'.

This done, Reynolds ordered the set from a Fort Wayne, Ind., manufacturer, had it shipped by air to the Johnson home and installed there at a cost of $42.50. He even had it serviced there. All of which just makes short shrift of the presidential denial.

Details of how a TV mechanic named Don Mulgannon serviced the famous stereo at the Johnson home were given by Dom Bonafede of *The New York Herald Tribune* in a dispatch from Washington, dated February 6, 1964: 'Don Mulgannon recalled: "I went back there (to the former Johnson home) six or seven times about the set, whether it was working properly or not. They wanted other speakers throughout the house and we put them in, but it was a brand new set with new diagrams and they felt it didn't sound good enough."...It was Mr. Reynolds who paid the repair bills, reported Mr. Mulgannon. The repair bills, it was learned, are in the possession of the Senate Rules Committee...'

In the matter of the TV station kickback, Johnson gave preference to an indirect denial, and in the process got himself into even deeper water. He left it to his faithful Texan aide, Walter Jenkins, to refute Reynolds' allegations in a manner so conspicuously untruthful that a whole string of complications ensued.

On December 11, 1963—i.e. at a time when Reynolds had already testified on the matter behind closed doors, but no inkling of it had yet become public—the Rules Committee's chief counsel, Mr. McLendon and its chief investigator, W. Ellis Meehan, met with Walter Jenkins at the Executive Office Building next door to the White House. Shortly before, Jenkins had been promoted from the comparatively modest position as business manager of the LBJ Company to the post of chief administrative assistant to the President.

At the end of this interview, Jenkins signed a sworn statement that he had read the memorandum drawn up by the investigators and that the statements therein were true to the best of his knowledge and belief.

The point that Jenkins signed this affidavit cannot be overemphasized because the question as to who perjured himself in the case, Reynolds or Jenkins, was to become one of the cardinal issues of the Baker affair—one that has remained unresolved to this day, at any rate ostensibly.

For, Jenkins' sworn statements made on this occasion are absolutely irreconcilable with the testimony Reynolds gave to the Committee and was to give again, under oath, at another session on January 9, 1964. He was questioned once more by the Committee on January 17.

Jenkins denied all of Reynolds' allegations, saying specifically that he did not have 'any knowledge of any arrangements by which Reynolds purchased advertising time on the TV station'. He also declared he was positive he had never heard from any source 'that there was a business connection between Robert G. Baker and Don Reynolds in the insurance agency operated by Mr. Reynolds or that Mr. Reynolds had any connection whatever with the record player gift'.

There was, thus, a clear conflict of testimony between Jenkins and Reynolds and also a clear basis for perjury proceedings. The Justice Department, however, adopted a wait-and-see attitude, possibly because a stronger case could be made against either man if Jenkins were called upon to repeat his denial in sworn testimony before the Committee itself.

From this point on, the question as to whether or not the investigating committee really wanted to get to the bottom of the matter revolved around the issue of whether or not Jenkins should be called to testify. While the Republicans pressed for it, inside the committee as in public pronouncements, the Democrats were reluctant. Once more, evidently, they had that Pandora box feeling and preferred to keep the lid on at any price. And so the Committee, splitting along party lines voted 6:3 on April 3rd, not to call Jenkins at this time.

In the meantime, an unprecedented smear campaign against the embarrassing star witness, Don Reynolds, had got under way, clearly with the blessing of the White House. On February 5 and 6, columnist Drew Pearson, who has repeatedly performed as an LBJ hatchet-man, viciously attacked Reynolds as an unreliable witness, basing his charges on the insurance man's alleged record in the armed services.

While it was certainly Pearson's right to criticize a witness whose general conduct is certainly not above reproach, the columnist went far beyond normal limits by attaching to copies of his syndicated column a confidential note to editors containing what was represented as an Air Force memo, taken from closed files of the Defense Department. The memo was addressed to Air Force Secretary Eugene M. Zuckert and was signed by Benjamin W. Fridge, Special Assistant to the Secretary of the Air Force for Manpower and Reserve Forces.

The memo said in part: 'I feel you should be aware of some of the circumstances surrounding the military service of former Maj.

Don B. Reynolds, who testified before the Senate Rules Committee in the Bobby Baker case the day before yesterday'.

What the memo itself had to say about Reynolds has not been made public but can be gathered in substance from the two columns written by Drew Pearson on the subject. In them, the columnist alleged that Reynolds, while serving as an Air Force officer and consular official in Germany, between 1946 and 1953, had used his post to force German women seeking visas to have sexual intercourse with him and had engaged in black market sales with Russian military personnel. Pearson also contended that Reynolds had often brought charges of sexual perversion and communism against personal enemies.

On February 10, Sen. Hugh Scott announced that he would ask J. Edgar Hoover, head of the FBI, to look into the leak of confidential information from 'raw FBI files' that were used to damage Reynolds' credibility as a witness. In a telephone interview with the Associated Press, Sen. Scott said:

'The release of raw FBI files could only have occurred at the instance of some person or persons higher than the FBI in government.

'I am in agreement with the story in *The New York Times* that information derogatory to Reynolds was offered to at least three newspapers by White House aides'.

This reference was to a dispatch by Cabell Phillips, published in *The New York Times* of February 8. In it, Mr. Phillips stated that two publications had been approached by the White House staff in an effort to have them 'alter or suppress articles based on the testimony of insurance man D. B. Reynolds,' and that, in another instance, a White House aide had 'volunteered to a third publication' that the Reynolds testimony was not to be believed.

If Sen. Scott in his statement could say that this leak from raw FBI files could only have been ordered by 'some person' higher than the FBI in government, the implication is clear, for only the President can tell the FBI what to do or not to do. Thus the origins of the smear campaign against Reynolds can be traced to Lyndon B. Johnson directly. The whole thing is typical of the way LBJ has operated all along to hide his own wrongdoings and shield his subordinates, lest they turn against him some day.

Unfortunately for Jenkins, his opponent Reynolds was not only able to document his charges with bills and canceled checks, but he also produced corroborative testimony of the highest importance. For, unable to make any rational use of the advertising time he had been induced to buy on the Johnson TV station, Reynolds ceded his rights to a business friend, Mr. Albert G. Young, also of Silver Springs, Md. Young is president of the Mid-Atlantic Stainless Steel Co., and he did use the advertising time on station KTBC at Reynolds expense, as both he himself and Reynolds have testified. Young turned over to the Committee ten letters which supported Reynolds' story and, by the same token, put Jenkins on the spot.

Nevertheless, the Senate Rules Committee persisted in its refusal to call Jenkins as a witness, evidently because the

Democratic majority had received word from 'above' that such a contingency should be avoided at all cost. President Johnson was determined to hold his protective hand over his chief administrative assistant, even though this meant, in effect, interfering with the normal course of justice. For such a clear-cut conflict in sworn testimony as existed between Jenkins and Reynolds in the matter would normally have warranted the opening of perjury proceedings against one or the other.

As bad luck (for LBJ) would have it, Jenkins, a few months later, got himself into a mess that almost defies description. The basic facts are well-known and the sordid details are not relevant to the scope of the present book. What matters is that Jenkins was forced to resign on October 14, 1964, after he had been arrested, a week earlier, on a morals charge. Further investigation disclosed that this long-time trusted aide of Lyndon B. Johnson had a police record as a sexual deviant dating back to January, 1959.

So much for that particular pillar of the Great Society and keystone of Lyndon B. Johnson's inner Texas set.

Jenkins' forced resignation opened the door for new Republican demands that he be subpoenaed to testify before the Rules Committee. The latter now went through the motions of complying with that demand while still sticking, in reality, to its set purpose to avoid at all cost a Jenkins-Reynolds confrontation that might have resulted in a perjury trial.

After his resignation, Jenkins vanished into a hospital where he was supposedly treated for high blood pressure and a nervous breakdown. When the Committee's subpoena was served on him, he responded to it by sending his lawyer, Peyton Ford, instead, and the psychiatrist who had been treating him, Dr. Leon Yochelson, to explain on February 4, 1965, that a personal appearance would endanger his health 'and possibly his life'.

On February 15, *Newsweek* predicted, 'Chances are that Walter Jenkins will never appear in person before the senators investigating dealings of the former White House aide Bobby Baker'.

'Never' is a big word that ought to be used sparingly. The Bobby Baker case is likely to smolder for a long time to come. It might outlive Lyndon B. Johnson, or at least President Johnson. But Jenkins may still be forced to come clean under oath. If he still happens to be around by that time, that is.

Reynolds' testimony also brought to light the mutually fruitful relationship between Bobby Baker and Mr. Matthew H. McCloskey, long-time Democratic fund raiser and for eight years treasurer of the Democratic National Committee.

McCloskey, considered the champion fundraiser of the Democrats—among other things, he is credited with having conceived the $100-a-plate political dinner—is, in private life, a Philadelphia building contractor. He is also, as experience has shown, a leading U.S. jerry-builder.

'Did you receive a $4,000 kickback on a commission earned by Reynolds in connection with the building of the District of Columbia stadium?'

This was another question asked of him at the Senate Rules Committee hearing to which Bobby Baker responded with stony silence.

Here we come to another typical Baker deal, one so complex and devious that it could serve as a textbook example in a manual on 'How to Swindle Safely'.

The District of Columbia Stadium is a professional sports complex, home ground of the Washington Redskins and Senators. In order to invest taxpayers' money in this project—and that kind of money is what a fellow in Bobby Baker's position likes best to manipulate—there has to be an Act of Congress authorizing it.

So Baker, having first explored the possibilities, with a number of pals, of making big money for himself, his friend and the party, launched the operation by pushing through Congress a bill authorizing the expenditure of $17 million on the Stadium. With considerable help from the Clerk of the House Committee on the District of Columbia, William N. McLeod, Jr., Bobby safely steered the bill through the committee and the House.

Even at that stage of the proceedings, it was a foregone conclusion that no one was better qualified to get the contract for this profitable building enterprise than Matthew McCloskey, the deserving, champion fundraiser for the party. But the outward forms of legality, i.e. the solicitation and examination of bids from various contractors had to be respected.

The questions of how to safeguard appearances and still make sure that McCloskey got the contract, and of how much should be distributed in kickbacks to all concerned, were discussed in detail at a meeting held in the spring of 1960 (none of the witnesses who testified on the matter appear to be able to remember the exact date) at Baker's Senate office.

Those present at the meeting included, besides Baker himself, his close associate Don Reynolds; the helpful William N. McLeod; and, of course, the man who was to get the contract, McCloskey.

Still another important personality attended the conference: Congressman John L. McMillan, Chairman of the District Committee.

He later issued a statement saying that the purpose of this meeting was simply to 'meet Mr. McCloskey and look over the plans for the stadium'.

When the bids from prospective contractors were opened, in June, who should turn out to be lowest bidder but Mr. McCloskey! So, of course, he got the contract.

His gratitude to all concerned found expression in two ways. First, he bought the required performance bond from the insurance agency headed by Don Reynolds (with Bobby Baker as a silent partner). On this transaction, Reynolds earned a commission of $10,031.56, of which he kicked back $4,000 to Baker. Reynolds, who revealed all this in his subsequent testimony, also testified that he paid $1,500 from the same commission to the then clerk of the District of Columbia Committee, McLeod, for promoting the bill in the House. What McMillan got, we have seen in Chapter 14.

That much of the operation came out in an early stage of the Baker investigation. When Bobby took the stand, in February 1964, the Committee already had these details in its files.

In the fall, another big skeleton came rattling out of the closet. In further testimony before the Committee, Reynolds, describing himself bluntly as the 'bagman', revealed that he had received a total of $35,000 in commissions from McCloskey, of which he channeled $25,000 into the 1960 Democratic campaign fund, while he kept for himself the remaining $10,000, half of which he distributed to his pals in the above-described manner.

Testifying before the Rules Committee on December 2, 1964—after the investigators and Bobby Baker had gone through another round of challenging questions and silent responses—McCloskey heatedly denied that there was any campaign pay-off involved in the Stadium deal. He also denied—under oath—that the meeting at Baker's Senate office, as reported by Reynolds, ever took place: 'That is not correct. Such a conversation never took place—at no time ever. I never heard of it'.

In view of the above-quoted statement by Congressman John L. McMillan, confirming that the meeting in question did take place, even though he denied the nature of its purpose, McCloskey's all-out denial would seem to make a good case for an investigation of possible perjury.

Nor is that all. For McCloskey subsequently acknowledged that his company had made a $35,000 overpayment on the insurance written by Reynolds, but explained it by saying that 'someone in our firm goofed'.

In an editorial entitled 'The $35,000 Goof', *The New York Times*, on December 5, 1964, commented on this excuse as follows:

'Matthew H. McCloskey, the Philadelphia building contractor and champion Democratic fundraiser, says that "someone in our firm goofed" in making a $35,000 overpayment on the insurance for the District of Columbia Stadium. It was never his intention, Mr. McCloskey explains, to use the ubiquitous Bobby Baker and the latter's free-talking insurance partner, Don Reynolds, as conduits for an underground contribution to the 1960 Democratic campaign. Absolutely not.

'It is good to have Mr. McCloskey's explanation of this curious transaction on the record. Making expensive "goofs" is not characteristic of him, but presumably anyone can err. It will be interesting to see whether Mr. McCloskey does, in fact, sue Mr. Reynolds to recover the money he states he paid erroneously...'

So far, nothing has been heard of such a lawsuit, one that alone could vindicate McCloskey's position—provided he came out of it the winner. In the absence of positive proof of an overpayment made by mistake—on the face of it a most unlikely explanation—McCloskey's admission that Reynolds did get the exact amount the latter claims to have received as 'bagman' is firm evidence of a pay-off.

As if to compound this sorry performance by a top Democratic party official, it was revealed at the same time that the Justice Department was pressing a claim for $4.9 million in damages against McCloskey and two other contractors for grave defects that turned up in a Veterans Administration hospital constructed by them in Boston.

On top of it all came the disclosure (in a UPI dispatch from Washington, January 22, 1964) that McCloskey's 'low bid' on the Stadium contract was a phony, too. His bid had been for $14 million and the performance bond posted by him guaranteed completion of the project at that figure. Later, however, the cost of the stadium was increased by another $8 million, for a total of $22 million—five million more than originally allowed by Congress.

On the strength of such merits, McCloskey, in June 1962, was appointed ambassador to Ireland, succeeding Grant Stockdale. At the end of 1963, with the Baker storm clouds gathering over his head, he resigned and went home to resume fundraising and jerry-building.

CHAPTER 25 - Master of the Cover-up

'THE Senate investigation of the Robert G. Baker case is going forward without interruption despite President Kennedy's assassination, Rules Committee Chairman B. Everett Jordan said today,' reported an AP dispatch from Washington on November 26, 1963. The next paragraph read:

'"I see no reason to make any changes in our plans," said the North Carolina Democrat, who has pledged a full-scale inquiry following up any leads regardless of who may be involved'.

That was the stately facade behind which the political charwomen were already busy sweeping all the real dirt under the carpet, even though, as 'Cassandra' of the London Daily Mirror jibed on March 2, 1964, 'trouble is they don't really make rugs big enough for so much dust'. Cassandra, I'm afraid, had a poor conception of the capabilities of the U.S. rug industry and seemed to be totally ignorant of American sweep-it-under-the-carpet techniques.

The New York Times, in a pen portrait of Senator Jordan, 'Investigator of Baker', which it published on November 1, 1963, noted that Baker was a protégé 'of one of the men Senator Jordan most admires, Vice-President Johnson'.

'Mr. Jordan was a strong Johnson for President supporter in 1960,' the *Times* went on to say, describing the Senator, in the same context, as 'a man who likes to be liked by everyone—some liken him to a friendly puppy dog'. I don't know whether it is considered sportsmanlike to launch a puppy dog hot on the trail of a pack of wolves and jackals, but I am sure it is not the most effective method of hunting.

And, to appoint an ardent Johnson admirer and Johnson henchman as chairman of a committee investigating a Johnson protégé was hardly the best way to get at the truth about Johnson's own involvement in the case.

If Senator Jordan, after President Kennedy's death, saw 'no reason to make any changes in our plans,' the only plausible explanation of the remark is that a whitewash had been planned from the start and was going to be accomplished.

Maybe Jordan, at the beginning of the affair, had been a little worried about how President Kennedy would react to such an unmitigated whitewash, but now his worries were over. According to *The New York Times* of December 7, 1963:

'Asked if Mr. Johnson's long association with Mr. Baker would "cause you to de-emphasize the investigation" now that Mr. Johnson is President, Senator Jordan replied that it was "an embarrassing question". He quickly added, however, that "I am not embarrassed, because we are going ahead—there is no change"...'

In *The New York Herald Tribune* of December 1st, 1963, Dom Bonafede noted a 'Shifting Emphasis on Baker Probe' and reported:

'Hard-crusted habitués here will lay two-to-one that the Rules Committee, and its overwhelming Democrat majority, will go through the motions and let the investigation die a natural death rather than embarrass the Johnson administration. While "King of the Senate", Mr. Johnson was political godfather to Mr. Baker...'

The hard-crusted habitues were dead right, just as the hard-crusted *Time* magazine was right when it predicted, in its issue of February 14, 1964, exactly what the verdict of the Warren Commission was going to be—at a time when that august panel had heard only one of the 552 witnesses who were going to testify before it.

They were parallel and coupled sham investigations: the Warren Commission's pseudo-inquiry into the assassination of President Kennedy and the Rules Committee's less than half-hearted probe into the Baker affair. And they were masterminded by the same political genius basically for the same purpose and toward the same end.

In both cases, too, the same slanted—and frequently downright dishonest—investigative techniques were employed: important witnesses were not heard, or downgraded, or shunted aside; eye-catching evidence was not 'found' by the investigators, because it had already been swept under the carpet ; every form of camouflage, from smokescreens to shadow-boxing was used to hide the true facts; trivia were blown up, the most irrelevant details were given a big play while essential facts were ignored or brushed aside.

The cover-up technique, in America, has been developed to unprecedented degrees of perfection. It has been successfully employed by 'investigators' who were in fact puppets dancing on

Lyndon Johnson's strings in at least five more-or-less concurrent and interrelated affairs: the Kennedy assassination; the Bobby Baker scandal; the Billie Sol Estes scandal; the case of the indiscreet Secretary (Fred Korth and the TFX); and the security aspects of the Walter Jenkins affair.

That the Baker 'investigation' was in fact a planned cover-up has been widely realized across the nation.

Here is a sampling of editorial opinion on the subject : Roscoe Drummond on 'The Baker Non-Investigation' in *The New York Herald Tribune* of May 3, 1964:

'The Democratic majority of the Senate non-investigating committee is showing positive genius in finding ways to prevent itself from getting the evidence in the Bobby Baker case. I don't mean that the Senate Rules Committee has been idle in its non-investigation. It has worked arduous hours in thinking up ways not to do its work.

'It has been quick and alert. When its principal potential witness—Bobby Baker himself closed one door in its face, the Democratic majority of the committee knew exactly what to do. At its own initiative it closed all the other doors of profitable inquiry and went right back to its work of not getting the facts.

The New York Times editorial on 'The Baker Non-Investigation' (March 19, 1964) :

'...the public will be short-changed if this slipshod inquiry is brought to an end while the many unanswered questions about Mr. Baker and his transactions remain unanswered.

'Senator B. Everett Jordan of North Carolina, who is in charge of the investigation, argues that the committee's authority is limited. This is a lame excuse. We do not believe in a Congressional committee exceeding its own authority; but the fact is that Mr. Jordan's committee has been uncommonly timorous and ostrich-like in the scope of its inquiry... More information is needed on what, if anything, the Murchison interests in Dallas and the late Senator Robert Kerr may have received for providing gifts and credit to Mr. Baker...'

The New York Herald Tribune editorial on 'Chicanery in the Senate' (March 5, 1965):

'In its non-investigation of the Bobby Baker case, the Senate Rules Committee has gone beyond even the ordinary limits of Political cover up; in its effort to discredit the embarrassing testimony of insurance agent Don Reynolds, the committee's Democratic majority—through chairman Jordan—has sought to pass off is an FBI report, a document actually prepared by Justice Department lawyers from raw (and unsworn) FBI files. Its getting to a point where the Senate ought to investigate its own Rules Committee'.

Richard L. Strout in *The Christian Science Monitor* of March 14, 1964: 'The investigation by Democrats of Robert G. (Bobby) Baker has cleared up everything except what Washington most wants to know...'

Editorial in *The Christian Science Monitor* of March 16, 1964, entitled 'Comfort for Cynics':

'...Yet it is not just politics to represent a wide public feeling that the investigation has been inconclusive. The suspicions raised about senatorial behavior, as well as Mr. Baker's, are not diminished by the appearance of a less than forthright confrontation of the suspicions by the Senate itself. This is one way to comfort the cynics about "politicians".

'Why was Walter Jenkins, White House aide, not questioned after his affidavit conflicted with the testimony of a central witness? Why, after all the talk about alleged "party girls," were the facts not pursued, as Sen. Carl Curtis suggested?...'

Newsday editorial 'Baker Probe Must Go On' (13-3-64) :

'The unseemly haste with which the Senate Rules Committee is attempting to close out its investigation of the malodorous machinations of Robert G. (Bobby) Baker is a discredit not only to the Senate, but to President Johnson himself...'

The New York Herald Tribune editorial 'Who's Hiding What?' (17-2-64):

'To say that there has been a lack of candor in official circles on the more explosive ramifications of the Bobby Baker case is to put it mildly...'

Columnist Henry J. Taylor in the *New York World-Telegram and Sun* of June 3rd, 1964: 'President Behind the Baker Hush':

'...From the very beginning, in his role of a political man, Johnson has condoned the committee's stalling tactics (or they couldn't have occurred), the refusal to summon at least 20 additional witnesses produced by Sen. John J. Williams of

Delaware, and others, the spiriting abroad of the German girl who gave another phase of the smelly mess, its British Profumo case odor.

'His power to reverse all this cover-up—unused—makes Johnson the decisive participant... A mere one-minute phone call by Johnson to the committee could take the lid off the investigation and let the chips fall where they may. This would be bad politics but, in truth, the lid is on only because Lyndon Johnson permits it. This is bad enough in Johnson, the political man, but in Johnson, the President, it is intolerable...'

And what about Johnson, the man, period?

Charles Mohr in *The New York Times* of October 15, 1964:

'Denver, Oct. 14—Senator Barry Goldwater charged today that President Johnson was blocking an investigation of Robert G. Baker because Bobby Baker's affairs lead right straight into the White House. "That's a pretty harsh accusation", Mr. Goldwater said...

'Mr. Goldwater said that President Johnson was "in effect telling the American people to go whistle—that so long as he does not want the truth known in the Bobby Baker case, the truth will not be known."

'The Senator charged that, instead of standing on the side of truth, Mr. Johnson "is standing firmly and coldly on the side of deceit and cover-up"...'

So much for the flagrant, conspicuous, and generally recognized cover-up in the Bobby Baker affair.

It has also been widely realized that much the same type of organized cover-up occurred in the Billie Sol Estes case, at least in so far as it concerned Lyndon B. Johnson.

Let's turn now to the TFX controversy and the role played by Fred Korth in this and related matters.

If Texan Johnson and his boy from Pickens, S.C., were in deep trouble with President Kennedy in 1963, so were a number of other prominent Texans. The one most heavily compromised, next to the Vice-President, was Secretary of the Navy, Fred Korth, who was, in private life, and now again is, a prosperous banker from Fort Worth, Texas.

Mr. Korth had incurred the President's displeasure on at least two counts:

1— He had been publicly charged, in Congress as well as in the press, with 'conflict of interest', a Washington euphemism for something that generally falls under the heading of corruption.

This is an extremely complex and intricate matter which would fill a book all by itself if exhaustively dealt with. In a nutshell, here is what happened:

Two of America's giant corporations, Boeing of Seattle, which operates mainly on the West Coast, and General Dynamics of Fort Worth, Texas, were vying for the Defense Department's award of the TFX contract. The TFX, at that time (1962/63), was a supersonic fighter-bomber in the experimental stage. Eventually, 1,700 planes of this type were to be built, at a cost of $6.5 to 7 billion. A prolonged battle raged over this plum, with each side trying to get as much help as possible in Congress as well as from their men in the Pentagon.

In December 1962, a decision was made by the Pentagon in favor of General Dynamics although the Boeing Company had been the lowest bidder and had had the backing of most military experts. While the final decision was made by Secretary of Defense Robert McNamara, it developed that his action was taken at the prompting of three personalities in particular, all of whom had a personal or political stake in the matter, to wit:

Vice President Lyndon B. Johnson, whose great influence at the Pentagon was derived from his previous position as head of the Senate Committee on Aeronautical and Space Sciences and of the Preparedness Subcommittee, while he also was a member of the Senate Armed Service Committee.

In the words of *The New York Times* military expert, Hanson W. Baldwin (November 28, 1963): 'When Mr. Johnson was Vice-President, many observers saw his "hand" in decisions about defense and space contracts. He was believed to have been instrumental in winning for Texas the great space center being built at Houston. Some observers thought he was involved in the Pentagon's award of a multibillion-dollar contract for an Air Force-Navy fighter plan, the TFX (F-III) to the Convair plant of General Dynamics at Fort Worth, Tex...'

The other two were Navy Secretary Fred Korth, about whom Baldwin wrote in the same article that he was 'tabbed as a Johnson man' and that his bank in Fort Worth was 'a minor partner in a consortium that had made loans to General Dynamics', and Roswell Gilpatric, Deputy Secretary of Defense, who, it later turned out, had received $126,000 from General Dynamics for legal work he had done for this corporation before he took his Pentagon post in 1961.

These facts were brought to light by a Senate subcommittee headed by Sen. John L. McClellan which opened hearings on the matter on February 26, 1963, after Boeing's charges of favoritism had found a wide echo in the press and public.

2— In the course of the same investigation, it was also disclosed that Korth, while Navy Secretary, had carried on private business on Navy stationary and on his official yacht, the *Sequoia*. Incredible as it may seem, Korth, on August 13, 1962, had written a letter to his former (and future) associate, G. E. Homstrom, at the Continental National Bank of Fort Worth—the same bank which, as has been noted before, had close business ties with General Dynamics—about his plans to 'have a little party aboard the *Sequoia*, primarily for my Texas friends... I am just wondering whether you and some of my other friends at the Continental may be coming through; likewise if you have some extra good customers that it would be nice to have'.

'This and much more evidence of misuse of the Secretary of the Navy's office came to the attention of the Congress, and shortly thereafter Korth resigned,' wrote James Reston of *The New York Times* after quoting the above excerpts from Korth's letter in his column of November 1st, 1963.

Although Korth's sudden resignation, on October 14, had been clearly forced by these revelations, President Kennedy went to the limit in trying to exonerate this peculiar 'Texas friend'. At his press conference of October 31, 1963, he even warned reporters against hasty judgments. He said he had 'no evidence' of improper action by Korth but added that this judgment 'has nothing to do with any opinion I may have about whether Mr. Korth might have written more letters and been busier than he should have been in one way or another'.

Clearly, President Kennedy wanted to spare Texas feelings as much as possible, for the appointment of this 'Johnson man' to his high defense post evidently had been made to accommodate LBJ; Texas didn't reciprocate.

Let's see now what happened to this investigation after President Kennedy's death. On this subject, Laurence Barret reported in *The New York Herald Tribune* (Paris) on December 11, 1963:

'The Senate investigation of the TFX warplane contract award has been quietly laid aside and there is speculation it may never be revived.

'Sen. John L. McClellan's investigations subcommittee held its last hearing November 20, two days before the assassination of President Kennedy. The next round was to have been held the following week.

'In the immediate aftermath of the murder there was an obvious desire on Capitol Hill to stifle unseemly controversy. Now things are getting back to normal. However, Senate sources indicated there are no plans to hold new TFX hearings before mid-January, and even that date is tentative.

'The main basis for speculation that the ten-month-old investigation may be dead is that it has taken on vastly greater political connotations now that Mr. Johnson is President...

'Throughout the hearings there have been hints that there was improper influence exerted to get this business for General Dynamics and Texas. At one of the last hearings, a Republican Senator sought to link Mr. Johnson with this suggestion...

'Even if President Johnson's name is kept out of the formal proceedings, it would be impossible to exclude Fred Korth, the former Navy Secretary, who resigned in embarrassing circumstances. He was scheduled to be the next witness. Mr. Korth and Mr. Johnson have been friendly for years and Mr. Korth, too, is a Texan...'

It is a matter of fact that this investigation was quietly buried. Korth was never called on the carpet and no effort was ever undertaken to determine the amount of improper influence that had been used to get the $7 billion contract for the Texas firm.

Thus the change of administration brought about by the murder of President Kennedy put an abrupt end to at least one current investigation and changed the nature of two others—Bobby Baker and Billie Sol Estes probes—from half-hearted investigation into wholehearted cover-up.

Now for a look at the fourth of the five interlocking cover-ups. When it became known, in mid-October 1964, that President Johnson's top aide, Walter Jenkins, had been arrested on a morals charge and it was learned further that he had a police record as a pervert dating back to January 1959, a gasp of horror went through official Washington. Not only because of the enormity of this situation, from the political and moral view-points, but even more because it is axiomatic that sexual perverts are great security risks. They are forever subject to blackmail by hostile intelligence services and there is an established rule that they cannot be employed in any sensitive work. And Jenkins had received top secret clearance for Air Force classified material on April 5, 1956; Department of Defense top secret clearance on December 23, 1957; Atomic Energy Commission 'Q' clearance on February 20, 1958. He sat in, after his boss had become President, on meetings of the National Security Council. As top presidential aide, he was a potential fountainhead of the most secret information in the land.

This fantastic situation, moreover, came to light as the election campaign of 1964 neared its climax; Johnson was now in a hell of a fix. The night he learned about Jenkins's arrest, and the nature of the charge that had been brought against his business manager, bosom friend and White House majordomo, LBJ looked as though the roof had fallen in on him. He's never lost that haggard mien since.

With the Republicans doing their utmost to exploit the issue—it was the only scandal at hand in which some of their own people weren't in any risk of getting caught—President Johnson again sought, and got help, from the man who has been the chief architect of all the big cover-ups of the Johnson Administration: J. Edgar Hoover, Director of the so-called Federal Bureau of Investigation.

Hoover got busy right away and in record time produced a whitewash of Jenkins which *The New York Times* of October 23, 1964 summarized in these headlines: REPORT BY F.B.I. ON JENKINS FINDS NO SECURITY SLIP - NO EVIDENCE IS UNCOVERED THAT EX-PRESIDENTIAL AIDE COMPROMISED NATION - SENT TO WHITE HOUSE - JOHNSON DIDN'T KNOW OF '59 ARREST WHEN HE ASSUMED OFFICE, AGENCY ASSERTS.

So now we can all go back to sleep. When J. Edgar Hoover, grand shield of the USA against all internal risks for 41 years, assures us that a twice-caught sex deviant with access to all top secrets never compromised the nation, everything must be okay. That's how public opinion was expected to react—and it did.

In sending his report on Jenkins to the White House, Hoover proudly announced that his minions had interviewed 'more than 500 persons' in the matter, between October 14, when Johnson ordered the investigation, and October 22 when the FBI came through with its product.

That was quite a performance, really. By contrast, it took the Warren Commission about eight months to dispose of the 551 witnesses still on its list after it had slipped the gist of its forthcoming verdict, based on the testimony of the first, to *Time* magazine.

This brings us again to the biggest cover-up of them all. Reread everything that has been quoted above from editorials published in the country's most distinguished newspapers about the cover-ups engineered by Lyndon B. Johnson in the Bobby Baker, Billie Sol Estes, Fred Korth & TFX and Jenkins cases and apply the same criteria to the Warren Report. It is all part and parcel of the same overall pattern.

There seems to be positively no limit to the amount of covering up two cunning schemers at the levers of maximum power, like Lyndon B. Johnson and J. Edgar Hoover, can put over jointly on an unsuspecting nation. It was easy, of course, in four out of the five cover-ups that have been discussed here.

But, to cover up the true facts in the assassination of a President of the United States is something else again. It takes all the power, authority and prestige of the presidency itself to make that kind of cover-up a success.

CHAPTER 26 - The Trial of Bobby Baker

WHEN long-delayed justice at last catches up with a conspicuous rogue, in the United States, it is usually in the shape of the income tax collector.

While it is as easy as child's play, in America, to get away with murder (in the literal sense), provided one is a big shot in politics or a member in good standing of the Mafia, it is very difficult, in the long run, to cheat Uncle Sam out of his due.

Scores of affluent gangsters, who, with the help of high-powered lawyers and plenty of backstage pull in City Hall, were able time and again to beat the most glaring murder raps, finally wound up behind bars as convicted evaders of federal income tax.

In politics, too, this nemesis is hard to escape, as the case of Bobby Baker—among many others—shows. He came out as nearly unscathed as possible, under the circumstances, of the Senate investigation, but the publicity engendered by this inquiry set the IRS sleuths at his heels, and they finally got their man, as they usually do.

As early as November 7, 1963, the Finance Office of the District of Columbia let it be known that it was looking into the District income-tax status of every person mentioned in connection with Baker's business activities.

That was the time when the Baker investigation really seemed to swing into high gear. It was also two weeks before President

Kennedy, who had pushed this inquiry, conveniently met with his death in Lyndon B. Johnson's bailiwick.

After the assassination, the Internal Revenue Service, well aware of the explosive potentialities of the case, chose to tread warily.

It bore down first on the most vulnerable of Baker's associates, the lobbyist Fred Black who was accused of failing to report about $140,000 in income in 1956, 1957 and 1958. On May 5, 1964, Black was convicted in the Washington Federal District Court of having evaded $91,121 in federal income taxes over the said three-year period and on June 18 he was given a 15-months to-four-year prison sentence and fined $10,000.

By contrast, it took the IRS more than three years to bring Bobby Baker to trial. True, there were other crimes to consider in his case, even though the prosecution carefully sidestepped any approach that might have lead them into really deep water.

When the Baker case finally came up for trial, in Washington on January 10, 1967, before Federal Judge Oliver Gash, a tall, thin, bespectacled disciplinarian, the indictment was more noteworthy for the charges it did not contain, than for the nine counts it listed.

As a matter of fact, these criminal proceedings were almost completely divorced from everything that had been brought out during the Senate investigation. There was no mention of 'Serv-U', of 'payola' or of MAGIC; not a whisper about the $100,000 North American Aviation had shelled out 'to get our man elected'; McCloskey and his stadium contract were just as taboo as the

Murchison deal; and, of course, the fair specter of Elly Rometsch had been banned rigorously from the courtroom. Nobody dared to introduce the 'sex angle'— though it really is the heart of the Bobby Baker case—into the proceedings which, on the whole, were handled like a routine matter.

Bobby Baker's 'Carousel' did pop up in the case, but in a different context from anything the Senate investigation had brought to light. And one of Baker's best friends and financial 'angels', the late Senator Kerr, was unexpectedly cast—by the defense—into the role of chief Villain, but then he was no longer there to defend himself.

Of the nine counts in the indictment, two charges of evasion of income taxes and one preparation of a fraudulent income tax return for an associate; two counts alleged grand larceny; two more, larceny after trust; one, transportation of stolen money in interstate commerce; and one, conspiracy to commit fraud.

At the start of the trial, William O. Bittman, chief Government counsel, introduced a matter that had not previously figured in the Baker investigation and had never been ventilated in the press. He told the jury that Baker, in 1962, had collected a total of $100,000 from several California savings and loan associations, ostensibly for the election campaigns of several Senators, but that he had kept approximately $80,000 of that money for himself.

'He had invested heavily in the Carousel Motel in Ocean City, Md., and was desperately in need of cash,' Mr. Bittman stated. He added that Baker, after collecting the supposed campaign funds from the California bankers 'within five weeks, spent $50,000 in cash, mainly on the Carousel Motel'.

As this story gradually unfolded in court, it provided a fascinating insight into the inner workings of the Great Society. In the background loomed, as so often, a wrangle over the preservation or abolition of special tax privileges

One of the goals of the tax reform bill which President Kennedy introduced in 1962 sought to end the special treatment long enjoyed by saving and loan associations by reducing the amount of earnings they could hold as a tax-free reserve against bad debts.

The House of Representatives approved a provision that would allow both stock and mutual companies to hold 50 per cent of earnings in tax-free reserves. However, the Senate, on August 7, 1962, approved an amendment proposed by Sen. Robert Kerr of Oklahoma that would have discriminated between the two groups of saving and loan associations. While the mutual companies (owned by depositors) were to be allowed, under this amendment, to hold 60 per cent of earnings in tax-free reserves, the stock companies (owned by stockholders) were to be allowed only 40 per cent.

The Senate version would have cost the stock companies about $10 million a year more than the House version. However, at a conference, on September 25, of the House Ways and Means and the Senate Finance Committees, the Senate conferees gave way and agreed to the House version. The latter was passed by both

Houses on October 2 and signed into law by the President on October 16, 1962.

So much of the story had been dry finance history before the Baker trial filled in the juicy details.

According to the indictment, Bobby Baker, shortly after his close friend and patron, Senator Kerr, had introduced his amendment, alerted its intended victims, the stock companies, to the dire risks they were facing. He told leading executives that the industry, in his view, was 'politically naive' and 'backward' and that it would be well-advised to become 'politically more active'.

The Savings and Loan executives took the hint and started to grease Baker's outstretched palm, apparently in the belief that the money would go to a bipartisan assortment of influential senators and help them change their minds. In that respect, and irrespective of how the about-face was accomplished, the operation proved successful.

The prosecution put on the stand, as its key witness, one Kenneth Childs, an S-&-L stock company executive and a leader in the field, who testified that, after Baker had advised him of his political naiveté he and other executives in 1962 handed over to the defendant a total of $100,000 in cash, in unmarked envelopes. No receipts were asked or given.

Specifically, the prosecution contended, one California savings and loan association executive by name of Stuart Davis, on October 21, 1962, handed over to Bobby Baker $50,000 in 100-

dollar-bills; and another, John F. Marten, likewise paid him $17,000 on October 3.

Those amounts were intended for senators, the prosecution contended, but Baker put them into his own pockets, and that was larceny.

Baker, ably assisted by Edward Bennett Williams, one of the most high-powered attorneys to be found in the United States, didn't deny that he got that money, but he indignantly rejected the idea that he had put it into his own pocket.

Did you steal that money?' Williams several times rhetorically asked his client.

'No, sir, I sure did not', Baker replied every time.

As *Newsweek* put it on February 6, 1967: 'One of the classic ploys of the criminal lawyer with a hard-pressed client is to pin the rap on somebody else'.

That's what Williams tried to do, with a vengeance.

After Kenneth Child's testimony, the defense put on the stand eight prominent lawmakers who had been named as potential beneficiaries of the $100,000 Democrats as well as Republicans. They were: Wilbur Mills, chairman of the House Ways and Means Committee; and seven senators, to wit: Everett Dirksen of Illinois; Frank Carlson of Kansas; Thurston Morton of Kentucky; William Fulbright of Arkansas; Wallace Bennett of Utah; Carl Hayden of Arizona; and George Smathers of Florida.

The lawmakers, needless to say, were indignant and for once they seemed to be on the right side of integrity. After Mills and

Fulbright had testified under oath that they received no funds from Baker in 1962, the defense was ready to concede the innocence of the others as well. There were, however, two possibly significant interludes. When Baker's attorney, Williams, asked Rep. Mills whether he had ever received funds from Sen. Kerr, Judge Gasch ruled the question out of order. And when Senator Dirksen was excused from taking the stand, the judge sardonically commented: 'I'm sorry, sir, to be deprived of hearing your golden voice'.

Having failed in his bid to extract from eight living lawmakers any admission that they had received any part of the $100,000 in question, the defense concentrated its efforts on the dead one, Senator Kerr. This attempt set off some real fireworks which almost elevated the sordid case to the heights of real courtroom drama.

Attorney Williams certainly had a point when he poured scorn on Childs and the other savings and loan association witnesses for the prosecution for claiming that they had turned over to Baker $100,000 without receipts and, more importantly, without any guarantee, that they would get anything in return.

Were these the sort of people, Williams asked the jury, to hand over huge sums of money without being sure of its actual use and destination? Why, the prosecution, Williams told the jurors, was 'asking you to believe that six of the leading executives in the savings and loan industry in California put together $100,000 for the benefit of some senators whose names they didn't remember...'

These executives, Williams continued with sparkling rhetoric, were not 'gullible farmers, slack-jawed country bumpkins', but were 'flint-eyed, marble-hearted tycoons' who couldn't be taken for suckers.

'You would have a better chance to walk out of the Louvre with the Venus de Milo under your arm,' Williams exclaimed, 'than you would have getting $100,000 out of those men, unless they knew where it was going, why and whether it got there'.

To the tantalizing questions of where that $100,000 was going, what is was for and whether it got there, the defense gave a devious, but nonetheless clearly understood answer. Without ever spelling out the word *b-r-i-b-e* in so many letters, Williams unmistakeably implied that the money had been a pay-off to Senator Kerr and that Bobby Baker had merely been the messenger boy who took it to him.

In September 1962, Williams told the jury, savings and loan officials descended on Congress 'like locusts on a lettuce patch'. Prominent among the 'locusts' was the president of the Home Savings and Loan Association of Los Angeles, Kenneth Childs, who was received by Senator Kerr. One day after this interview, the defense attorney contended, Kerr withdrew the amendment he had sponsored and 'the stock companies won the day'.

Williams pointed out that, after Sen. Kerr's death, $43,000 had been found in one of his safety deposit boxes. This, he suggested, was part of the boodle Kerr had gotten for his change of heart on the S & L tax issue. When the late senator's son, Robert Kerr, Jr., a key witness for the prosecution, heatedly denied that the $43,000 had come from that source, Williams countered by saying: 'I won't quarrel with any son coming into court to speak well, though falsely, to save his dead father's reputation... But not when a live man's liberty is resting on the testimony'.

Williams' presentation of this matter also drew an angry response from Prosecutor Bittman to whom the alleged Kerr affair was simply a red herring wantonly drawn across Baker's trail.

'Whatever wrongs Robert Baker has committed in his life,' Bittman exclaimed, 'they are small compared to what he has attempted to do in this case [defaming the name of the dead senator who had been his friend]. I think this is the real tragedy'.

There were other moments of tension and dramatic suspense when Baker, on January 20, took the stand in his own defense. He had quite a story to tell as to how he did get money, late in 1962, to keep the Carousel going, without stealing any of the $100,000 campaign funds, as alleged by the prosecution. In doing so, Bobby quite casually dropped the bombshell everyone had expected would explode at the trial. But it proved to be little more than a dud.

Yes, Baker conceded, it was true he had been in pretty desperate financial straits, late in 1962, due to the unexpectedly heavy cost of building the Carousel Motel. But he didn't have to steal money from anybody in order to bail himself out, for he had friends.

And then, without specifically using a name, Baker declared that in his need he had gone to see 'the best friend I had around Capitol Hill—the then vice-president'.

He didn't have to be specific. The United States has only one vice-president at a time and the name of the one who held that office in 1962 was Lyndon B. Johnson.

'I told him I had a very serious financial problem and asked his advice,' Baker went on to relate. 'He picked up the phone and called his friend and my friend, Sen. Kerr, and then advised me to go immediately to Sen. Kerr's office, which I did'.

After listening to his story of financial woe, Kerr, according to the defendant, telephoned the president of the Fidelity Bank and Trust Co., in Oklahoma City and arranged for Baker to be given a loan credit of $250,000. Kerr also promised to lend him $50,000 personally —and that was the money that went into the Carousel, Baker claimed.

Later, near the end of four hours of testimony, Baker once more reverted to his tender relationship with Senator Kerr. On Christmas Eve 1962, he related, Kerr, who had suffered what was to be a fatal heart attack, called him to forgive the $50,000 loan he had made to Baker.

According to the defendant, the ailing and moribund oil tycoon told him over the phone that he 'wanted to wipe the slate clean of the money,' so Bobby could forget about the loan. 'He asked me what kind of a tax loss I was going to have (in 1962), and I said $60,000,' Baker added and then quoted Kerr as telling him,

'Well, just put down that you got a fee from me for all the wonderful things you've done for me'.

It would have been interesting to learn just what were 'all the wonderful things' Bobby Baker did for the multimillionaire oilman who, after Lyndon B. Johnson's move to the vice-presidency, was for two years The Power on Capitol Hill; but, alas, death has sealed the senator's lips and wise discretion has sealed those of Bobby Baker.

However, there are limits to the discretion that can be expected from a harassed person like Bobby Baker. When he invoked in his testimony 'the best friend that I ever had around the Capitol,' without dropping the name everybody understood anyhow, Bobby no doubt gave fair warning to Whom It May Concern that he wasn't going to let himself be pushed around too much. He never lost one iota of his self-confidence and he has good reason to be self-assured, at least for a while. As long as Lyndon B. Johnson sits in the White House, nothing really serious can befall Bobby Baker, provided he keeps out of traffic accidents and keeps his nose clean—especially of carbon monoxide poisoning.

Bobby Baker made two more passing references to his 'best friend' in his testimony.

On one occasion, he related how the then Vice-President and Mrs. Johnson gave him a ride in their plane to and from the funeral of Senator Dennis Chavez of New Mexico, on November 21, 1962.

On the way, the plane also picked up Senator Kerr at Oklahoma City.

More significant, indeed, full of innuendo, was another story Baker coyly told as the courtroom spectators pricked up their ears. In 1960, while Johnson was Senate leader, Baker testified, one of LBJ's staff members, a man named Jeffrey Minto, rented a plush, $250-a-month apartment in a glass-fronted River House across the Potomac River in Washington. Minto paid for the place out of campaign funds, for it was to be used for 'speech-writing and conferences'.

The next year, i.e. in 1961, Baker took this apartment over personally for business, political work and a number of meetings, he said.

The matter came up at the trial because the IRS had questioned a $1,200 tax deduction which Baker had claimed for 1961 for 'office space'. The defendant sought to establish that he had paid this amount toward the rent of the River House apartment. He deducted only $100 per month in his tax return, he said, because he used the place for 'political and personal' matters and couldn't justify the whole $3000 rent for business.

It further developed during the proceedings that the late Carole Tyler had had a hand in preparing some of Baker's income tax returns and through 'oversights and mistakes' failed to report part of his income, in particular a sum of money he had earned from a land deal made in partnership with Sen. George Smathers of Florida. Carole also forgot the deduct the rent for the River House apartment on Baker's 1964 income tax return, or so Bobby claimed.

The 12-man jury (including one woman) was not impressed by Baker's explanations and they did not wither either under the drumbeat oratory of Attorney Williams. On January 29, 1967, they found the defendant guilty on seven of the nine counts he had been indicted for.

The jury declared Robert Baker guilty of having evaded $1,042.61 in federal income taxes in 1961 and $22,048.36 in 1962; of having stolen the $50,000 he had received from Stuart Davis as well as the $17,000 which John F. Marten had handed over to him; of transporting in interstate commerce another stolen amount, to wit $33,000 received in Los Angeles on November 9, 1962, from Sidney M. Taper, California savings and loan executive; of assisting Wayne L. Bromley (a middleman who had collected illicit fees for Baker) in the preparation of a fraudulent 1963 income tax; and of conspiring with Bromley and Clifford Jones, former Lieutenant Governor of Nevada, to defraud the United States in its tax collection function through concealment and misrepresentation.

The two counts on which the defendant was acquitted had charged larceny after trust.

On April 7, 1967, Baker—who could have drawn up to 48 years in prison and a $47,000 fine on the seven counts he was convicted for—was sentenced by Judge Oliver Gasch to serve from one to three years on each of the seven counts, the sentences to run concurrently.

The judge allowed the defendant to remain free under $5,000 bond, pending appeal, which Attorney Williams promised to carry 'all the way to the Supreme Court'.

Bobby Baker, according to the UPI, 'left the courtroom smiling'.

CHAPTER 27 - The Ways of a Usurper

LET us now revert to the darkest stain on Lyndon B. Johnson's somber record and examine it in some detail: the assassination of his predecessor, President John F. Kennedy.

Even if it should not be possible to prove, to the complete satisfaction of a court of law, that Lyndon B. Johnson instigated the murder, there cannot be the slightest doubt that he did condone it. His every action after the deed bespeaks complicity with the assassins.

The evidence that Johnson, at a minimum, became an accessory after the fact, which will be amply documented in the following pages, is overwhelming. I do not think that it could be dismissed by any independent tribunal when the day of reckoning comes.

With the President, a victim of foul murder, dead, whose duty was it to take immediate and drastic action in order to ensure the capture and trial of all possible assassins and their accomplices?

It was the duty of Lyndon B. Johnson, the new Chief Executive.

What did he do? Did he launch the biggest manhunt in history? Did he use every means at his command to make sure that the Crime of the Century be fully investigated and every participant brought to book? Did he give strict orders to the FBI and the Secret Service, relentlessly to pursue every lead, to grill every suspect, to check minutely every conceivable angle, to close all loopholes, to bar all escapes?

He did nothing of the sort. As soon as one poor little fellow had been caught Johnson decided that Oswald, the 'Marxist', was good enough for him as the 'lone assassin'. He immediately called off the chase for the real murderers, although District Attorney Jim Garrison of New Orleans and others even then were hot on their trail.

At least fifteen suspects already in the net—several of them confronted with *prima facie* evidence of their guilt—were released. Every single clue not pointing to Oswald was systematically wiped out. Material evidence of utmost importance, which from the first day revealed a conspiracy, was suppressed. Witnesses who could have exposed the plot were shoved aside, intimidated, harassed, bullied and even murdered. A fraudulent autopsy was performed on the body of the President. A fake re-enactment of the crime was staged. An innocent scapegoat was sacrificed. And, on top of it all, the records of this sham investigation were withheld from public inspection through burial in the National Archives where access is limited and a large portion of the materials relating to the assassination has been 'classified'.

Who was responsible for this shameful travesty of justice?

Lyndon B. Johnson. Everything the FBI and the Secret Service did or did not do in the case, everything the CIA has been doing lately to block the Garrison inquiry, these federal agencies have been doing under orders from the White House. None of them could have acted as they did without such authority.

'The buck stops here,' President Harry Truman used to say, referring to the Executive desk. It does indeed. Lyndon B. Johnson will have to take the full responsibility for the fact that all the law enforcement agencies under his control joined forces in suppressing the truth about the assassination of President John F. Kennedy.

Their first step was to hunt down and sacrifice the pre-ordained fall guy, Lee Harvey Oswald, and to make the world believe that he was the assassin. The story of this vicious frame-up has been related in detail in my book *Oswald: The Truth* and need not be recapitulated here. After the book had gone to press, Garrison confirmed the correctness of my thesis in every respect. He has on at least three occasions publicly asserted that Oswald neither killed the President nor Patrolman Tippit—as I have always held, from my first book on the subject.

In a television interview on May 21, 1967, Garrison declared: 'No, Lee Oswald did not shoot President Kennedy. He did not fire a shot from the Book Depository Building... he did not touch a gun on that day. He was a decoy at first. And then he was a patsy and then he was a victim'.

Just let this statement sink in and ponder the enormity of its significance. The 'lone assassin' certified by the Dallas Police, the FBI, the Secret Service and finally the Warren Commission, never fired a shot on November 22, 1963. He was just a decoy, a patsy, a victim.

And this statement comes from a District Attorney, after an exhaustive inquiry. Can one imagine a bigger bombshell? Yet the world press, almost in its entirety, paid no attention to it. One need not search far for the reasons of this unusual reserve. Those editors who are now engaging in a conspiracy of silence about the sensational results of the Garrison inquiry, just as they previously conspired to suppress the disclosures made in my first book on the subject, *Oswald: Assassin or Fall Guy?*, published in June 1964, know what they are doing. They know that they must keep the Oswald Legend alive at all cost or face the inescapable conclusion that this monstrous hoax was aided and abetted by a President of the United States. And just as inescapable is the next question: WHY?

* * *

Nothing incriminates Lyndon B. Johnson more devastatingly than the fact, now established on the judicial level, that no genuine hunt for the murderers of President Kennedy ever took place, although there were plenty of clues available from the start. Before I go into the details of this scandalous omission, let me quote a significant remark by Senator Russell B. Long of Louisiana who, as is well known, prompted the Garrison inquiry. According to an UPI dispatch from Washington, February 21, 1967:

'Senator Russell B. Long, D. La., said today "the New Orleans district attorney has something" that the Warren Commission investigators failed to uncover about the assassination of President Kennedy... Sen. Long said that Mr. Garrison had arrested a person he thought to be involved in an assassination plot shortly after the assassination. "But when the press media came out and said there was no one connected with Oswald, Garrison let the person go," he said'.

Senator Long, given his eminent position in the Senate, is evidently reluctant to express himself too clearly. After all, the reputations of two of his colleagues in the Senate, who were members of the Warren Commission, are at stake in the Garrison inquiry. His statement, therefore, is vague and in two respects inaccurate.

For, it shifts the blame to the press media which of course had no power to obtain the release of any person arrested as a suspect in the assassination. If the press 'came out and said there was no one connected with Oswald,' it was because reporters had been misled, from the start, by the official investigators. And, secondly, it is not correct to say that Garrison 'let the person go'. The fact of the matter, confirmed by Garrison himself, is that the suspect in question, David Ferrie, had been turned over to the FBI by the New Orleans district attorney and it was the FBI who turned him loose.

While information on this subject is still sporadic and therefore almost certainly incomplete, it is an established fact that arrests of suspects took place, after the assassination of President Kennedy, in at least four different places—Dallas, Fort Worth,

Miami and New Orleans—and involved a total of at least fifteen persons.

To begin with Dallas, scene of the crime, the little known fact of the matter is that it was known from the first day that two, if not three, potential suspects had been taken into custody there before Oswald was captured in the Texas Theater. I called attention to this important matter in *Oswald: Assassin or Fall Guy?* and the Warren Commission, therefore, has no excuse for having failed to look into these cases.

As stated in Chapter 7 of that book, the *Dallas Times Herald*, in its first edition to hit the streets after the assassination at 2:30 p.m., i.e. at a time Oswald was still unheard-of—reported:

'Patrolman W. E. Barker saw workers in the Texas School Book Depository pecking on a window from the third floor and pointing to a man wearing horn-rimmed glasses, a plaid coat and rain coat. The officer immediately arrested the man for questioning and placed him in a room of witnesses in Sheriff Bill Decker's office across the street from the Depository.

'With the young man protesting, the crowd all along the way jeered at him as he was escorted across the street. One woman said to the man: "I hope you die." Another screamed hysterically, "Is that him? Is that him?" An unidentified photographer shot a picture of the arrested man and then said bitterly, "I hope you burn." Officers on the case would not explain what connection the man might have with the shooting nor would they identify him'.

Note the detail of the account and the liveliness of the scene which rule out any possibility that it could have been made up by a reporter. The officer who made the arrest is identified by his name and initials; three persons are quoted as witnesses and a picture was taken; the suspect was placed in the custody of the Sheriff, at a given location, and there were 'officers on the case'.

It does not matter in the least whether this young man actually had anything to do with the shooting. What matters is that once a person has been arrested—and in a case of such gravity as this!—his case must be disposed of one way or another. Either he is released, having been able to prove his innocence, or he is bound over and arraigned. But he cannot simply drop out of sight without a trace, as this man did.

It is a matter of record that the Warren Commission carefully studied my book *Oswald: Assassin or Fall Guy?* With a minimum of honest intention to search for the truth, the Commission could not have failed to investigate this matter. All they had to do was to ask Patrolman W. E. Barker on what grounds the suspect in question had been arrested and to inquire from the Sheriff's office how his case had been disposed of. Yet, Patrolman Barker's name does not appear on the official list of witnesses and there is no record that the matter was discussed between the Commission and the Office of the Sheriff. None of the three persons who had shouted their spontaneous anger at the suspect was questioned and no attempt was made to identify the photographer or to get hold of the picture he had taken. The whole incident was simply treated as though it had never happened, and a person suspected of having shot at the President, or of having been an accomplice on the spot, simply vanished into thin air.

Why? Does not this off-hand treatment of an important lead, to say the least, bespeak a clear-cut intention not to look for the truth about the assassination?

Nor was this the only arrest made on the spot, as is shown by another report in the *Dallas Times Herald*, on December 8, 1963, which I also quoted in *Oswald: Assassin or Fall Guy?* and thus presented to the Warren Commission on a silver platter, for easy further investigation:

'It was also learned Saturday that an early suspect in the assassination of President Kennedy was still in jail—but no longer as a suspect in the killing. The man, a 31-year-old...who gave a Knight Street address, was arrested minutes after the assassination when officers swarmed railroad yards near the assassination scene. A man was reported seen in that area carrying a rifle...'

The fact that this man was arrested in the area of the railroad yards indicates that he is not identical with the young man in a plaid coat and rain coat, for the latter was seized close to the Book Depository. The hair-raising thing about this second case is that the never-identified 31-year-old man with the Knight Street address was still in jail weeks after Lee Harvey Oswald had been buried, and the case against the Kennedy murderers with him. Wrote the *Times Herald* on this score:

'The suspect was unarmed when arrested but booked, along with others arrested in the hectic hours following the assassination, on charges of "investigation of conspiracy to commit murder. The investigative charges were dropped Monday morning but the man was held in jail on "city charges."'

This case is so outrageous it truly cries out for investigation, yet the Warren Commission paid no attention whatsoever to it. Here we have a suspect other than Oswald who was actually charged with conspiracy to murder the President. Better still, these charges were not dropped until early December, long after the whole matter had been officially buried, as far as the public was concerned! And finally, a man first charged by the State of Texas with being an accomplice in the assassination of the President of the United States winds up, without explanation, being still in jail on 'city charges'—no doubt, for littering the railroad yard.

It should also be noted that the above-quoted report speaks of 'others' arrested in the hectic hours following the assassination, which suggests at least a third suspect in custody in Dallas that day, in addition to the young man with the horn-rimmed glasses and the man with the Knight Street address. What became of all of them?

Another, no less interesting case in point has come to light more recently. On September 29, 1964, *The New York Herald Tribune* published an UPI dispatch from Strawn, Texas, that ran as follows:

'Donald Wayne House laughed about it a little yesterday at his home here, but he failed to find a thing funny about it last November 22 when he was mistaken for the accused assassin of President Kennedy. The fact that Mr. House was arrested as a suspect in the assassination, questioned three hours and held in jail an hour in Fort Worth has never been told before.

'Last November 22 he visited Dallas, caught a glimpse of President Kennedy, then started back home. He did not know Mr. Kennedy was assassinated until he turned his car radio on well out of Dallas. When he stopped in Grand Prairie for gasoline, a woman asked him whether he had heard what the killer looked like. He gave her the description he had heard on the radio without realizing it also fitted him.

'The woman noted the similarity, however, and telephoned the police. "What am I being arrested for?" Mr. House said he asked. "You are being arrested for the assassination of President Kennedy," a policeman said. After three hours of denying he was the assassin, he was put in a cell. Finally, a policeman came to the cell door and said: "They've caught another boy. He is Lee Harvey Oswald. They are pretty sure he did it."'

Again, it is not a question of whether D. W. House had anything to do with the assassination. Rather, what matters is the way his case was disposed of. The ostensible grounds for his arrest were no mote than the fact that he looked somewhat like the (extremely vague) description broadcast by the police. According to the Warren Report, the radio alert sent to police cars at approximately 12:45 p.m. described the suspect as 'white, slender, weighing about 165 pounds, about 5'10" tall, and in his early thirties'. As I have pointed out in my previous books, this description did not fit Oswald in several respects. I have no way of knowing whether it did fit Mr. House, but in any case there must have been thousands of young men in the Dallas area, at that moment, to whom this description would have applied just as well.

Therefore, it stands to reason that when the police picked up House and, despite his protestations of innocence, questioned him for three hours and then put him into a jail cell, they must have had more solid grounds for doing so than just the young man's apparent similarity to the description broadcast in the radio alert.

What grounds? It is easy enough to guess. Remember the time: it is just past 12:45 and Lee Harvey Oswald, having escaped from the Book Depository is still at large. The police are frantically searching for him, not because they really have anything on him, but because they need him as a scapegoat. They realize that he is most probably on his way to Fort Worth where his mother and brother live, and, indeed, the Texas Theater, where Oswald was arrested, is close to the main highway that leads from Dallas to Fort Worth, only half an hour away by car. So it is obvious that all police cars in the area had been ordered to keep a sharp eye on that road and to hold any young male traveling in that direction who might conceivably be Oswald. Donald Wayne House seemed to fit the bill.

No less significant than his arrest is the way Mr. House was released. For three hours he had been arguing in vain that he was not the assassin. Did he have an airtight alibi? Apparently not, since he was sent to jail. Yet suddenly the door opens and the suspect is set free.

Why?

For no better reason than that the police has 'caught another boy' and that 'they are pretty sure he did it'.

How could the Dallas police at that early moment be 'pretty sure' that Oswald was the assassin? Remember: Mr. House was arrested shortly after the radio alert had been sent out, i.e. around 1 p.m. He was questioned for three hours and held in jail an hour, for a total of four hours. his release, then, took place around 5 p.m., at a time when Oswald had not even been told that he was suspected of presidential murder (as is well known, he was originally picked up and questioned on charges of killing Patrolman Tippit).

If the Dallas police were so sure of Oswald's guilt, even before they started to question him—so sure, indeed, that orders went out to release other suspects, without further ado—one can only conclude that it was all part of a cut-and-dried scheme to pin the blame on Oswald and nobody else.

Even if the police were 'pretty sure' Oswald did it, within three hours after he had been caught, how could they be sure that he did not have any accomplices? How could the fact that one person is picked up on suspicion of murder—especially in the assassination of a president!—be considered an alibi for another? If Mr. House couldn't prove his innocence during three hours of grilling, how could it be proven by the mere fact that somebody else was arrested in a case that could very well involve several people?

Viewed in conjunction with the other cases discussed above, the House affair clearly proves that the police were interested only in Oswald, not in any other possible suspect, unless a link to Oswald was indicated. This attitude again proves that there were no orders in effect to hunt down all possible suspects and to pursue all possible leads.

For his part, Jim Garrison, the District Attorney of New Orleans, has recently added some important details to the foregoing information which until then had been exclusively presented in my books *Oswald: Assassin or Fall Guy?* and *Oswald: The Truth*.

In an interview published by *Playboy* magazine in October 1967, he stated: 'As it happens, a man was arrested right after the assassination as he left the Dal-Tex Building [this is an evident reference to the man who was arrested by Patrolman Barker, see above] and was taken away in a patrol car, but like the three other men detained after the assassination—one in the railroad yard behind the grassy knoll, one on the railroad overpass farther down the parade route, and one in front of the Book Depository Building—he then dropped out of sight completely. All of these suspects taken into custody after the assassination remain as anonymous as if they'd been detained for throwing a candy wrapper on the sidewalk...'

Subsequently, in his '*coup d'etat*' statement of December 29, 1967 (see Chapter 33, below), Garrison charged that 'the American people have never been told the names of 10 men (some of whom we have identified as participants in the assassination) who were arrested in Dealey Plaza minutes after the assassination. They later were quietly released after the murder of officer Tippit, in another part of Dallas, provided the necessary diversion to cover their release'.

The same pattern shows in the arrests made outside the Dallas area. Just as Donald W. House was released, not because he could prove his innocence in the assassination, but merely because it had been established that he was not Oswald, other suspects were promptly set free simply because no link to Oswald could be proved in their cases.

Records at the New Orleans Police Department show that three men were arrested in that city, two days after the assassination of President Kennedy, when the District Attorney received information that they were involved in the crime. They were David W. Ferrie, a former airlines pilot and jack-of-all-trades who at that time was working as a 'private investigator' for the notorious mobster Carlos Marcello, top man in the New Orleans Mafia; Patrick Layton Martens, then 21 years old, and Alvin Roland Beauboef, who was 18 at the time.

No sooner had the arrests been made, than the FBI and the Secret Service stepped into the picture and demanded that the three suspects be turned over to federal authorities for further investigation. Garrison complied, with the result that all three were promptly 'checked out' and released after having satisfied the FBI agents that they had no connection with Lee Harvey Oswald. At no time did the federal agents concern themselves with even the hypothetical question of whether Ferrie and his friends might have had something to do with a conspiracy to kill the President, without Oswald being involved.

Clay Shaw, principal defendant in the present, early stage of the Garrison probe, had also been questioned by the FBI and then 'checked out' in the days immediately following the assassination, after the lawyer, Dean Adam Andrews, had put the finger on him. That makes another total of at least four persons in the New Orleans area, all of whom have subsequently been re-implicated in the case as a result of the new inquiry launched by Garrison. Independently of how their cases may be disposed of in court (with the exception of Ferrie, who died under highly mysterious circumstances just as Garrison was about to re-arrest him), the solid grounds for suspicion which have now been revealed make it plain that the FBI, in November 1963, failed in its duty. These suspects were 'checked out' not because their innocence had been established, but because Oswald was dead and no further complications were wanted. This is only one of many instances (many others are documented in my book *Oswald: The Truth*) where the FBI conspicuously demonstrated its aversion to finding the truth about the assassination.

The gravest case of them all is that of the white-supremicist terrorist who, in a secretly tape-recorded talk with a Miami police informer, revealed not only the existence of a plot against President Kennedy but even important details of the manner in which the assassination could be accomplished—two weeks before it happened.

The matter has already been discussed in some detail in *Oswald: The Truth*. What needs to be emphasized here is this paragraph from the AP dispatch, datelined Miami February 3, 1967:

'...the man who described a possible assassination on the tape was picked up by the FBI five days after President Kennedy was killed in Dallas, and questioned. The Secret Service and the FBI in Miami would not comment...'

Of course they would not. How could these federal agencies ever explain what they did? They actually had in their hands a man who had unwittingly betrayed to an informer the very blueprint of the assassination when it was still in the planning stage—and they let this self-confessed terrorist go—five days alter the President had been killed in just the way he had said it would be done.

In all these pseudo-investigations by the FBI as well as by the Dallas Police, the sole criterion of suspicion was some kind of link to Oswald. If the suspect had nothing to do with Oswald, he was automatically 'checked out'.

In order to correctly appraise this nonchalant attitude of the federal authorities, one has to envisage only the theoretical possibility—always present when a case goes to court—that the accused slayer, in this case Oswald, might have been able to prove his innocence and would therefore have had to be acquitted.

What then? With all alternative solutions of the crime eliminated beforehand by the FBI, there would have been no one left to prosecute nor any lead that could he followed. Under the circumstances, the murder of the President was bound to remain unavenged. What an unexpected stroke of luck Oswald was killed by Ruby, so the case could be closed!

There is no escaping the hard fact, unpleasant as it may be: just as the Secret Service closed both eyes when Kennedy was killed, the FBI closed both when it was supposed to be looking for the assassins.

And, just as the delinquent Secret Service men escaped any kind of sanctions, the delinquent FBI got away with murder— literally and figuratively speaking.

If Lyndon B. Johnson's conscience had been clear, he could not have tolerated such scandalous police procedures. He would have cracked down hard on the federal agencies under his control for being so remiss in their duties. The fact that he did not only condone such outrages but rewarded them— in the case of the FBI, its chief J. Edgar Hoover was continued in office after the normal age limit—speaks volumes.

The full responsibility for the fact that no real hunt for the murderers of President Kennedy was ever set in motion and that, as a result, they are still at large, falls squarely on Lyndon B. Johnson.

His failure to avenge his slain predecessor cannot be explained on any other premise than that he himself was involved in the crime.

CHAPTER 28 - Johnson's Phony 'Red Conspiracy'

IN the political jungle, it is standard practice to blame one's own foul deeds on the ideological adversary. When the Nazis, early in 1933, set the Reichstag on fire as a means of seizing uncontrolled power in Germany, they promptly came up with an obscure little Communist whom they charged with the crime and then liquidated. When the Texas gang assassinated President John F. Kennedy, to seize a power denied to them by the American electorate, they had an obscure little Communist (and, in this case, not even a genuine one) ready to take the blame and then be sacrificed.

This is not the only existing parallel in the Van der Lubbe and Oswald cases. Nor is it the only existing parallel between Hitler and Johnson, both advocates of the Big Lie as the all-purpose expedient in politics. And that's not the end of the similarity either.

If the American people were not so incredibly gullible, if they were not so pathologically steeped in anti-communism, the coarseness of the "Red Plot" tale spun by the Dallas conspirators as a cover-up for their own crime would have alerted them to the fact that something was terribly wrong.

The record shows that it was Lyndon B. Johnson himself who took the lead in spreading the notion that the murder of President Kennedy could only have resulted from a Communist plot and that there could be no other motivation. The first inkling of Johnson's active part in concocting this legend came in an UPI dispatch from

Washington, December 24, 1963, which started with this paragraph:

'President Johnson ordered the news of President Kennedy's death withheld until he could leave the hospital on the chance the assassination was part of a plot to kill all the officials in line for the presidency, a White House spokesman said yesterday'.

The story itself is well-known. Minutes after Kennedy had been pronounced dead at 1 p.m., Assistant White House Press Secretary Malcolm Kilduff, told Johnson: 'I have to announce the death of President Kennedy. Is it all right with you?'

'And he reacted immediately,' the UPI dispatch goes on. 'He said, "No, Mac, I think we had better wait for a few minutes." He said, "I think I had better get out of here and get back to the plane before you announce it." He said, "we don't know whether this is a worldwide conspiracy, whether they are after me as well as they were after President Kennedy, or whether they are after Speaker (John) McCormack, or Senator (Carl) Hayden. We just don't know'.

The key word in this paragraph is 'worldwide'. It indicates without doubt that Johnson was thinking, or rather, pretending to think, in terms of a Communist conspiracy. For, if he thought it was, or could have been, a plot say by the Ku-Klux-Klan or the John Birch Society, it evidently would not have been a 'worldwide' conspiracy. There is no other conceivable political force today, than the Communists, that could engage in a 'worldwide' conspiracy. The suggestion, clearly expressed by Johnson in the same context, that the plotters might be planning to kill all the officials in line for the presidency, points in the same direction. For, obviously, no person or group in America could have had an interest in wiping out all organized government in Washington, while this could be, theoretically, the design of a cunning foreign enemy. Besides, Johnson, in later pronouncements (see below) has left no doubt that he was indeed referring to a Communist 'plot'.

Now, it is again important to keep the time element in mind. It is just a few minutes past 1 p.m., and Oswald is still at large. At that early moment, then, no one—neither the Dallas police, nor the FBI or the Secret Service, least of all the then Vice-President Johnson—possessed any information whatsoever on which to base any kind of judgment concerning the motivation of the assassination. Not ostensibly, anyway. Only somebody in the know would venture to emit such a judgment for the purpose of blurring the tracks. That is exactly what Johnson did. By jumping to the conclusion—publicly—that this could be nothing else but a Communist plot, he gave the show away. This was the false pretense the real conspirators had agreed upon in advance.

Note also how confused and absurd Johnsons remarks are—indicating a troubled conscience. Why should the news of Kennedy's death be withheld, until the man who was now Acting President had left the hospital? Why shouldn't he be safe there? With all the forces of law and order now on the alert, were there not enough guns at hand to protect the new chief of government against a second assassination attempt? Does anyone in his right mind believe that the 1,500 men already mobilized for the parade by the Dallas police, plus the Sheriff's deputies, the Secret Service and the FBI did not represent a force strong enough to beat down any attempt at violent overthrow of the government—if, indeed, it was a Communist attempt?

This consideration leads to another one which shows even more strongly how preposterous the 'Red Plot' theory, or rather pretense, fostered by Johnson and his friends, really was. Dallas has had for decades the reputation of being America's most conservative big city where every lever of power is in the hands of staunch anti-communists. Moreover, it is located in an area geographically far removed from any conceivable base of support for Communist agents. Is it plausible to allege that a Communist attempt at overthrowing the government of the United States could be made in Dallas of all places? Now, if the seat of action had been New York, or San Francisco, or even Miami, such an assertion might be barely believable. But in Dallas—

How liars expose themselves! The bigger the lie, the more certain is eventual exposure, even if it takes a long time. The 'credibility gap', which by now has become a sort of trademark of the Johnson Administration, began at Dallas, on November 22, 1963, at 1 p.m. But for an incredibly abject and servile press, the American people would have known, or at least guessed, the truth long ago.

The phony nature of Johnson's Red Plot fears and his every move that followed the assassination is also brought out clearly in

William Manchester's account of the historic telephone call which Johnson put through from the Presidential plane to Robert Kennedy in Washington because he needed advice from the Attorney-General about how to take the oath and by 'cruel mischance' (Manchester) that official happened to be the dead President's brother. After he had gotten Robert Kennedy on the line, Manchester writes, 'Johnson began by expressing his condolences. But he had just become the busiest man in the world, and after a few compassionate sentences he plunged into business. The murder, he said, "might be part of a worldwide plot." In his statement to the Warren Commission seven and a half months later Johnson suggested that the Attorney-General had agreed with this interpretation and had "discussed the practical problems at hand—problems of special urgency because we did not at that time have any information as to the motivation of the assassination or its possible implications."

'In fact, Robert Kennedy was unresponsive. He was not among those who suspected a grand conspiracy, and he didn't understand what Johnson was talking about,' Manchester goes on to say. Given the well-known sources of his information, there is no reason to question the accuracy of his account on this point. Kennedy's rebuttal makes Johnson out the unabashed liar he is and has always been.

Elsewhere in his book, Manchester quotes Supreme Court Chief Justice Earl Warren as explaining thus why he had accepted to serve as head of the Presidential Commission against his will:

'The President told me how serious the situation was. He said there had been wild rumors and there was the international situation to think of. He said he had just talked to Dean Rusk, who was concerned... He said that if the public became aroused against Castro and Khrushchev there might be war...'

This is a humdinger. Johnson, the man who was the first to set 'wild rumors' going, pressuring the Chief Justice to take a very much unwanted assignment in order to stop those rumors. The brazen liar who had talked about a 'worldwide conspiracy', the moment the martyred President's heart had stopped beating, being concerned about public feelings that might lead to war against the Communist powers! Was there ever a hypocrite in high office to match such a performance?

The most revealing item in the case, however, is a dispatch from Dallas by Dom Bonafede of *The New York Herald Tribune*, published in that paper on May 19, 1964, under the headline 'U.S. Gagged The Oswald Plot Talk,' which read in part as follows:

'Plans by Dallas police to link the Nov. 22 assassination of President Kennedy with an international conspiracy were headed off by Washington officials a few hours before the arraignment of Lee Harvey Oswald, the suspected assassin, *The New York Herald Tribune* has learned. The disclosure was made by a high-ranking law official here and confirmed by David Johnston, the Justice of the Peace before whom Oswald was arraigned.

'"Washington was anxious not to have the assassination tied in with an international plot because of the harm it would do to U.S. foreign relations," the official commented'.

The anxiety of Washington is understandable only on the premise that there was no international plot, yet the impression that such a plot did exist was being created by interested parties. For, if such a plot really had existed, i.e. if a Communist power had actually been responsible for the assassination, then things had reached a point where U.S. relations with that power certainly could not be harmed any further.

'He [the official] said that after the arrest of Oswald, Dallas County District Attorney Henry Wade received an urgent telephone call from Washington requesting him to make certain that the charge was one of straight murder—avoiding the mention of possible foreign complications,' the *Herald Tribune* dispatch went on to say.

'Mr. Johnston reported that Mr. Wade informed him prior to writing the complaint against Oswald that the call came from the Stare Department following consultation with the Justice Department'.

This shows how the Oswald case was stage-managed throughout, without the slightest regard for due judicial process. The possibility that the man might be innocent apparently never entered anybody's mind, not even in Washington, although at that early moment no proof of any kind could be said to exist against him. The question being debated between officials was merely whether to pin a 'straight' murder rap on him, or to present him as the tool of Communist conspirators. The Dallas police were all in favor of the latter course of action, as the following paragraph shows:

'Mr. Johnston nonetheless recalled, "Enough evidence had been collected after his arrest clearly to show the man [Oswald] was a pink. The police got a little excited and talked about drawing up a complaint indicating the assassination was part of an international conspiracy. I talked with Wade about it, and he asked if there was any basis for an international conspiracy. At that particular point, I could see nothing to prove it. To say it is one thing, but to prove it in court is another"'.

What did the Dallas police get so "excited" about that they jumped to the conclusion an international plot was afoot? The dispatch says on this score:

'Mr. Johnston said that immediately after Oswald's capture, he (Judge Johnston) and assistant District Attorney William Alexander and several police officers were sent to search Oswald's quarters in a Dallas rooming house. He said:

'"The boy [Oswald] was like a pack rat; he never threw anything away. There was a pile of Communist material. Most of it was from the Fair Play for Cuba Committee, and there were four or five letters from a Communist group in New York. Potentially, this was pretty strong stuff."'

Judge Johnston here is engaging in gross double-talk. On one hand he affirms that the material allegedly found in Oswald's room was 'pretty strong stuff'; on the other, he says that he could see nothing in this material to prove an international conspiracy.

Actually, what was discovered in Oswald's room was nothing more than some routine correspondence between Oswald and Arnold S. Johnson, director of the information and lecture bureau of the Communist Party in New York, concerning the 'entirely fictitious'—as the Warren Report itself concedes— FPCC chapter which Oswald 'purportedly' (again, this term is used by the Commission) formed in New Orleans. And Judge Johnston himself states that most of the 'pile of Communist material' found in Oswald's room was from the FPCC which, as the published correspondence shows, had no ties with Oswald's spurious, one-man 'chapter' and disapproved of the way he handled it.

I have maintained all along, starting with *Oswald: Assassin or Fall Guy?*, that Oswald was never a genuine Communist or Marxist, but an undercover agent and stool-pigeon serving the CIA and the FBI. In my book *Marina Oswald*, this thesis is fully documented. It has received powerful support, from Epstein, Lane and others as far as the FBI is concerned, and, more importantly, from Garrison as regards Oswald's relationship with the CIA. Garrison has made it perfectly clear that Oswald's ostentatious 'pro-Castro' activities in New Orleans were nothing more than a 'cover' for his role as an undercover agent working against Castro. In his television interview of May 21, 1967, Mr. Garrison stated explicitly that Oswald had been working for the CIA in New Orleans and castigated that agency for its 'criminal activities' in trying to conceal this fact from the Warren Commission and even from the FBI.

If Oswald never threw away any of the phony Communist material he kept in his room, he did so on orders from his taskmasters in the CIA and the FBI. The fact that such material was found at all constitutes further proof that Oswald was no assassin, for a man who is about to commit a crime of such magnitude does not leave his room cluttered with stuff that is bound to incriminate him. All this is part and parcel of the official frame-up of which Oswald was a victim.

The fact that the Dallas police promptly sought to exploit this bogus propaganda stuff in drawing up a complaint that was to present the assassination as the handiwork of international (i.e. Communist) conspirators is powerful proof of their own involvement in the 'Crime of the Century'. Those gentlemen who went to search Oswald's room knew beforehand what they were going to find there, for they were working hand-in-glove with the local bureau of the FBI which knew all about Oswald's real face and the true nature of his political activities. The whole nefarious scheme is now being exposed, step-by-step, as a result of the New Orleans investigation and the picture that gradually emerges fits exactly the thesis first propounded by this writer about the real background of the assassination.

Precisely because I have been proved right in every other important aspect of the case, I feel completely confident that further developments will also prove right my contention that Lyndon B. Johnson was behind the whole scheme.

It was he who started the 'wild rumors' of a worldwide conspiracy, minutes after the guns of Dallas had propelled him into the presidency—the biggest sounding board in the world. Then the Dallas police picked up the cue and got all set to belabor this false issue. But Robert Kennedy in Washington immediately realized—if perhaps only instinctively—what had really happened and put on the brakes. In concert with the State Department, which could not but realize the damage to the national interest that was bound to result from this wild scheme, the Department of Justice moved to quash it by phoning District Attorney Wade in Dallas. Then, 'following a conference with the District Attorney's office, the Dallas police agreed to drop the reference to an ideological plot' to quote once more from the *Herald Tribune* story.

All of which represents another strong link in the already long chain of circumstantial evidence which proves that there was, indeed, a grand conspiracy to kill the President of the United States. But it was not an international, much less a worldwide one. It was an all-American plot in which Lyndon B. Johnson, acting in cahoots with the Dallas oligarchy and with the local branches of the CIA, the FBI and the Secret Service, played the leading part.

CHAPTER 29 - What's the Hurry, Mr. Johnson?

THE moment President Kennedy expired, Vice-President Johnson became Acting President. In this capacity, he was empowered to take all measures, especially all emergency measures, dictated by the needs of the hour.

This simple statement of incontrovertible fact takes the wind out of all the pious baloney with which the advocates of the Usurper have been trying to justify the unseemly haste of the swearing-in aboard 'Air Force One'.

When Arthur Krock in *The New York Times* of January 10, 1967, wrote that 'the perils of these exigent times sustain Mr. Johnson's decision to reduce to the lowest possible minimum the period in which the Presidential office was vacant,' the distinguished commentator either didn't know what he was talking about or else he was abetting the final touch of 'The Crime of the Century'.

The presidency is never vacant as long as any of the four officials constitutionally in line for succession is alive. Will Arthur Krock deny that Johnson, as Acting President, was in a position to meet the challenges of the atomic age which Krock underscores in his piece? What additional powers did he acquire by having the oath administered to him on the spot, instead of in Washington?

The American news media, which have with rare unanimity collaborated in putting over on the American public and world opinion the greatest fraud in modern history and which still exert every possible effort to prevent the truth from coming out, have also done their best to gloss over the sinister significance of Johnson's rush to get sworn in at the murder scene, in his pre-eminent domain.

William Manchester, in *The Death of a President*, has given a graphic and disgusting account of this abominable ceremony, even though the published version only represents a much watered-down variety of the original manuscript. *Newsweek*, in its issue of December 26, 1966, gave a preview of what was in the book before it underwent editorial surgery:

'Sources say Manchester has Mr. Johnson calling Attorney-General Kennedy in Washington for a ruling on when he should take the oath of office. RFK was noncommittal—but LBJ was already convinced in his own mind that the oath-taking must be held before Air Force One could be airborne for Washington. The new President reportedly feared a Soviet attack, but the stunned Kennedys apparently interpreted his actions as an impatient desire to seize power'.

This last sentence, of course, is phrased incorrectly. The seizure of power was already an accomplished fact and could hardly be undone in any conceivable way. Nevertheless, it is clear enough that the Acting President feared some kind of challenge, perhaps from the Kennedy camp.

That is why he displayed such indecent haste in getting sworn in. Johnson has always been a great believer in appearances, as distinct from reality. When Johnson, immediately after the

President's death, put through his first call to the Attorney-General Kennedy, in Washington, he said, according to Manchester: 'A lot of people down here think I should be sworn in right away. Do you have any objections to that?'

'Kennedy was taken aback,' Manchester writes (in the published version of his book.) 'It was scarcely an hour and a quarter since he had first heard of the shooting, less than an hour since he had learned that the wound had been fatal. As Attorney-General he couldn't understand the need for a rush, and on a personal level he preferred that any investiture be deferred until his brother's body had been brought home'.

If the Attorney-General didn't feel there was any need for a rush, there was no such need. He was the law officer most qualified to pass on this issue. Johnson's pretended fears of a 'Soviet attack' were nothing but a subterfuge contrived *ad hoc*. In any case, as has been stated before, he could have coped with such an attack just as well in his capacity as Acting President.

What followed next—the long distance argument about who could administer the oath and what text should be used (it's prescribed by the Constitution)—borders on the grotesque. When Robert Kennedy and his deputy, Nicholas Katzenbach, had reached the conclusion that any Federal Judge could administer the oath, including a District Court Judge, Katzenbach displayed remarkable intuition. 'I imagine he'll want Sarah Hughes,' he said, according to Manchester.

'Sarah Hughes was from Dallas, and he [Katzenbach] remembered Johnson's vigorous lobbying for her appointment,' Manchester goes on to say, but he fails to mention several important things about this lady who had been a great friend of Lyndon B. Johnson since 1943. Sarah Hughes' knowledge of the law has always been very limited. She is a graduate of one of those obscure diploma mills which flourish down south; this one went out of business long ago. Without Johnson's vigorous lobbying for her, she would never have gotten anywhere near a federal judgeship.

If Sarah has never been much of a jurist, she had, besides her friendship with the powerful Congressman Johnson, other useful connections. *Newsweek*, in its issue of February 27, 1967, has disclosed quite casually that Sarah Hughes is a member of the board of trustees of the Hoblitzelle Foundation of Dallas, which has been identified as a CIA conduit, i.e. one of those innumerable make-believe foundations which channel CIA funds into political parties, cultural organizations, labor unions, religious groups, students' associations and so forth. Anybody who sits on the board of such an out-and-out CIA affiliate as the Hoblitzelle Foundation must be looked upon as being an undercover agent for the CIA.

It is certainly not by chance that Johnson called upon his CIA friend Sarah Hughes to swear him in, at the murder scene, in such haste, for Jim Garrison, in his television interview of May 21, 1967, openly accused the CIA as the agency which executed and covered the assassination. Garrison said he had identified five men as the killers of Dallas and he stated that they were all former employees of the CIA. His use of the adjective 'former' does not mean anything under the circumstances, for naturally the CIA wouldn't keep on its payroll, ostensibly anyway, five of the men who had assassinated the President of the United States.

These statements of Garrison's leave no doubt that President Kennedy was killed by the CIA on behalf of Lyndon B. Johnson, with the Dallas police helping to set up the ambush, with the Secret Service looking the other way and with the FBI covering up. That is the hideous truth about the assassination.

That Robert Kennedy grasped this truth instinctively from the first hour appears also from the irony he put into his advice to Johnson:

'Anybody can swear you in. Maybe you'd like to have one of the judges down there whom you appointed. Any one of them can do it'.

As one of the most influential figures on Capitol Hill, Johnson had been packing the federal judiciary for years with his friends. He was no less active on the state and regional levels, as the incredible performance of the Dallas judges in the Oswald and Ruby cases has strikingly demonstrated.

CHAPTER 30 - Why All This Secrecy?

Nothing could demonstrate more conclusively the utter falsehood of the official version of President Kennedy's assassination than the extraordinary precautions the Johnson regime has taken to conceal the evidence from public inspection and scrutiny.

In March 1967, *The New York Post* ran a series of articles on 'The Warren Report and Its Critics,' by Michael J. Berlin, which, in keeping with that paper's previous attitude, was generally favorable to the Report and skeptical about the criticism that had been leveled at it. In the sixth and last article, however, the author appears to have undergone a curious change of heart. What made him reconsider? A peep at the National Archives did. Let's listen to him:

'The Warren Commission papers are stored in the stacks of the National Archives, behind a door numbered *6 W 3*. To enter, the archivist uses both a key and a combination. Inside, all the visitor sees is aisle after aisle of metal shelves, filled with cardboard file boxes, legal size, five inches thick'.

Thus are guarded the treasures of a bank, the nation's gold stock in Fort Knox, the military secrets of the Pentagon. Is this the way to guard the records of a Commission entrusted with the task of establishing the truth about the assassination of a President of the United States? If the official truth is the truth, why should it be so jealously kept from public scrutiny? Is truth the sacred privilege of a handpicked few?

'Stacked on both sides of one long aisle, and in part of another, are 900 of these file boxes—300 cubic feet—filled with the 1,555 Warren Commission documents,' Mr. Berlin goes on to relate. 'Some documents are just a page or two, some make the file box bulge. About a third are classified.

'According to the archivist, somewhere in that long aisle are the photographs and X-rays of the autopsy of John F. Kennedy. And somewhere in that 300 cubic feet there may be—there just may be the information that can either ease the minds of the 59 per cent of the nation who today doubt the Commission, or cause enough new doubts to necessitate a new investigations of that day in Dallas'.

If any information that could possibly strengthen the official thesis were to be found in that aisle, it would long since have been dug out and given maximum publicity by the zealous advocates of the Warren Report. A government that is faced with a vast percentage of incredulity among its people—the Louis Harris Poll of May 29, 1967, showed that 66 per cent of all Americans believed the assassination resulted from a plot—does not neglect a chance to improve its image, *if it can*.

Not only is a large proportion of the material classified, i.e. it will not be made available to any researcher without official approval, but the documents that may be freely inspected are full of gaps and deletions. Mr. Berlin writes on this score:

'(Archivist Michael) Simmons produces a document at random: No. 7,809 pages, dated 12.10.63, at Dallas, Re: Lee Harvey Oswald, "Report of FBI Special Agent Robert P. Gemberling." Some of the pages are missing. In one spot, 150 pages are withheld, sequestered in another file box, and a pink slip in the gap says: "Pages... through... being withheld by order of the FBI." The topic: "Interviews" relating to "other persons," "identified" and "unidentified" in the Dallas area.

'Standing in that room, the urge arises, barely controllable, to sweep Simmons aside, run down that aisle, and grope among the file boxes for The Whole Truth'.

It is just as well Mr. Berlin controlled his urge to sweep the archivist aside and to make a dash for The Whole Truth. Such an action would certainly have brought official reinforcements to the spot quickly, for the kind of 'truth' that has to be kept behind a combination lock is apt to be defended also *manu militari* against inquisitive probers. Johnson knows only too well what is at stake for him on those inviolable premises. The moment he loses control of the National Archives in Washington, he will be done for.

Further on in his article, Mr. Berlin relates how even Wesley Liebeler, a former staff member of the Warren Commission, ran into a stone wall when he tried to do a little sleuthing on the side.

Asked if he felt as frustrated by the inaccessibility of the files as are the critics of the Warren Report, Liebeler exploded:

'Frustrating? I think it's a goddamn outrage. I can't even look at my own goddam memos any more, and neither can anybody else. When the Commission disbanded, it sent the files to the Archives and didn't go through them to determine which should be made public and which shouldn't. The question wasn't resolved until August, 1966, when the Justice Department ruled that the Archives had the obligation to go through these papers and decide which should be made available.

'I think that this kind of determination should not be made by the Archives. Seeing the way the government people think, it's obvious that there would almost be an instinctive desire to withhold. [At this point, Mr. Berlin inserted in parentheses: "Apparently, the Archives, in picking and choosing, has depended on the requests of such agencies as the FBI on which of their documents should be withheld". So now its Johnson's all-purpose FBI that is in full charge of The Whole Truths. It has been handling this sacred trust in a manner reminiscent of the Gestapo under Hitler.—J. J.]

'I don't know what's to become of all this,' (Liebeler continues), 'but some people have become interested in it and are taking steps to try to do something about it... It's premature to discuss it... I don't know if we're going to get at [the classified documents] or not, but there's a good chance that we will...' So much for Liebeler, a maverick among the Commission counsels who has since embarked upon a private inquiry into the assassination evidence. Not that Liebeler has become a 'critic', but his faith in the Report he helped to fabricate appears to be somewhat shaken.

Columnist Henry J. Taylor, previously also a fervent believer in the official version of the assassination, appears to have had some second thoughts, too. In the *World Journal Tribune* of January 30, 1967, Mr. Taylor published a column entitled 'Mysteries Hide Truth About Kennedy Death,' which contained these significant passages:

'But when you move outside the independent authority of Parkland Hospital into what happened at the Federal Government's Naval Medical School at Bethesda, Maryland, where President Kennedy's autopsy was performed, everything changes. Preciseness disappears, clarity and completeness vanish, official documents become burned or rewritten. These mysteries started with an affidavit by the chief autopsy surgeon, a Naval commander, buried in Vol. 17 of the Warren Report: "I, James J. Humes, certify that I have destroyed by burning certain preliminary draft notes relating to Naval Medical School Autopsy A 63-272." A naval officer taking any such action without orders would be court-martialed. Who ordered this, and why?'

Here, Mr. Taylor is being a bit naive. Who ordered this? Well, who is Commander Humes' Commander-in-Chief? President Johnson is. Even if the order was handed down through some admiral, as it presumably was, no naval officer, no matter how highly placed would dare take such action on his own authority. In this case, too, the buck decidedly stops at the President's desk.

Why did Johnson order Commander Humes to destroy his original notes and then write a completely fictitious and fraudulent autopsy report? (See the Chapter 'The Autopsy Fraud' in *Oswald: The Truth*) Because that was the only way to hide the indisputable fact that Kennedy was shot from the front. And if that point were established beyond a shadow of doubt, there would be the devil to pay for all the participants in the Oswald Hoax, including, and above all, Johnson.

For the same reason, nobody is permitted to examine the 22 color photographs, 18 black-and-white prints, 11 body X-rays and a roll of film made during the autopsy. They were immediately seized by the Secret Service, disappeared for three years and finally wound up in the classified section of the National Archives. The Warren Commission itself never saw them.

The whole argument about how many bullets hit Kennedy, and from which direction they were fired (for details, see *Oswald: The Truth*) could be promptly and easily resolved through public examination of these documents by a number of independent experts. Why doesn't the Johnson regime bow to the oft-made demand for such an examination? If the official story is true, the government has nothing to fear. The fact that it does fear, and has taken great care to prevent, public inspection of these photographs and X-rays, proves all by itself that the official version is untrue.

On December 12, 1967, Garrison released to the press (which displayed scant interest in the matter) a set of previously unknown photographs which show a federal agent picking up a large-caliber bullet from the lawn on the south side of Elm Street, at the spot where Kennedy received his mortal wound. The bullet, which was positively identified by Garrison's ballistic experts as a .45—which could not possibly have been fired from Oswald's gun—was found amidst splotches of dark grey matter which came from Kennedy's head; in the immediate vicinity, a little later, a large portion of Kennedy's skull, which had been torn off by that bullet, was found.

The clock above the Texas School Book Depository, clearly visible in one of these pictures, reads 12:40, indicating that this bullet was discovered within ten minutes of the shooting. A uniformed policeman and a deputy sheriff are seen in these photos watching the federal agent as he picks up the bullet and then carries it away in his cupped hand. After that, this immensely important piece of material evidence simply vanished. The Warren Commission never saw it, nor did it mention it in the Report.

Here are some of Garrison's comments on this extraordinarily telltale discovery:

'These photographs indicate that long before the fraudulent announcement describing Lee Harvey Oswald as the lone assassin, the federal government had to know that this large caliber bullet was used in the assassination. Consequently, the federal government had to know that—inasmuch as it is impossible to fire a .45-caliber bullet from a 6.5 Mannlicher-Carcano—there had to be a number of individuals firing at the President'.

The District Attorney went on to say that when Oswald was shot by Jack Ruby the federal government 'had to know that the real assassins of the President were simply getting rid of the patsy so that he could not testify against them—as well as federal employees and officials who might be involved'.

Garrison then turned to the systematic suppression of evidence in the case which could never have taken place without the sanction of Lyndon B. Johnson.

'This is just another instance,' he said, 'of the pattern of deception by the federal government in which evidence has been systematically concealed or destroyed. In this instance, however, the fraudulent activity of federal agencies and officials is here exposed by these photographs'.

'These photographs explain,' he went on to say, 'why the federal government has so long concealed the autopsy photographs—the 22 color photographs and 18 black and white photographs—and has kept them under lock and key in concrete vaults'.

The photographs also explain, he added:

—Why not a single member of the Warren Commission dared to look at these autopsy photographs—because they knew that they would see wounds caused by gunshots from a number of directions.

—Why the United States Justice Department under Ramsey Clark has worked so diligently to obstruct any legitimate investigation and to interfere with any trials connected with this case.

—Why the President of the United States, by executive order, concealed vital files and important evidence so that no one could see them for 75 years.

Then, summing up his case against Lyndon B. Johnson—or, rather, that fraction of it which rests on the concealed .45 caliber bullet—Garrison said these photographs also indicate that the President 'must know that the Warren Commission's conclusion is a fraud and that the people of the United States have been fooled'.

There was no alternative but to conclude that the entire assassination investigation and the Warren Commission inquiry comprised 'an elaborate camouflage designed to protect the assassins of President Kennedy as well as the men behind them,' Garrison pointed out. He could hardly have been more specific.

Also 'classified' are, among many other items, Mrs. Jackie Kennedy's deposition before the Warren Commission (presumably because she blurted out something that was incompatible with the official version); a substantial portion of Marina Oswald's testimony relating to her life with Lee Harvey in the Soviet Union (because of telltale details that give away the true nature of Oswald's assignment to the USSR as a spy for the CIA—for details see *Marina Oswald*; a major portion of the FBI report on David Ferrie, one of the principal suspects in the Garrison enquiry until he died under mysterious circumstances; and many other FBI reports that cut too close to the truth.

Oswald's rifle is also out of bounds to the public. In this case the Johnson regime went to the extreme of whipping through

Congress a bill awarding permanent custody of the 'assassination rifle' to the federal government. This was done because a Denver oilman and gun fancier, John J. King, had sought to acquire this rifle which, after Oswald's death, belonged to Marina, under the normal rules of law. King had paid Marina outright $10,000 for this rifle and promised an additional $35,000 on delivery, but she was never able to regain possession of the weapon which had been seized by federal authorities after the Dallas shooting.

Why did Johnson and his obsequious Department of Justice go to such lengths to secure possession of this rifle, even though, in the process, private property rights had to be brutally disregarded? Again, the answer is: in order to hide the truth. For the fact of the matter is that the rifle found in the Book Depository was not Oswald's Carcano, but a Mauser. And Oswald that day 'never touched a gun', as Garrison confirmed on May 21, 1967. The story of how the Dallas Police switched rifles in order to incriminate Oswald against their better knowledge is fully told in *Oswald: The Truth* and need not be recapitulated here. The fact that the federal government used every means at its disposal to back up this fraud, and then spirited away the evidence, speaks for itself.

Total Secrecy is the best friend of Total Fraud.

Since this chapter was written and the proofs corrected, interesting developments relating to the autopsy photographs and x-rays have occurred. On May 9, 1968, Garrison's office issued a subpoena for them as it required them for use in preparing its case against Clay Shaw. Garrison's assistant, Alcock, was reported in the *Times-Picayune* the following day to have said that his office had evidence that the material would reveal that Kennedy had been struck by bullets fired from three different directions. He also said that it would reveal that the fatal head wounds had been inflicted from the front.

The subpoena was later returned on the grounds that the archivist in whose name it had been prepared had recently been replaced. A new subpoena was accordingly issued with the name of the archivist amended, but the United States Attorney's Office in the District of Columbia returned it on the grounds that it could not represent Garrison's office in this matter, exactly as it had done over the subpoena issued to Allen W. Dulles, the former head of the CIA and Warren Commissioner, to testify before the Grand Jury in New Orleans.

CHAPTER 31 - Why Do the Kennedys Hate Lyndon Johnson So Much?

When one of her entourage suggested to the young widow that she should change her blood-stained clothes before the flight back to Washington with the Johnson party already installed on Air Force One, Jacqueline Kennedy fiercely resisted. No, she was not going to change, she replied, 'So they can see what they've done'.

Who, Oswald? Or any other nameless assassin? It stands to reason that Mrs. Kennedy's insistence on wearing her blood-caked clothes on the plane could not be meant to show to the actual snipers what they had done to her; none of them could possibly be on that plane. Who, then, was 'they'? Is there any other possible explanation than that she meant Lyndon Johnson and his party?

This terrible phrase 'so they can see what they've done', constitutes positive proof that Mrs. Kennedy instantly guessed what lay behind the tragedy; that she knew deep down in her heart that her husband had been killed at the instigation of Vice-President Johnson.

Nor is that all. When Johnson later, in his incomparably hypocritical manner, tried to 'comfort' the widow, she pushed him back. 'I don't want that man to touch me,' she cried out to her entourage. So does a sensitive woman shrink from a murderer.

Unwilling to admit the truth, yet at a loss to explain the intensity of such feelings, officialdom and the press have blamed the highly emotional, even hysterical state Mrs. Kennedy was in at the time. Yet, when she poured out her heart to William Manchester, in April 1964, the shock of her terrible experience had worn off long before. Since then, years have gone by and there is no sign that Jacqueline Kennedy's hatred of Lyndon Johnson has in any way abated.

Why does she hate him so much? The fact itself is conceded by all informed observers, yet few ponder its significance. Is it normal for the widow of a president to be consumed with burning hatred for his successor? Did Eleanor Roosevelt thus detest President Truman?

Manchester and others who, in spite of the overwhelming evidence to the contrary, persist in defending the official version of the assassination, as laid down in the Warren Report, that Mrs. Kennedy was upset at Johnson for trivial reasons. They pretend to believe that these harsh feelings resulted from Johnson's uncouth behavior after he and his party had taken possession of Air Force One. But, could a state of mind lasting for years be induced by such trivia?

If it were just a question of dislike, the argument might be tenable. But the extraordinary depth and intensity of the hostile feelings which the Kennedy family, in particular Jacqueline and Robert, nourish toward Johnson, cannot thus be explained away. This is not just the slightly superior attitude of proper Bostonians toward a Texas hick; this is a blood feud that defies all attempts at reconciliation.

To be sure, the Kennedys have kept up appearances rather well. For reasons of their own which the outsider cannot fathom they seem to have put off the Day of Reckoning to a convenient but uncertain day in the future.

Robert Kennedy, in particular, displayed a considerable talent for face-saving and make believe harmony. He stayed with the new President as Attorney-General for nine months, swallowing any number of humiliations along with his suppressed anger. He chose a Polish city of all places to proclaim the guilt of Lee Harvey Oswald, knowing full well that the story wasn't true. He refused to read the Warren Report (as did all other members of the Kennedy clan), but nevertheless "accepted" it. He announced and repeated his intention to vote for a Johnson-Humphrey ticket in 1968, until Senator Eugene McCarthy proved to him that LBJ could be beaten.

In considering the seemingly strange case of Robert Kennedy, which Barbara Garson perfectly parodied in *Macbird!*, one little-known fact has to be taken into account. Robert Kennedy always had a close connection with the CIA; he was his brother's personal liaison officer with that intelligence agency. In a strange way, Robert Kennedy, acting on behalf of the CIA, unwittingly helped to make the assassination of his brother possible when he intervened with the Dallas Police, several months prior Kennedy's fateful visit to Dallas, in order to prevent the arrest of Oswald and Ruby (for details, see *The National Enquirer* of May 17, 1964, as quoted briefly in *Oswald: Assassin or Fall Guy?* and extensively in my German-language book *Die Warheit uber den Kennedy-Mord*)

It seems that Johnson has been holding this indirect and innocent involvement of Robert Kennedy in his brother's death as a club over Robert's head. Certainly, he has made good use of the fact that Robert Kennedy belonged to the higher councils of the CIA to make sure that the truth about the CIA's role in the tragedy of Dallas should not come out. In this respect, then, Robert Kennedy is a prisoner of his own past.

Yet for all his self-restraint and his professions of loyalty, the bad blood runs deep between Robert Kennedy and Lyndon Johnson. When the repressed feelings come to the surface, as happens every now and then, the results are spectacular as during that famous clash over the peace feelers Kennedy had brought back from Paris early in 1967. According to *Time* magazine (March 17, 1967) there was quite a scene:

'During a 45-minute meeting in his White House office on February 6, Johnson castigated Kennedy for his stance on Vietnam. "If you keep talking like this, you won't have a political future in this country within six months," the President is said to have warned. "In six months, all you doves will be destroyed." At one point, Johnson used the phrase, "The blood of American boys will be on your hands." Finally, the President told Kennedy, "I never want to hear your views on Vietnam again." He also reportedly said to the Senator: "I never want to see you again."'

Under such extreme provocation—imagine Johnson, his own hands dripping with blood, berating Kennedy for wanton bloodshed!—Robert Kennedy's self-control cracked. Says *Time* of him:

'Bobby, for his part, is said to have called the President an s.o.b. and to have told him at one point: "I don't have to sit here and take that (shit).'"

I wonder if it has ever happened before in the history of the United States that a President has been called a son-of-a-bitch by a Senator in the presence of witnesses. Only a sudden and uncontrollable upsurge of long-repressed rage can have prompted the normally cool Robert Kennedy to go so far.

On substantive issues, there have been more virulent clashes between Johnson and other Senators like Fulbright and Morse, but there is nothing to match the intensity of bad feeling, on a distinctly personal level, that has existed for years between LBJ and Robert Kennedy.

Is there any other plausible explanation for this mutual hate than that Robert knew Johnson was the murderer of his brother, and that Johnson knew the younger Kennedy had vowed to destroy him?

On the whole, the American press, despite its usual fondness for political battle, has chosen to soft-pedal this deadly animosity between Johnson and Robert Kennedy, apparently on the theory that too many people might draw their own conclusions and guess the truth about the assassination.

It was left for a German reporter, therefore, to give the most graphic account of this blood feud I have seen anywhere to date. In a dispatch entitled 'The Festival Became a Battleground,' the correspondent of *Die Welt*, Heinz Barth, described, in the issue of May 29, 1967, of his paper, the launching of the carrier John F. Kennedy in these terms:

'If the prevailing mood at the baptism of the new aircraft carrier John F. Kennedy at Newport News last weekend can be taken as an omen, this youngest, 61,400-ton giant will sail under threatening skies and on stormy seas. It was a beautiful day and Jacqueline Kennedy wore an extremely elegant white spring dress of tolerable length. On the baptismal pulpit, however, the temperature between Lyndon Johnson and the complete Kennedy clan was well below the freezing point, in spite of the summer-like day. If this intense mutual aversion, which is steadily growing in depth, could be measured in nautical terms, it would displace a tonnage far in excess of that of the world's most modern carrier.

'The ceremony, normally the occasion for exalted feelings and national pathos, was marked by an unmatched sobriety. Only if the most rudimentary rules of good behavior left no other choice, did the President pay the slightest attention to the family of his predecessor... Here at Newport News, America's TV-spectators, for the first time since the embarrassing disclosures of the Manchester book, were able to view the antagonists together on the screen.

'Under the glaring sun of Virginia, millions of Americans were able to witness the spectacle of an enmity of shocking proportions which no longer affords any hope of reconciliation. Even more hopeless than with the rest of the family is Johnson's relationship with Jacqueline—which is understandable in the light of the judgment she had passed on his manners.

'The whole nation could see how he ignored her with studied indifference, while she in her turn cut him icily. He did not even abide by the rule of protocol and failed to accompany the widow of the last President and her children to the baptismal pulpit, across the crowd estimated at 25,000...

'The master of the White House couldn't have been more sparing in his personal tribute to John F. Kennedy. There was no trace of the usual Texan joviality in the President's speech. Normally, Johnson puts his heart into everything he talks about. He can speak feelingly even about waste disposal. Hence the monotonous indifference with which he reeled off his text was bound to attract attention. One could see how he loathed this command performance which he had arranged in such a way as to reduce the glorification of his predecessor to the barest minimum... His speech was brutally short... lasting only four minutes instead of the 20 minutes in the program'.

At the end of the ceremony, Herr Barth remarked, 'there was no hope left that the conflict between the Johnsons and the Kennedys, which burns with the fire of irreconcilable enmity, could ever be settled'.

Die Welt, in which these lines appeared, is a conservative newspaper, consistently friendly to Johnson. The editors, therefore, made no attempt to interpret for their presumably startled readers the meaning of this extraordinary feud. To most people, in Europe as in America, the bitter enmity between the Kennedys and the Johnsons is just one of those things that defy logic and reasoning. They are too blindfolded, or too thoroughly brainwashed, to see the very simple, plausible and, indeed, cogent explanation of it all. It is to be found in the sober definition the *Oxford Dictionary* gives of the term 'blood feud'—'between families one of which has spilt the other's blood'.

CHAPTER 32 - Sabotaging the Garrison Enquiry

Even at this late hour, Lyndon B. Johnson could effectively wash his hands of the Kennedy murder. All he would have to do is to let the new inquiry into the assassination that has been launched by Jim Garrison of New Orleans, take its normal course. Would it not be the duty of the President to assist a law officer investigating the assassination of a President of the United States?

Instead, Johnson has used, and is still using, every means at his disposal to discredit Garrison and to block his investigation. In this endeavor, he has even resorted to every shabby device in the *Book of Dirty Tricks*, the Bible of his favorite agency, the CIA. Witnesses are bribed, intimidated or murdered. Material evidence, again, is withheld, faked or suppressed. Torrents of abuse and slander are poured on Garrison's head every day by Johnson's servile press and TV networks.

To begin with, the insinuation was spread, through Washington channels, that Garrison's inquiry was 'politically motivated', that it was a hoax devised by an over-ambitious and publicity-seeking go-getter intent on feathering his own nest. This charge is really too stupid to warrant rebuttal. Since when is it conducive to the political career of a public prosecutor to make up a case out of whole cloth and then present it to a judge and jury at the certain risk of acquittal?

This is, indeed, the touchstone of Garrison's honesty and integrity: so far, he has been upheld, at every step, not only by one, but by three independent judges as well as by a Grand Jury. If he didn't have a case, as his detractors assert, how is it conceivable that the courts would go along with him?

At this point, Johnson's advocates switch to the no less silly argument that Louisiana is 'anti-federal'. There had never been previously any indication of such feelings, except perhaps on the civil rights issue, as everywhere in the South. But that issue is not at stake here.

The next move in this insidious smear campaign was to blame the Napoleonic Code, on which Louisiana's legal system is partly based, and to pretend that this Code does not afford the innocent (meaning Clay Shaw and company) the same protection as the Anglo-Saxon concept of justice. Those who are now bemoaning the harsh fate of a Clay Shaw, who can at least afford a battery of good lawyers, never shed any tears when Lee Harvey Oswald, poor and helpless in the hands of a ruthless police, was even denied, through trickery, assistance by legal counsel. If the way the Oswald affair was handled by the Dallas Police and District Attorney Wade is any tribute to the Anglo-Saxon concept of justice, I go for the Napoleonic Code.

At the start of his investigation, Garrison seemed to be anxious to placate the powers-that-be in Washington. But he remembered only too well that the FBI, in November 1963, had 'checked out' the suspects his office had already picked up on no better grounds than that they couldn't be linked to Oswald. Under the circumstances, it is hardly surprising that Garrison rejected the demand by Congressman Gerald Ford (a former member of the Warren Commission!) that he turn over any new evidence in his possession to the U.S. Attorney-General for forwarding to the President.

'I am running this investigation, not the President, not the Attorney-General,' Garrison declared. 'Now if they want to help me, I'll welcome their assistance. But I'm not reporting to anyone'.

Garrison knew only too well what would happen to the evidence he had painstakingly gathered if he were to turn it over to the Attorney-General 'for forwarding to the President'. It would have been suppressed, or doctored, like all the evidence in the Oswald case. The FBI and the CIA have developed extraordinary skill in the art of making evidence fit their preconceived notions and they have demonstrated, time and again, a total lack of scruples in interfering with the due process of law. (If this statement is doubted by any reader, I refer him to the numerous examples of such illegality given in *Oswald: The Truth and Marina Oswald.*)

It is probably not by chance that Johnson picked the precise moment the news of the Garrison investigation broke to place at the head of the Department of Justice a fellow-Texan and native of Dallas ('the murder capital of the world,' as Melvin Belli once said), the 39-year-old Ramsey Clark, son of Supreme Court Justice Tom C. Clark. The young man lost no time deploring the New Orleans inquiry in tones of chagrined surprise and indignation. 'I find it curious and I find it disturbing and I find it saddening,' he proclaimed and added pathetically, 'I believe in the Warren Report. I believe Lee Harvey Oswald was the lone killer of President Kennedy. I believe... I believe.... I believe...'

Mr. Clark's act of faith is touching, but as Attorney-General of the United States it is incumbent upon him to investigate, not to believe, especially in a matter of such gravity. Instead, he has done everything in his power to stop Garrison. He even instructed several FBI agents Garrison had subpoenaed for questioning to disregard the orders of the New Orleans court. An Attorney-General of the United States who aids and abets contempt of court is something of a novelty, but in this case there is nothing that can still surprise one.

From the start, and consistently ever since, America's leading news media, after having played an incredibly one-sided, biased and shabby role in reporting the assassination, took the side of the Johnson regime against the courageously non-conformist New Orleans District Attorney. *The New York Times*, *The New York Herald Tribune* (Paris), *The Washington Post*, *The Los Angeles Times*, the newsweeklies and the radio and television networks all outdid themselves in either not reporting the news from New Orleans or trying to discredit Garrison. I doubt that there has ever been, in the history of the American press, an organized, nationwide smear campaign of such scope and ruthlessness—and it was manifestly, almost blatantly, directed from Washington.

In an article on the 'U.S. Establishment' (unrelated to the Kennedy murder) in *The New York Herald Tribune* (Paris) of

March 22, 1965, John Crosby gave this apt description of current relations between the government and the press: '...Official guidance is, I should say, the greatest threat to press freedom in America... The Washington press corps cannot be bought but they can be conned and they are conned all the time by official guidance which is not much less strict than official guidance in Russia...'

Indeed, all the vicious outpourings in the American press against Garrison and his inquiry can be clearly traced to the Washington correspondents who are being 'conned all the time by official guidance'. Contrary to Mr. Crosby's opinion, I believe that quite a few of these gentlemen can also be bought, if not for cash then through official favors. There is no other way to explain the unbelievably shameful role of the American press in the Oswald drama and its New Orleans sequel.

When Garrison boldly attacked the officially sponsored Oswald Myth, as he did early in his public statements and with increasing emphasis, he became practically an outlaw as far as Washington is concerned. No wonder, for the apparent legitimacy of the Johnson regime is closely tied to the perpetuation of that fraud. Anyone able to prove that Oswald was framed saps the foundations of the regime and will in due course bring it down.

After Garrison, at his first press conference of February 23, 1967, had stated flatly, 'I have no reason to believe that Lee Harvey Oswald killed anybody in Dallas on November 22, 1963,' the die was cast. He might have been forgiven by the Establishment, had he merely sought to prove a conspiracy involving other persons beside Oswald. But to say, as Garrison did even more pointedly in the course of another conference on March 8, 1967, that Oswald was innocent of both the murder charges brought against him by the Dallas police is tantamount to saying that the police themselves were involved in the assassination of the President. On no other premise can their zeal in prosecuting and then sacrificing a scapegoat be adequately explained.

At the height of the Dreyfus scandal in France, at the turn of the century, a prominent French politician—who firmly believed in Dreyfus' guilt—exclaimed, 'If Dreyfus is innocent, our generals are guilty'.

Analogically, it is certain that Oswald's innocence documents the guilt of the Dallas Police. But then one thing leads to another. If the Dallas Police had a hand in the assassination, or the CIA for that matter, or both, FBI chief J. Edgar Hoover, who masterminded the cover-up, is an accessory after the fact not only morally, but in a legal sense.

Garrison has publicly vowed to prosecute all accessories after the fact in the assassination of President Kennedy, all those who had 'substantial knowledge' of the true facts and failed to disclose them. He has already specifically accused Richard Helms, Director of the Central Intelligence Agency, of being at least an accessory after the fact and he can hardly fail to consider J. Edgar Hoover in the same light. Both men, however, are only heads of federal agencies under the direct control of the White House. Indict Helms or Hoover in the assassination of President Kennedy and you are indicting Johnson. The buck stops at his desk.

After a particularly scurrilous attack made on him by the National Broadcasting Company, in a one-hour televised special report, on June 19, 1967, Garrison took off the gloves. He issued a statement saying, 'All the screaming and hollering now being heard is evidence that we have caught a very large fish'.

The name of that 'very large fish'? Garrison at the time refrained from putting a label on, but the implication was perfectly clear. There are many big fish in Washington, but the only one that dominates the picture is Lyndon B. Johnson.

CHAPTER 33 - The First *coup d'etat* in American History

On the 29th of December, 1967, District Attorney Jim Garrison, in a statement issued in connection with the subpoenaing of three material witnesses in the Kennedy murder, said: 'Each of the three witnesses was in a unique position to observe activities relevant to the assassination. None of them were questioned by the Warren Commission'.

Garrison then went on to say that this was because the Commission's real objective 'was to hide the fact that for the first time in American history, a *coup d'etat* had occurred, resulting in the carefully planned execution of a President of the United States'.

A *coup d'etat*. The execution of a President. That is a far cry, indeed, from the official version of a deranged loner shooting President Kennedy for no particular reason.

Never before had the true nature of the Dallas events been described so frankly or so accurately, at any rate not by any person in authority.

Yes—what really happened at Dallas, on Nov. 22, 1963, was a regular *coup d'etat* of the kind which, according to Warren Commissioner John J. McCloy, is practiced in the 'banana republics', but never, never in these United States. It couldn't happen here—but it did.

This *coup d'etat* was carried out with remarkable aplomb and co-ordination by a 'precision guerrilla team' of at least 8 and possibly as many as 15 persons, as Garrison has pointed out repeatedly in statements to the press and interviews. These snipers—partly Americans, partly Cuban exiles—had previously been trained at a special CIA camp near New Orleans, which is known to insiders as the 'assassins camp'.

'President Kennedy plainly was shot from a number of different directions,' Garrison stated in the same context, repeating his earlier assertion that bullets had been fired from the Texas School Book Depository, the adjoining Dal-Tex Building, the 'grassy knoll' and even from a manhole along the route of the motorcade. It was indeed, as Garrison told an interviewer from *Playboy* (October 1967) an 'overkill operation'.

And the purpose of this *coup d'etat*, this execution of the President by a firing squad, the killing of a trapped, defenseless man, betrayed *in extremis* by his closest friends and official protectors, was simply to put Vice-President Lyndon Johnson in the White House. That is the long and the short of the 'Dallas Mystery'.

Garrison had long shied away from this ultimate and inescapable conclusion. At the start of his probe he had scoffed at those who, like this writer, had long before openly accused Johnson of being the power behind the assassination. While he avoided directly pointing the finger at Johnson in the 1967 *Playboy* interview, Garrison did make one thing perfectly clear: the primary purpose of the assassination was to change the foreign policy of the United States by putting a more belligerent president in the driver's seat: 'President Kennedy died because he wanted peace'.

As well, Garrison believes that Johnson is also the main architect of the Oswald frame-up and of the elaborate cover-up that followed the assassination:

'President Johnson is currently the most active person in the country in protecting the assassins of John Kennedy,' he said.

Protecting an assassin is a very grave crime, as everyone knows. When it comes to shielding the murderers of a President, it is a felony second only in gravity to the killing itself. In the eyes of a high-ranking law enforcement official, then—and, mind you, one who has thoroughly investigated the crime in question—Lyndon B. Johnson is guilty of being an accessory after the fact, and a most active one at that, in 'The Crime of the Century'.

Could there be a more serious accusation, leveled against an incumbent President of the United States, than the charge publicly made by a District Attorney that he, the Chief Executive, was aiding and abetting the murderers of his predecessor?

And how did Johnson react to this grave accusation? He didn't.

For details, see my book *How Kennedy Was Killed.*

It is true that the President of the United States enjoys no special protection against verbal or printed attacks. However, this is no ordinary case of political mud-slinging. This is an open accusation, the charging of a most heinous crime. If ever there was a case in which official action on a charge of criminal libel was called for, this is it.

For, if Garrison cannot prove his charges, then the roles are reversed, and he is the criminal. And then he should be dealt with severely by the courts (and this writer), for to impute to an innocent President the monstrous felony of conniving at the assassination of another President would be a very grave offense of itself.

So far, Lyndon Johnson has refrained from taking any kind of legal action against Garrison, or against me, for that matter. (In at least three of my books—*Oswald: The Truth*, *The Garrison Enquiry*, and *How Kennedy Was Killed*—I openly accused Johnson of complicity in the assassination.) I'm sure he has excellent reasons for being so coy. But the matter cannot rest there.

At a minimum, Congress should threaten President Johnson with impeachment if he does not institute proceedings against his detractors and clear his name in open court. But I doubt Congress will act. Johnson has too many Senators and Representatives in his pocket.

In the last analysis, I feel, only a thoroughly aroused public opinion will be able to force the issue into the courts.

To go back to Garrison's press conference of December 26, 1967, he had quite a few more remarkable things to say, for instance:

'President Johnson must have known by the time of the arrest that Oswald did not pull the trigger'.

Perverting the course of justice is another grave felony. If Johnson knew by the time Lee Harvey Oswald was arrested that this man was innocent of the crime imputed to him by the Dallas police, yet condoned the tragic farce of his indictment and subsequent murder while in police custody, then he is also guilty of that crime.

Garrison's statement that Oswald did not pull the trigger was hardly news to me who had been the first writer to defend the thesis that Oswald was an 'impossible assassin' and a 'perfect fall guy'.

But even to me, hard-boiled cynic that I am, it came as a shocking surprise when Garrison disclosed at Monteleone Hotel press conference that it had actually had been Oswald, the 'presumed assassin', who, on November 17, 1963, warned the FBI that there was a plan afoot to kill President Kennedy at Dallas, five days later.

According to Garrison Oswald, who had long been an undercover agent for the FBI, had gotten wind of (or possibly attended) the 'final, definitive meeting' which the principals involved in the assassination held on that November 17th. His tip resulted in a TWX (inter-bureau message) sent to a number of FBI offices on that date. The message, of course, went right up to the desk of FBI Director J. Edgar Hoover, but the newsmen could judge for themselves, Garrison added 'what came down to President John Kennedy'.

Now here again the point must be made that Garrison, with this statement, has charged a top government official with a top crime. Either one of two things: Hoover was guilty of criminal negligence when he took no steps to avert the impending danger to the Chief Executive, and even allowed all normal security precautions to be relaxed on that day, or else he was guilty of complicity in the assassination. Hoover can no more afford to refrain from legal action against Garrison than Johnson himself can.

At one point, during this press conference, Garrison exclaimed: 'You are being fooled. Everyone in America is being fooled. The whole world is being fooled'. It was almost an understatement. 'Why?' he went on. 'Because of power—because if people knew the facts about the assassination they would not tolerate the people in power today. Keep in mind who profits most. Who appointed the Warren Commission? Who runs the FBI? Who runs the CIA? The President of the United States'.

On January 4, 1968, Garrison unmasked yet another disturbing aspect of the matter: the government's extraordinary solicitude for 'cooperative' witnesses. This came about as the District Attorney subpoenaed as a material witness one Janes Hicks of Enid, Oklahoma, currently a civil service employee at Vance Air Force Base. According to Garrison, Hicks was present at the assassination scene and 'may have special knowledge concerning the details of the assassination with respect to its planning and execution as well as personnel employed in the assassination of the president'.

Obviously, then, Hicks was, or should have been, a key witness. Yet the Warren Commission never questioned him. Instead, this man before very long found himself holding a cozy job with a government agency. He had been out of work at the time of the assassination.

'There is nothing unusual about the fact that witnesses of special interest and persons whose histories otherwise relate to President Kennedy's assassination, have been given jobs with the United States government,' Garrison remarked and then continued:

'Those who already had not worked with the Central Intelligence Agency, or were not working for it at the time of the assassination, consistently are found to have received jobs since in installations connected with United States defense operations' (where, of course, they can be watched more closely than in any other employment—J.J.).

Garrison added that all of the persons 'who participated in the assassination or who could be important witnesses, have profited one way or another. One after the other, their financial status has noticeably improved since the execution of President Kennedy in Dallas'.

In other words, not only did Lyndon Johnson not prosecute the real assassins of Kennedy—whose identities he knows—but he paid them off with government jobs and other benefits.

The District Attorney concluded by saying that 'the involvement of high officials of the United States government in the affair become more and more apparent'. And that is the understatement of the year.

So here you have the two sides of the medal: on one hand, sudden and mostly violent death has overtaken more than a score of eyewitnesses to the assassination and the related Tippit murder, and, on the other, the principals and the hired gunmen in the plot were richly rewarded after the foul deed was done.

And it all happened under the aegis and responsibility of the one person in the world who could and should have avenged the murder of President Kennedy—his successor, Lyndon B. Johnson, 'the man who profited most'.

Isn't it perfectly clear why Johnson chose to cover up for the assassins, and pay them off, rather than bring them to justice?

As the year of crucial decisions, 1968, wore on, Garrison became increasingly open about Johnson's role in Kennedy's murder.

A UPI dispatch from New Orleans, dated February 20, 1968, quoted Garrison as saying that United States Attorney-General Ramsey Clark was 'attempting to influence potential jurors by testifying for the defendant' in advance of the Clay Shaw trial.

'He was referring to Clark's statement Sunday that Garrison had uncovered nothing new in his investigation,' the dispatch went on to say.

This, I submit, is self-incrimination at the highest level. For, all the world knows by now—or will shortly know—that Garrison has uncovered a tremendous amount of official complicity in the assassination. If none of it is 'new' to Mr. Clark, then the only possible explanation is that the Attorney-General has conspicuously shirked his duty. And, what reason could he have for malfeasance so grave, but to protect his boss, Lyndon B. Johnson?

Garrison further accused Clark of 'doing his best to torpedo the case of the State of Louisiana' because 'apparently 'it is felt in Washington that if the truth of President Kennedy's murder can be kept concealed, President Johnson's promotion to the presidency will appear more legitimate'.

And on February 21, The Netherlands Television Foundation broadcast an interview with Garrison taken by radio reporter Willem Oltmans in which the fighting District Attorney bluntly stated:

'President Kennedy was murdered by CIA elements. Those who were involved in the murder worked laboriously to give such a presentation that the suspicion would rest on others. This manner of organizing a murder is standard procedure with the CIA'.

Garrison also said in this context that he had to assume that President Johnson knew that the CIA killed Kennedy because he appointed an investigation committee composed mainly of pro-CIA persons.

In this interview, Garrison further predicted that 'the next United States president who tries to put the brakes on the war machine' will also be slain.

Garrison was quoted in the Dutch interview as saying that he had to speak out in Europe 'because it is impossible in America. The U.S. press is controlled to such an extent by the CIA that we no longer can say the truth. They throttled us'.

To such a pass have things come in the once freest democracy on earth under the oppressive regime of America's first Usurper. But Lyndon B. Johnson's time is running out, and, unless he stages a last-minute second *coup d'etat*, one that will do away with the Constitution itself, he is inextricably doomed.

Johnson knows he is trapped. His predicament is of classic dimensions. If he chooses to be a candidate again, he risks exposure, if not by the Kennedy clan then by a determined Republican opponent, for, by the time he must make his choice, Garrison's enquiry will be far advanced. But if he does not make a bid for four more years of power he invites open disaster even before his present term runs out.

He may be impeached by Congress when eyes begin to open at last, but I doubt it. Johnson has too many Congressmen, and especially Senators, on a string, in both parties, to have to fear such a contingency. It is much more likely that his successor, whether he be another President Kennedy or an honest Republican like Nelson Rockefeller, will reopen the Kennedy murder case and let justice take its course.

Garrison stated, early in his inquiry, that in due course 'every individual involved', including all accessories after the fact, would be arrested and brought to trial.

'The only way they can escape is to kill themselves,' he added significantly. He wasn't just thinking of Dave Ferrie.

If Lyndon B. Johnson has any brains left, he'll blow them out before the law gets around to him. That way he could at least escape he pinnacle of infamy and save his country from foundering in an abyss of national shame.

Epilogue

So now Lyndon B. Johnson has taken himself out of the 1968 presidential race—or has he? Judging by his well-established record for double-talk and duplicity, the suspicion is warranted that he didn't really mean it, and that it was just a tactical ruse for him to say he wasn't going to run and wouldn't accept a draft.

At any rate, the total lack of skepticism which the press—especially in America and Britain—has manifested towards this seemingly momentous pronouncement is characteristic of our pre-Orwellian era of unquestioning acceptance. The word of Big Brother is as good as the gospel, whatever he says. When he mounts the pulpit and acts history, the 'credibility gap' suddenly vanishes and only blind faith remains.

As this book goes to press, the Democratic National Convention is still a few weeks away. No one can forecast with any degree of certainty what is going to happen in Chicago. The bare possibility that Lyndon B. Johnson was for once sincere and really does not have his eye on re-nomination, cannot be ruled out. But I, for one, do not believe that man will relinquish power of his own free will. Not the supreme power he grabbed so ruthlessly from the man who held it by the will of the people. I have a hunch, let us say, that at the critical moment Johnson will jump back into the race and will accept—oh, ever so reluctantly, of course—the draft which his henchmen are already busy preparing. And the trick may well work.

Meanwhile, it is fascinating to watch LBJ at a new game—that of peacemaker. Having failed miserably as a warlord, he is now banking his political future on the diplomatic skills of his troubleshooters. And, for once, one cannot help wishing him success in this endeavor.

Joachim Joesten

May 1968

THE MURDER OF ROBERT KENNEDY

Two weeks before Senator Robert Kennedy, brother of the assassinated President, was in his turn murdered in Los Angeles, *Time* magazine published a cover story entitled 'The Politics of Restoration' which opened as follows:

'To many enemies, he [Robert Kennedy] is more his father's son than his brother's brother. Indeed, it was old Joe himself who observed, "He hates just like I do." By this reckoning, Robert Kennedy is the spoiled dynast, reclaiming the White House as a legacy from the man he regards as a usurper...'

The attempted restoration was dealt with swiftly by the CIA in a matter reminiscent of the *coup d'etat* carried out in Dallas in November 1963. The chosen locale was the bailiwick of one of Lyndon Johnson's staunchest supporters—Mayor Yorty of Los Angeles.

In the process, another attempt to curtail the tax privileges of the U.S. oil industry was deftly averted. As *Time* had put it in the above-cited cover story on Robert Kennedy: 'He speaks for tax reform and attacks the oil depletion allowance, as others have for years, but Bobby might just be tough enough to get something done about it'.

He might have been at that. But the forces of darkness were tougher, and quicker on the draw.

So there will be no Kennedy restoration after all. And Texas once more emerges the winner, in its own inimitable style.

THE DARK SIDE OF LYNDON BAINES JOHNSON

Who cares? Nobody cares.

How blind is it possible to be?

ABOUT THE AUTHOR

Joachim Joesten, the son of a doctor, was born in Germany on 29th June, 1907. He attended Nancy University in France and the University of Madrid in Spain.

Joesten returned to Berlin where he worked as a journalist for the Weltbuehne. Joesten was also an active member of the German Communist Party.

After Adolf Hitler gained power Joesten emigrated to France. Later he moved to Denmark. His first book, *Denmark's Day of Doom*, was published by Victor Gollancz in 1939.

When the German Army arrived in Denmark on 9th April, 1940, Joesten fled to Sweden. After marrying May Nilsson, Joesten and his wife emigrated to the United States. Soon after arriving in New York, Joesten joined Newsweek magazine. In 1944 he became a freelance writer.

Joesten took a keen interest in the assassination of President John F. Kennedy and published *Oswald, Assassin or Fall Guy?* in 1964. Like other early authors who questioned the official version, Joesten was forced to get his book published in the England (Merlin Press). In the book Joesten claimed that the Central Intelligence Agency, Federal Bureau of Investigation, the DallasPolice Department and a group of right-wing Texas oil millionaires conspired to kill Kennedy. He openly accused Police Chief Jesse Curry of being one of the key figures in the assassination.

Other books by Joesten include *De Gaulle and his Murderers* (1965), *Marina Oswald* (1967), *Oswald: The Truth* (1967), and *The Garrison Enquiry: Truth & Consequences* (1967).